The Search for a Sense of Wildness

A Park Ranger's Adventures in Isle Royale, Everglades, and Glacier Bay National Parks

To All Those
Who Have Inspired Me
To Search For Wild Places

—·—·—·—·—·—·—·—

Isle Royale National Park

N

Lake Superior

Blake Point

Rock Harbor

Mott Island

Daisy Farm

Moskey Basin

McCargoe Cove

Todd Harbor

Minong Ridge Trail

Greenstone Ridge Trail

Lake Desor

Siskiwit Lake

Malone Bay

Siskiwit Bay

Windigo

Lake Superior

- - - Hiking Trail
X Fire Towers

Lake Superior

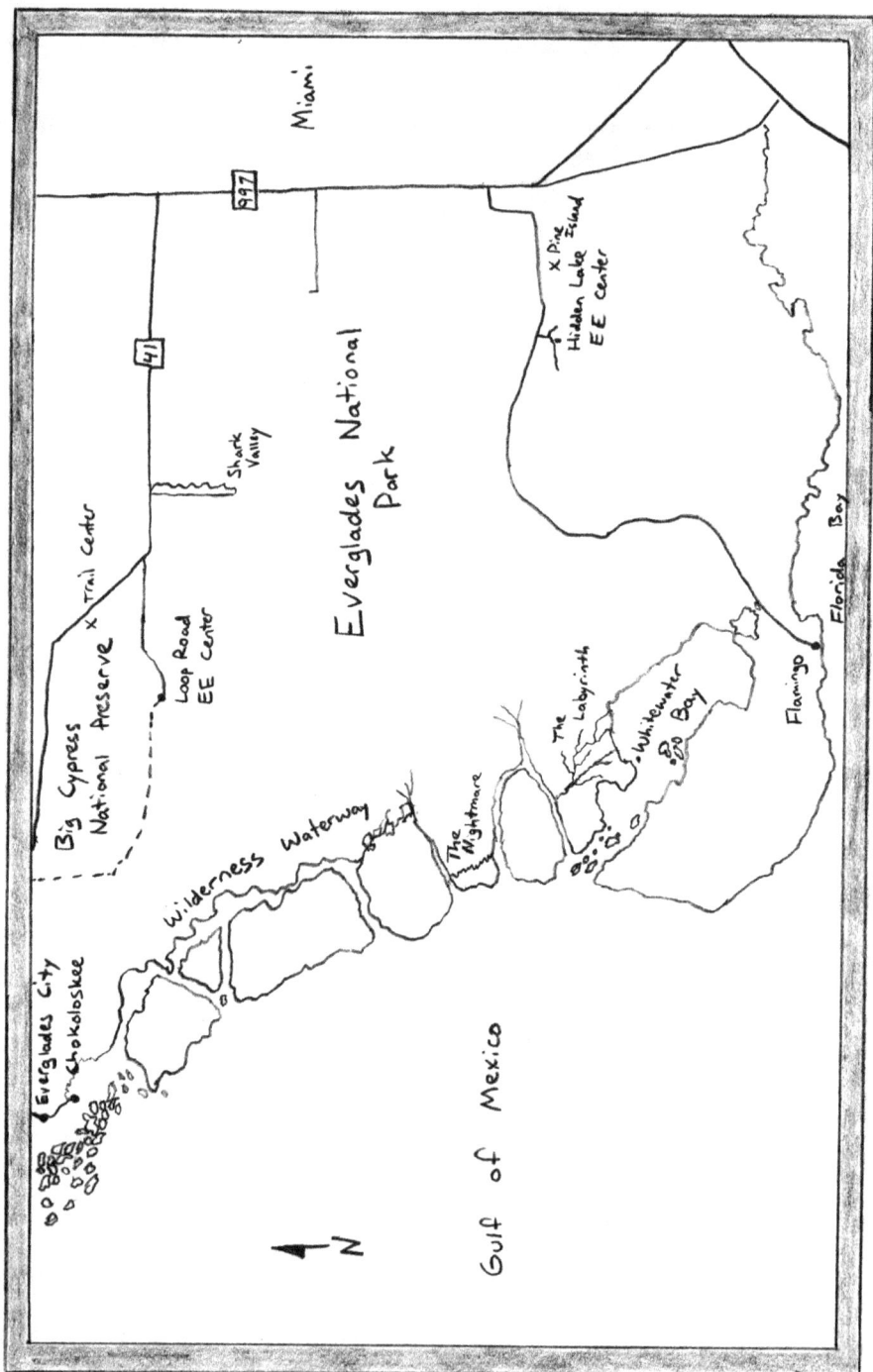

Miami

997

41

Shark Valley

Big Cypress National Preserve x Trail Center

Loop Road EE Center

Everglades National Park

x Pine
Hidden Lake Island
EE center

Florida Bay

Flamingo

The Labyrinth

Whitewater Bay

The Nightmare

Wilderness Waterway

Everglades City
Chokoloskee

N

Gulf of Mexico

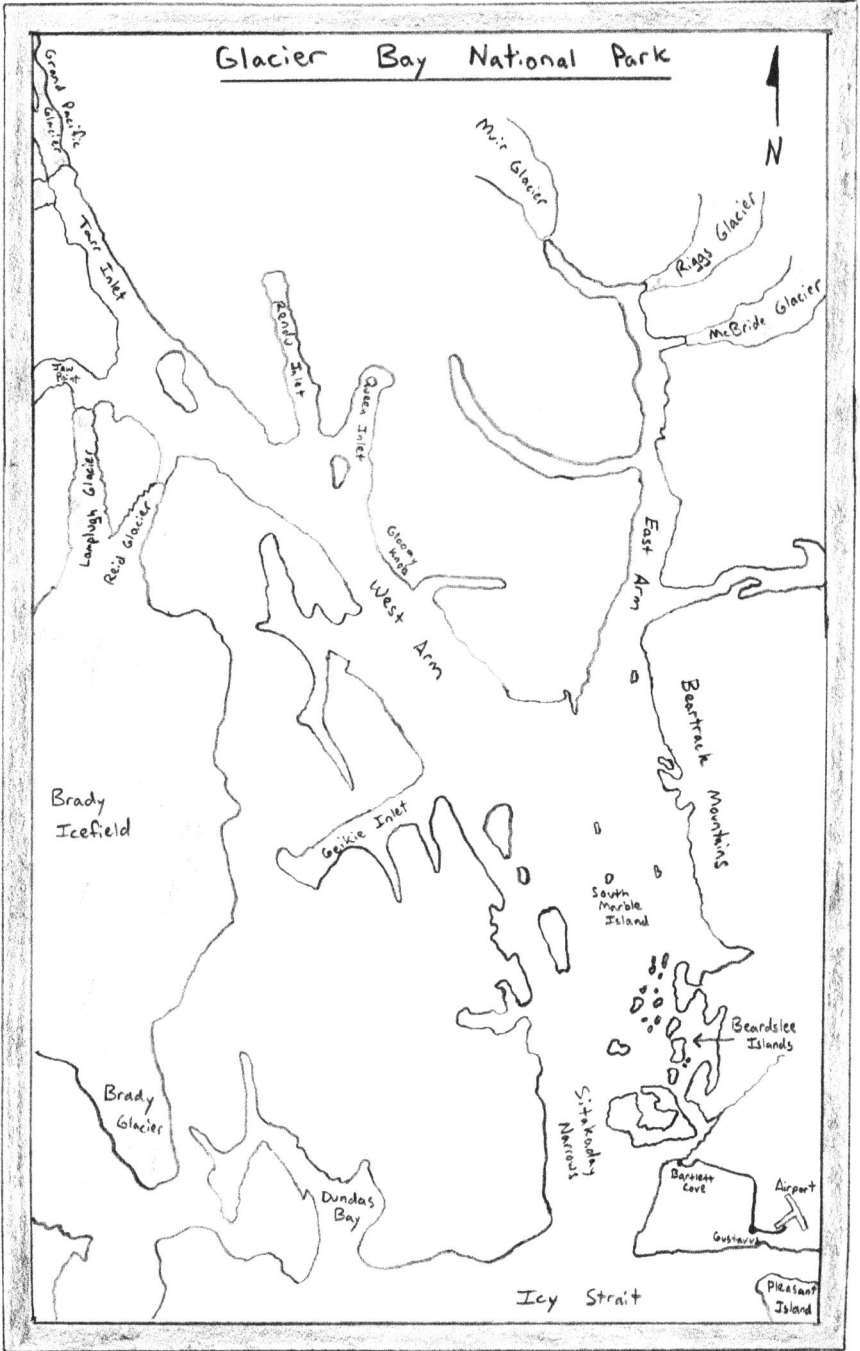

Glacier Bay National Park

N ↑

Grand Pacific Glacier

Muir Glacier

Riggs Glacier

McBride Glacier

Tarr Inlet

Jaw Point

Rendu Inlet

Queen Inlet

East Arm

Lamplugh Glacier

Reid Glacier

Gloomy Knob

West Arm

Beartrack Mountains

Brady Icefield

Geikie Inlet

South Marble Island

Beardslee Islands

Brady Glacier

Sitakaday Narrows

Dundas Bay

Bartlett Cove

Airport

Gustavus

Icy Strait

Pleasant Island

Table of Contents

Prologue:

Breathlessly, I raced out the cabin door into the cold darkness of a northern Michigan winter. A feeling of utter awe melted over me as I caught my first glimpse of the magic. A curtain of shimmering green light stretched across the black, star-filled sky. It pulsed and undulated like an ancient leviathan finally released from its grave. It was timeless, eternal.

Suddenly, I heard the creaking and groaning of shifting ice. The late winter breakup of the ice-choked Straits of Mackinaw was beginning.

The northern lights danced and soared for hours that night back in March of 1994. I stood in the frozen air, mesmerized by an overwhelming enchantment. It was the first time I had truly felt the whisper of a sense of wildness. This "sense" is not easy to experience. It is not necessarily something seen, smelled or even heard. It's more of a *feeling* of utter wildness found only in an incredibly wild and magical place. If you're fortunate enough to experience this sense of wildness, you'll never forget it.

Some people will say that true wilderness no longer exists. They may even laugh when you mention that you felt it. But it does exist. In the forgotten corners of this world, people whisper in certain circles of a sense of wildness so intense that all other feelings emanate from this one. It is in these utterly wild places that they sense the presence of the Creator. They feel love, peace, joy and absolute happiness. They feel an overpowering sense of awe that we live on a truly magnificent planet. These places are so rare that they are in immediate danger of becoming extinct. Too many people have forgotten how and where to look. What will happen if we lose this link to the heavens? Back on that cold, wintry night, I felt the sense of wildness. Like magic, it was gone the next morning. For several years, I walked around like a boy who had lost his kite. It took a long time, but I *did* find it again.

Chapter 1:

1997: Awakening a Dream

I had no reason to believe the day would be any different than any other. It was early April, 1997, and I was within one month of graduating from college. My plans had been made for the summer. I was going to live with my close friends somewhere near Grand Rapids, Michigan, and planned to spend another summer working as a deck hand on the Scrappy IV, a 40 foot sailboat owned by Seymour Padnos in Holland, Michigan. Spending hours on end silently gliding through the emerald waters of Lake Michigan certainly had its appeal. In the summer of 1996, I had been as happy as could be doing just that.

Everything I needed was within close proximity. I had a girlfriend, awesome friends, loving parents who lived in my hometown just 40 minutes away, and a fantastic job on a sailboat. My contacts at college had already given me some great leads on environmental jobs in Grand Rapids starting in the fall. My friends began talking about buying a house together. I should have been perfectly, one hundred percent content. But something was wrong. It was too orderly, too average, and too predictable. My life was barreling fast forward into a comfortable life in the region where I had always lived, safe and secure. I was restless, as I had been for months. It was becoming increasingly difficult to focus.

Day after day, I found myself in desperate dreams I longed to fulfill. Oftentimes, in the middle of my Cell and Molecular Biology class, I would close my eyes and suddenly find myself backpacking up some remote valley, watching eagles soar high above me. Or I'd be paddling breathlessly under a midnight sky smothered in ancient stars. Sometimes I'd zone out and find myself gazing upon unnamed mountains and waterfalls in a land far away. I dreamed of that elusive sense of wildness that I knew danced somewhere in the forgotten corners of the world.

It was five o'clock in the afternoon on a dreary, early spring day, and I was finally slipping out the back door of the classroom. I walked to my car in a chilly mist and slowly began driving toward the house in Jenison that I shared with three of my close friends. The 15 minute drive was my only time alone. With a deep sigh, I leaned against the window and drove down the road I had driven countless times before. Surrounding me, congested streets were filled with a myriad of cars, zipping past on important missions.

When I stepped into the house, there was already activity in the living room. Voices laughed over the hum of the TV. In the corner of the kitchen, a red light blinked on the answering machine. Like a moth drawn to light, I drifted immediately over to the machine. I could hardly have known that this message would change my life. My heart skipped a beat as I pressed the play button.

"Hello, this is Smitty Parratt from Isle Royale National Park calling for Mike Ausema. I am calling about a volunteer position we need to fill on Isle Royale. If you are still available and interested, please call me at 906-482-2654."

The cloud of bleakness that had been following me around for the previous months was just beginning to show its silver lining! Within a week, I had cancelled all of my other plans. Much to the dismay of more than one person, I accepted a job as a volunteer park ranger for Isle Royale National Park.

"You can't be serious," said my girlfriend. "Your life is here. What are you thinking?"

"What about insurance?" asked my dad, a concerned look covering his brow.

Their concerns fell on deaf ears. I was thrilled, filled with a growing sense of excitement. My job was to be a campground host stationed at Daisy Farm, the largest backcountry campground in the park. My responsibilities included presenting evening programs to backpackers twice a week, talking with visitors and answering their questions as they passed through or set up camp, maintaining the campground in working order, roving the trails, and serving as the first link in a backcountry emergency. I would live in a small log cabin with no electricity and no running water. A stove, refrigerator, and a couple of lights were the only appliances, and they operated on propane. My food would be delivered on a six hour boat ride from Houghton, Michigan to Mott Island, once a week. When my food arrived, I would have to drive a boat 20 minutes from Daisy Farm in order to pick it up. And to top it all off, for the first time in my life, not only would I be leaving my home, but I would also be completely on my own.

Over the next month and a half, I did as much research as I could about Isle Royale. The largest island in Lake Superior, Isle Royale became a National Park in 1931. Receiving only 18,000 visitors per year, the park is the least visited National Park in the lower 48 states. It is also the most remote. For the most part, there are only two methods to get to the park.

The first, and easiest (in sunny conditions), is to take a float plane from Houghton, Michigan. The trip takes only half an hour, unless it's foggy or inclement weather. These delays can last for days. The second way to get to Isle Royale is via a regularly scheduled passenger ferry from either Houghton or Copper Harbor, Michigan or Grand Portage, Minnesota. From Grand Portage it takes a little over two hours to reach the island. From Copper Harbor it takes about four and a half hours and from Houghton, six hours. The ride can be a pleasant journey across the deep blue waters of Lake Superior, or it can be a nightmare of tossing and turning amid the frothing waves of an angry freshwater sea.

Isle Royale is unlike any other park in the lower 48 states. Traveling to the remote island is such a challenge that once they've arrived, visitors spend an average of three and a half days. Compare that to an average of about four hours spent in most other National Parks. Getting to the park in the winter is practically impossible due to snow and ice, and the park is closed from the end of October until mid April for the protection of the wildlife. There are no cars. The only way to traverse the land is on foot, and the water, by boat.

Biologically, the island is one of a kind. There are just 15 mammal species living on Isle Royale, compared to over 50 species on the Canadian mainland just 14 miles to the north. The island is home to the highest concentration of moose on the planet. Researchers continue to conduct the longest ongoing predator/prey study ever attempted involving wolves and moose.

The more I read, the more excited I became. A whopping 99% of the park is designated wilderness. With 165 miles of trail and countless miles of paddling, I'd be able to lose myself for days. Isle Royale is saturated with a sense of wildness. To top it all off, the island is far enough north that I'd have a 20% chance of seeing the Aurora Borealis, or northern lights, on any given, clear night. These mysterious, glimmering curtains of green, white, red and even purple are caused by magnetic disturbances from the sun. No other element of the north filled me with such mystery and longing as this magical display of heavenly lights. I knew the adventure of a lifetime was just around the corner, but little did I know just how much of an adventure it would truly be.

The Island

May 28th dawned cool and sunny. The small amount of gear I owned was loaded onto the Ranger III, a 165 foot, sky blue vessel, the largest craft owned by the National Park Service. After a few passengers climbed aboard, we left Houghton at nine in the morning, hummed along the Portage Canal and quietly skimmed the mirror-like surface of Lake Superior. I couldn't help but stare as we passed the last few cars, the last signs of civilization. Ever so slowly, the cars and soon the mainland of Michigan disappeared behind us into the vastness of Lake Superior.

It began as an odd, undulating horizon to the Northwest, but grew bolder by the minute. Soon, I could make out deep green hills and jagged ridges, and then a rugged shoreline guarded by massive, lichen covered rocks. Finally, I could see individual trees and a brilliant white lighthouse, gleaming in the sunlight. This was Isle Royale, the place I had been envisioning. I held my breath as we gracefully slipped through Middle Islands Passage, a narrow opening amongst unforgiving rocks. Beyond that was Rock Harbor channel, a deep blue fjord-like channel protected from the big lake by a string of rocky islands to the south and the bulk of the main

island to the north. Finally, after six hours of travel, the Ranger III was tied up on the dock at Mott, a small island that houses park headquarters.

With a smile on my face, I stepped off the boat and onto a wilderness island nestled in a desolate corner of an even greater wilderness: Lake Superior. My gear, a pitifully small amount that needed to last me three and a half months, was unloaded and I was led to a tiny boat cove where the Lorelei, a 26 foot boat, was awaiting my arrival. Bob Whaley, the district ranger, and Smitty Parratt, the chief of interpretation, helped me aboard and off we motored into the clear blue water with a destination of Daisy Farm.

As we pulled up to the dock at Daisy Farm, I noticed a small, well-used cabin about 50 yards from shore with a thick northern forest beyond. Smitty explained that this was to be my home for two weeks until the construction of a new cabin, about a quarter of a mile away, was finished. It took the three of us just one trip to bring all of my belongings to my new home. It suddenly began to dawn on me that I was going to be utterly alone in the middle of this wilderness in just minutes. Frantically, I searched my mind for something clever to say to keep my new friends with me as long as possible.

"Hey Mike, I'll pick you up for training tomorrow morning at 7:30, okay?" said Bob. Before I could say anything, they were back on the boat and speeding away toward Mott. Silence. It was so quiet; I wasn't sure what to do. Had I ever before experienced true silence?

I was alone. It was a 20 minute boat ride to Mott, and I didn't have a boat. Rock Harbor, the main portal for backcountry campers, and the residence of several other rangers, was seven rough trail miles from my cabin. There were no campers in sight. It took me just 15 minutes to move in. Now what?

I then began to do what would later become one of my favorite things to do in wild places: I began to listen. At first, I heard nothing. Then, with a deep breath, I began to shed my fast paced way of life. Subtle sounds, at first blending together, broke the silence. I heard the gentle lapping of waves along the shoreline, then a slight breeze rustling the needles of a nearby white pine, and the tentative buzzing of a mosquito too cold to do much else.

After a hearty dinner of macaroni and cheese, I decided to take a walk. Slowly, I ambled up the Mount Ojibway trail, which eventually led to an old fire tower on the ridge. The wildness enveloped me instantly. Brilliant white birch trees contrasted with the darker color of the surrounding evergreens. Massive webs of hanging green lichen draped off the branches like flowing beards from an ancient tribe of tree people. The nearly constant song of white throated sparrows penetrated the air. After about half an hour, a loud "CRACK" brought me to a standstill. What was that? Just then, I remembered I was in moose and wolf country. I had never seen either species, and wasn't really excited about seeing one for the first time by myself in an unknown wilderness with darkness approaching.

As if on queue, the entire forest seemed to come alive. Strange sounds emanated from hidden predators lurking in the deep shadows. I turned around just as a large creature faded like a ghost into a stand of thick spruce. Was it a wolf? Without realizing it, I had been following something for quite some time; beneath my feet I saw a myriad of moose prints and a single, large set of canine prints.

With a bit of relief, I stepped back into my little cabin, shutting the door tightly to keep out the rapidly descending chill of night. As I wrote in my journal by candlelight, a single loon began a mournful wail from some hidden corner of the bay. This set off a chorus of several other loons in a perfect echo across the still water. I was home.

Death in the Cabin

Despite temps hovering around freezing, I awoke at four o'clock in the morning in a heavy sweat. I sat up in bed, feeling incredibly nauseous. "How could a simple meal of macaroni and cheese make me feel this sick?" I wondered. After three more restless hours, I awoke feeling even worse. I stepped outside and tried to drag myself to the outhouse, but I could barely move. Crawling and stumbling, I crashed back into the cabin and onto a chair. "Bob is due to arrive any minute," I said out loud. "I'm just going to have to tell him I can't make it to training today. Maybe I can sleep it off." Drowsiness threatened to pull me back into a deep sleep.

About 20 minutes later there was a knock on my door. "Are you ready?" asked Bob.

"I'm sorry, Bob, but I feel really sick. It might have been something I ate. Maybe I should stay here and sleep it off."

Bob took one step into the cabin, and with a strange look on his face said, "Why don't you come with me. We'll put you on the top of the Lorelei to get some fresh air. If you still feel sick after our 30 minute ride to Rock Harbor, then you can hang out in my house. You'll probably feel better with a bit of fresh air."

Miraculously, I did begin to feel better. After a nice, cool boat ride, I even felt like taking part in training. Shortly after lunch, one of the maintenance employees approached me with some frightening news. "Your cabin had a propane leak," he said in a gruff voice. "You're lucky. Another hour in that cabin, breathing carbon monoxide, and you would have been a goner…Welcome to Isle Royale."

Backpacking Solo

It took me a few days to get up enough courage to stay in my cabin again. The leak had been repaired, but trusting that the cabin was safe enough to sleep in was a whole different matter. The next time I spent the night in the cabin, I propped every window and even the door wide open. During the time that my cabin was airing out, I took advantage of two days off and had another life changing experience.

At six o'clock in the evening on May 30th, I stepped onto the Rock Harbor trail with a full backpack and unbridled energy. For the first time in my life I was solo backpacking. A sense of limitless freedom pulsed through my veins. I could walk whatever speed felt most comfortable, take breaks and eat snacks whenever the desire surfaced, and travel wherever the wind blew me. It was sunny and warm, and I was as happy as I'd ever been.

The trail led toward Moskey Basin, a small bay at the far end of Rock Harbor channel. With every step, new treasures were unveiled before my eyes. Ancient rock ridges covered in bright orange lichen; tiny, bright green birch leaves; an unimaginable silence in the depths of a cedar swamp; each a new awakening in my mind. Red squirrels chattered high above in the trees, a far-off loon let out an eerie wail and the calls of white throated sparrows saturated the forest.

Beyond Moskey Basin, I left the shoreline and plunged deep into the heart of the forest. The sun was just above the treetops by the time I had hiked six miles and arrived at one of four campsites along tranquil Lake Richie. The last ten minutes along the trail were so riddled with moose tracks that I nervously assumed there must be hundreds living around the lake. My tent was set up in a matter of minutes and soon I was sitting along the shoreline, ready to experience the sunset. As the fiery glow in the west began to fade, a sudden, sharp "snap!" brought my attention immediately down to the water's edge where a massive, shaggy creature was hauling itself out of the lake with impossibly tall legs. My heart raced and my eyes widened as I watched my first wild moose appear from the dark waters of Lake Richie. It calmly ambled away, following the lakeshore for the next 20 minutes.

Ever so slowly, the shadows lengthened across the lake. One by one, a million frogs began croaking their songs into the surrounding darkness. Between loon calls, the frogs and the absolute solitude, I felt like the little boy who had once again found his kite.

I woke up raring to go. It was another perfect day, blue skies with temperatures rising into the 70s. After studying the map, I noticed that the Indian Portage Trail bisects the island and its numerous ridges. Up and down those ridges and past beautiful inland lakes I walked, six miles, toward secluded McCargoe Cove, on the north shore of the island. At one o'clock in the afternoon, I wandered into a backcountry campsite nestled in the forested bluffs along the crystal clear water of this narrow, hidden cove off of Lake Superior.

I had never before had so much time to do whatever my heart and mind desired. As the minutes crept by, the excitement faded into an uneasy feeling. What was I going to do? "I know," I said to the nearby birds, "I'll explore the campground!" It was one forty-five when I left and two o'clock when I returned. Now what? I decided to take a nap and after that, I explored the campground again. At three thirty I was so antsy that I decided to take a longer hike up the Minong Ridge trail. For the rest of the afternoon,

I explored the ridge. When I arrived at an open, rocky hilltop called Pine Mountain, I decided that I'd return in the evening to watch the sunset.

After dinner, another nap and a third jaunt around the now-very-familiar campground, I decided it was time to hike back up to my recently discovered sunset spot. It was eight forty-five when I arrived. Dismayed, I saw the sun still high in the sky. I wandered back and forth, not sure quite what to do, until after ten o'clock, when the sun finally dropped below the distant hills of Canada, painting the sky with brilliant hues of purple and orange.

The following day, I hiked back toward Daisy Farm along the Greenstone Ridge, the more popular of two ridgeline trails that extend the length of the island. As my feet traveled the well-marked trail, I began to reflect on the last couple of days. Perhaps solo backpacking isn't that great after all, I thought to myself. I just spent two days and two nights alone, without anybody to talk to, nobody to share my thoughts with…I thought about college life and all my friends and family back home. Slowly, something seeped into my consciousness; I didn't know how to be alone. Growing up with three brothers and two family-oriented parents, I was never alone. Throughout my college years, I always lived with roommates and spent lots of time with my friends. I was never alone, and I hadn't realized it until this moment. I didn't know the innermost part of myself and I wasn't even remotely comfortable being alone. Long ago I remember hearing that in order to find inner peace and happiness, you had to get to know yourself and be comfortable with what you discovered. Deep down, I desperately wanted to discover who I was and what my path in life would be.

Just then, I saw a flash of movement behind me. Two hikers were cresting the hill I had just climbed. Despite longing to find people to talk to over the last two days, I found myself in no mood to talk, much less be overtaken on the trail. I picked my pace up a notch. After a few minutes, I turned around and was surprised to see them just 100 yards behind me and closing in fast. Faster and faster I hiked through the forest.

"Excuse us," a voice probed from behind. They had caught up with me! Unbelievable! I had always been very athletic, and far outpaced my backpacking buddies during college. Who *were* these people and *where* had they come from? "Mike, is that you?" came the same voice. Startled, I turned to see my boss, Smitty, and his wife, Shawn.

At that moment, a strange connection shot through my mind, straight to my soul. It felt as if I had known these two people my entire life. Is that possible? We ended up hiking together to the Ojibway Tower, an old stately fire tower on an exposed section of the Greenstone Ridge, where we enjoyed a leisurely lunch, and then continued down the trail to Daisy Farm. The few hours that we spent together that afternoon cemented a lifelong friendship that would take me on some of the wildest adventures I could ever imagine.

The Marathon

The morning of June 29th began at an insanely early hour, in Windigo, a small community located at the western end of Isle Royale. It was three o'clock in the morning, and I leaped out of bed faster than a lightning bolt. A buzz of excitement filled the air as the four of us stuffed a few necessities into our light backpacks. Kyle, a law enforcement ranger from Windigo, wolfed down his customary oatmeal breakfast as Smitty and Shawn ate some high energy granola with milk. I grabbed a couple of Pop Tarts and was pacing like a caged animal by the door within minutes. Shortly after three thirty, four headlamps began bobbing along silently as we melted into the black forest heading northeast from Windigo. Soon, the first glimpses of dawn appeared and slowly the darkness surrounding us began taking on the form of trees, shrubs and flowers. We reached the ridge just as dawn was breaking. The brilliant orange and pink sky looked as if it had been painted by an unseen hand. Lake Desor lay below us like a brilliant sapphire nestled among a sea of emerald trees. We had already hiked 14 ½ miles by the time we stopped for a second breakfast at Ishpeming tower.

The idea behind this adventure had begun almost a month before, while I was hiking with Smitty and Shawn on the Greenstone Ridge. One of my favorite things about a long hike with friends is the storytelling. That day, Smitty and Shawn told me so many stories about wild and crazy hikes that I was intrigued beyond belief. Smitty then unveiled his plan to hike the island in a day.

"Is that even possible?" I had asked in disbelief.

"Sure it is," was his confident reply. "We'll have to get up really early and hike with headlamps until daylight, and then plan on hiking well into the evening. The Greenstone Ridge trail stretches almost 41 miles from end to end, nearly the entire length of Isle Royale. We won't have to hike exceptionally fast, just steadily and with lots of high energy food. Water is the only other issue that we'll have to worry about. We'll need to drink a lot of water and stay really well hydrated throughout the day. My plan is to start in Windigo, hike 41 miles following the Greenstone Ridge trail until arriving at Lookout Louise, hike one mile down to Hidden Lake, and then paddle the canoe that we'll stash there back to Rock Harbor. Want to come along?"

"That sounds like an amazing challenge," I said, as the extremity of the hike sunk in. "Count me in!"

As the days of June crept by, I became more and more excited about the prospect of such a challenge. It might have been an impossible feat, but Smitty's confidence made it seem attainable.

By the time we took a break under the Ishpeming Tower, only pausing long enough to chow down our second breakfast, I was certain I would be able to hike the entire distance. My legs felt strong and my determination was unstoppable.

Mile after mile slipped by, as we glided along the spine of the island. Twice, we spooked moose that were only a few feet off the trail. They jolted, cantered a few yards, realized that there was no apparent threat, and then stopped to stare inquisitively at these four hikers who had stumbled into their world. Cool, overcast skies gave way to a blisteringly hot, summer sun. Further and further we hiked. We talked about everything and nothing at all, just to get our minds off of the incredible distance ahead of us. I began to laugh more and more as the day progressed, starting with a crazy game Smitty decided to play.

"Have you ever heard of Molly McGee from Tennessee?" he asked.

"No," I replied hesitantly.

"Shawn and I will tell you about Molly and you see if you can catch on and tell us a few things about her," said Smitty with a sly smile on his face. Shawn just rolled her eyes. "Molly likes trees, but she doesn't like forests."

"Excuse me?" I said.

With a big laugh, he continued. "Molly likes pizza, but she doesn't like popcorn."

"Hmmm…" I said. "Continue…"

"Molly likes swimming, but she doesn't like water."

"Actually, she doesn't like to swim," chimed in Shawn.

"Good point," said Smitty. "But she does like swimming!"

I was totally confused at this point, but the expectant smiles on their faces kept me intrigued. "Molly likes Smitty, but she doesn't like Mike," laughed Shawn.

"She doesn't like Shawn either!" retorted Smitty with a long laugh.

"That's not very nice," I said. This seemed only to encourage them.

"Molly likes beer, but she doesn't like alcohol," Smitty continued. The conversation degraded from there with uproarious laughter. "Molly likes boobs, but she doesn't like breasts!" Tears were flowing down Smitty's face and he was clutching his stomach.

I was laughing so hard just watching Smitty that I could barely breathe. Suddenly, I caught on and I began laughing even harder, until I collapsed next to the trail. "Molly McGee from Tennessee only likes words with double letters in them," gasped Smitty and the game continued.

Time passed slowly, joyously. Our bodies fell into a rhythm and we had just one thing on our minds: walking. It was glorious. By mid afternoon we had reached the Ojibway Tower, 33 miles into our journey. Fatigue was beginning to set in, but determination won over.

The shadows were lengthening as we passed Mount Franklin, an outstanding viewpoint toward the far-off wilds of Canada. We marched through meadow after meadow bursting with wildflowers. Finally, when I was sure my feet were ready to fall off, I saw a small sign ahead marking the end of the Greenstone Ridge Trail. Smitty and I scampered up to Lookout Louise, a mind-boggling view of lonely islands, bays, Lake Superior and the far-off, surreal view of Canada. We had hiked just over 40 ½ miles. Our bodies were aching, but again, the mind can be unbelievably powerful. For the last mile down the steep, rugged trail to Hidden Lake, the rhythm of walking took over, my mind skipping between dizzying exhaustion and exhilaration. Before I knew it, we were crossing a rickety boardwalk through a small swamp on the edge of Hidden Lake. One leg of the journey remained, a simple paddle across the calm waters of Tobin Harbor. We dragged the canoe out of its hiding place and happily sat on the seats as we drifted out into the harbor. The loons seemed to serenade us as we cut through the water toward Rock Harbor. Success was within sight!

"You know," said Smitty, as we glided through the dark water, "our bodies can do so much more than we realize. I wonder how many people think what we just did was impossible? It's that way with so many things in life. Most people put limits on what they can do. If you just open your mind, it's amazing what you can accomplish."

I couldn't help but stare back at the Greenstone Ridge. What an adventure. One thought kept entering my mind. My eyes went blank and I was once again a little kid happily running around our backyard in Grant, Michigan, with an exceptional amount of energy. My mom and dad had just excused us from the dinner table after reading a Bible verse from the book of Isaiah, chapter 40: *"but those who hope in the Lord will renew their strength. They will soar on wings like eagles; they will run and not grow weary, they will walk and not be faint."* I hadn't thought of this verse in years, but suddenly it was so fresh in my mind that it was as if I had just read it moments ago.

A shiver ran up and down my spine as I realized someone else had been with me all day. I smiled, imagining myself soaring with the eagles and not growing weary. For the first time in my life, I truly felt the presence of God.

After we returned to Mott Island that evening, I ate so much pizza that I thought I would burst. Stomach full, I climbed into bed. My head hit the pillow in utter exhaustion. Mission accomplished.

With my heart racing, I sprinted down the steps of my cabin and over to my floundering boat. The "Pickerel," as my little 14 foot, 30 horse power boat was called, was being lured into the jaws of an angry sea. Winds nearly flattened me and rain pelted my face as I ventured out from the protection of the trees and into the full wrath of the gale. The winch system, which normally brought my boat up onto shore, had already been dragged into the frigid water and the Pickerel rammed continuously against the rocks of the shoreline with a sickening smack. I leaped into the water and dragged the heavy winch system onto the rain-soaked land. Inch by agonizing inch, I pulled on the water-logged boat until the mighty lake finally relinquished its grip. For the next hour, I painstakingly bailed bucket after bucket of water until the boat sat upright again.

Finally, I had a chance to look around. I could just catch a glimpse of the open water of Lake Superior beyond Middle Islands Passage and the scene that met my eyes sent a shiver down my spine. Waves as tall as houses rolled in and violently crashed onto the rocky islands with a thunderous roar, sending spray high into the air. Even in the protection of the harbor, white caps could be seen in every direction. Temps hovered in the mid 40s. "How could this possibly be July 2nd?" I wondered.

The rest of the morning and most of the afternoon I spent holed up in my cabin, reading books, drinking hot tea and watching the storm pummel the land. Finally, in late afternoon, I ventured out into the campground. The three-sided, wooden shelters were filled with shivering, drenched campers. A few hearty souls attended my evening program on loons, which I presented under the cover of a shelter that evening. Afterwards, several of the campers returned with me to my cabin for some dry blankets and hot chocolate.

It was ten thirty, and darkness had enveloped the forest and the lake. The last few campers were leaving my cabin, heading back to their own shelters, and I was exhausted. I was surprised to hear a knock at my door.

"Are you the ranger here?" asked a quivering voice. Two bedraggled campers nearly collapsed on the floor. Before I could say anything, they continued, "We just hiked three and a half miles from Moskey Basin because our friend there is hypothermic and having trouble breathing. Please, can you help her?"

I began calling on my radio in an attempt to contact an emergency medical technician (EMT) either in Rock Harbor or Mott. The calls were met with silence on the other end.

"Well, if you don't mind helping me push my boat back into the water, we can go to Moskey Basin now," I hesitantly said as I relit one of the candles in the window.

Outside, the rain still fell in buckets and white caps continued to churn in the harbor. With the help of the two campers, we inched back into the water and were soon on our way to Moskey Basin. The next time I tried the radio, I connected with someone at Rock Harbor who promised to be underway within minutes.

The EMT from Rock Harbor beat me to Moskey Basin. His lights helped me find the dock and with four extra hands on board, I was able to tie the boat to the dock in the heavy chop.

On the far side of the campground, we found the hypothermic woman who was gasping for air. We decided to bring her out of the campground on the litter and get her to the electric heat of Rock Harbor as soon as possible. It took six of us to carry her to the dock and load her onto the larger boat which was already raring to go. The two campers thanked me, and then plodded back to their tents. By the time I got the Pickerel's motor started and had turned around to return to my cabin, there was only a distant light from the rapidly retreating boat in the distance, heading toward Rock Harbor.

As quickly as they had come, they were gone. Darkness enveloped me as I bounced over the white caps, into the howling wind and driving rain. All sense of direction abandoned me. The return journey would have to be by a mixture of instinct and luck.

It was then that the seriousness of my predicament hit me, and I began to pray. Moskey Basin is quite wide, but a mile or so down the channel I would encounter an area referred to as the Narrows. During the daylight, or with radar, it was easy enough to pass through as long as the captain stayed equidistant from either shore. However, I had neither radar nor daylight to guide me. On either side of the Narrows were sandbars and submerged rocks that could end the life of a boat. Waves were splashing against the bow and I had to continuously wipe the rain off my face using my hands as windshield wipers. I slowed the Pickerel to a crawl and turned my running lights off to improve my night vision. Each minute that passed felt like an eternity. Suddenly, trees loomed right in front of me. A feeling of sickness overwhelmed me as I realized that I had veered too far to the south. I was nearly on top of the submerged rocks!

I turned the boat hard to the left and listened for the telltale crunch underneath me that would indicate the tragic end of the Pickerel. Miraculously, I didn't hear it. The boat continued to putter toward the north, bringing me back to the middle of the channel. Hesitantly, I continued to inch along, and then made my turn back toward Daisy Farm.

Just when I thought I had lost my way again, I saw a faint light on the northern shore just a couple of hundred yards away. The candle in the window of my cabin glowed like a ray from heaven. I was home!

Unfortunately, I had pulled my winch system onto the shore, so there was no safe way to tie up the boat at my cabin. The main campground dock was located just a quarter of a mile away, so I headed in that direction instead.

Again, I slipped into the gloom. Creeping forward, I knew the dock was right in front of me, but I couldn't see it. I swung my flashlight back and forth trying to catch a reflector. Finally, a metal cleat glinted in the darkness. With a huge sense of relief, I grasped the dock and in the blink of an eye had two lines firmly attached. It was two o'clock in the morning by the time I fell into bed, utterly drained of strength.

By the middle of the next day, the storm had begun to lift and sunlight filtered through broken clouds. I found out that waves had been measured at 15 feet in the open lake and winds had been listed as a strong gale (47-54 mph according to the Beaufort scale). The hypothermic camper had fully recovered and life for all of us was returning to normal.

It wasn't until the early morning hours of July 5th that I truly felt my sense of peace return. I was spending the night on Davidson, a small, rocky island where the park's researchers lived. The night before we had celebrated; delicious potluck delicacies filled our stomachs, and stories and music filled the air as everyone gathered together. I had fallen asleep on the couch next to the fireplace. Everyone else had returned to their homes. At one thirty in the morning, a chill overtook the room and I awoke to embers in the fire. Suddenly, I was no longer tired and I wanted nothing more than to wander around outside. When I closed the door quietly behind me, I saw more stars in the dark sky than I ever imagined existed. They hung like sparkling diamonds in the moonless sky. Lake Superior lapped quietly along the rocky shore, and the fear and excitement of the previous days drained away, becoming a mere memory. The peace and tranquility of the island seeped back into my blood.

"Are you the ranger here?"

It was ten thirty at night on July 14th, not even two weeks since the last time I had been approached with that panicky question. I had just been rehashing the story of the previous medical emergency to Randy, my best friend, who had arrived on the island for a week-long visit that afternoon.

"A pot of boiling water fell on our scout leader and he's in a lot of pain," came a scared voice from a 13 year old boy.

I grabbed the radio, reported the emergency to Bob in Rock Harbor, and then ran down the trail to the campground. The scout leader was on the shore, writhing in pain. A pot of boiling water had fallen off the table and poured down his leg, pooling into his boot. It took a while to calm him down, but the soothing coolness of Lake Superior helped ease the pain. Blisters had already angrily erupted on his foot and leg, and I knew he would have to leave the island. Bob arrived on the scene and treated the wound as best as he could with the limited medical supplies available. The next day the scout leader sadly returned to the mainland of Michigan, unable to complete his trip as planned.

The following day, Randy and I escaped on foot into the backcountry. The weather was hot and sunny as we worked our way to Lake Richie, where we enjoyed a lunch of cheese and crackers on the edge of the glistening water. We continued hiking through the vast coniferous forest and cedar swamps until we reached West Chickenbone, where we had decided to set up camp. Chickenbone Lake, shaped like a boomerang, is surrounded by a dense mixture of trees and wetlands. It's prime habitat not only for moose, but also for mosquitoes. That afternoon, we sat in the shade of a beautiful white pine and compared life here on the island with life in the outside world.

"I've only been on the island for a month and a half but it's already difficult to imagine life on the mainland," I said while absently staring out across the deep blue ripples on the lake. "Everyone and everything that's not on the island is just kind of a fuzzy memory. I feel like I've been here for a year and a half...in a good way. When I was a kid, summers used to last forever, and this is the first summer in years that time has slowed to a crawl. Life is so simple. There is no alarm clock to wake me up. There are no cars speeding frantically up and down the streets. There are no crowds of people."

With a smile, I began to realize how much I had learned about myself. I had already spent many days comfortably alone, listening to my thoughts. I was beginning to hear the heartbeat of this island and it echoed my own.

"I need to live in a wild place," I continued. "It's where my soul is. I've never felt so free, so alive and so at peace with the world around me." We let an easy silence fall between us as the first few mosquitoes of the evening began hungrily searching for something to sate their appetites. Randy knew all along that this newfound aspect of my personality had been hiding within me. Abruptly, I continued, "The other day it suddenly occurred to me that I can do this for a living. I could work as a ranger for the National Park Service and always live and work in these wild places! I can't imagine going back to that other world now."

From that moment on, I knew what my goal would be. More than anything else, I wanted to return to the island the next summer as a paid ranger. Not so much for the money, but because I loved the job. I wanted to return as a paid ranger to prove to myself and to my family that this was not just an unrealistic dream; it could truly become a career.

By evening, the mosquitoes were swarming with unbelievable strength, forming thick clouds around our heads. Grimly, I imagined a mosquito picking me up and transporting me to a hidden swamp in the middle of nowhere. As we walked down to the edge of Chickenbone Lake, a strange phenomenon occurred. Hundreds of dragonflies came out of hiding and began to dart back and forth, just above the surface of the water, devouring mosquito after mosquito. Cautiously, we took off our head nets and were shocked to discover that there were almost no mosquitoes around us. If only we could have our own troop of guardian dragonflies to protect us wherever we went!

The distant cumulous clouds turned an unfathomable shade of pink and the lake mirrored the beauty, as dusk settled on one of the wildest places in the lower 48 states. One by one, the dragonflies disappeared, replaced by angry mosquitoes determined to drink their share of blood before we escaped into the protection of the tent.

Several nights later, Randy and I decided to climb up to the Ojibway Tower from Daisy Farm. It was nearly eight o'clock in the evening by the time we made our decision and packed our gear, with a plan to spend the night in the fire tower on the ridge top. The sun had nearly slipped below the horizon by the time we glimpsed the tower through the stands of birch and aspen. Once at the tower, we climbed the column of stairs leading to a single room with windows on all sides, which was previously used by fire lookouts who spent days on end living alone in the tower. Looking out the windows, we had a commanding view of the entire eastern half of the island, miles of Lake Superior and the distant cliff of the Sleeping Giant in Canada.

The summer dusk settled ever so slowly and one by one the distant lights of Thunder Bay, Ontario, blinked on. In a surreal sort of way, it was like looking into another world. I couldn't help but wonder what life was like there. An orange glow began to lighten the sky just over the eastern horizon. A massive, full moon seemed to rise directly out of the depths of Superior. An equally impressive thunderstorm was pummeling far-off Canada with luminous bolts of lightning. Time stood still. Mesmerized, we stared at the world around us. The experience reached a dramatic climax two hours later when a green curtain of light began dancing above the thunderstorm to the north. For the next hour, northern lights undulated back and forth in a magical, silent dance.

Meeting the Locals

The warm days of summer crept by in blissful solitude. I began to recognize certain animals near my cabin: the pileated woodpecker that often clung to the dead birch trunk near the outhouse, and the moose that sometimes wandered through the trees just beyond the trail which led to the campground. More and more, I became tuned into everything around me. I would often nestle into the comfy chair on the porch of my cabin, feet propped on a cardboard box that my food order had been delivered in, and listen to the complex array of nature's sounds for hours on end. Perhaps my favorite pastime was listening to the loons as dusk settled, their calls echoing back and forth across the harbor.

In early August, I made a startling discovery which proved to be one of the most interesting wildlife encounters of the summer. The hot days of late July and early August began tempting me to take afternoon swims. It was refreshing to jump into the invigoratingly cold water, and then sit on the steps of my porch while letting the warm sun and light breeze dry my skin.

One of those pleasant afternoons, as I was sitting on the steps letting the sun perform its magic drying act, I noticed a bee fly by and disappear beneath the step I was sitting on. I didn't think much of it until I noticed several more flying in the same direction. Curious, I began watching the hole that the bees were entering. Soon I lost track of the number of bees flying back and forth. I leaned closer and peered between the cracks of the steps. There, in plain site, was the largest, busiest bee hive I had ever seen. Thousands of bees swarmed over a massive honeycomb. My heart jumped into my throat as I recalled stories Smitty had told me, about hikers inadvertently stepping onto hives and dying from hundreds of bee stings.

I couldn't move for the next hour. Now that I was watching, it seemed like a bee was flying by every few seconds. "How could I have missed this?" I muttered under my breath. "It's been here all summer, and I've walked by, completely oblivious to it, hundreds of times."

Gradually, as I sat in stunned silence, a thought began to swirl around in my mind. "They've been here all summer," I said to anything that would listen. "They know I'm here and yet they haven't done anything!" I lingered a few more minutes, then slowly stood and walked away, half expecting to get bombarded by bees. Nothing happened. They just continued about their business.

As the days passed, I became more and more curious. Every day, I would sit on the same step and stare at this enormous, growing nest that was located just a few feet from my front door. Every day, the bees seemed as busy as before. There were thousands, perhaps millions of bees swarming around the nest, but never did they appear hostile toward me. They would sometimes fly within inches of my face. Perhaps they were as curious as I was. Little by little, I began to feel a connection I had never felt before. They knew I lived in the cabin, and I knew they lived under the steps. Each of us could be deadly to the other. We were so different, yet we had our similarities. We were simply neighbors on a wild and beautiful planet with a mutual respect for one another.

One of the great excitements of living on a remote island is the anticipation of guests arriving from the outside world. August 12th was a day I had looked forward to for quite some time. In the late morning, I jumped into the Pickerel and motored over to Mott Island. With lunch in hand, I wandered to the south side of the island to enjoy a sweeping view of Lake Superior.

My eyes strained across the gigantic body of water, anxiously awaiting the first glimpse. Suddenly, it appeared. Like a tiny toy boat in a massive bathtub, the Ranger III bobbed up and down with the waves, heading toward Isle Royale. It grew larger by the minute and soon hummed through Middle Islands Passage and into the protected waters of Rock Harbor channel. The Ranger III was our lifeline to the outside world. Tuesdays and Fridays, it arrived with mail and once a week it brought the food that we had ordered a week before. It was my only contact with the outside world. Today's boat was even more significant. I raced to the dock, a feeling of excitement nearly boiling over in me. I could feel a huge smile light up my face when I spotted my dad and my brother, John, leaning over the railing with cameras in hand.

My dad had been skeptical when I accepted a volunteer position as my first job out of college. A lot of people had been. Volunteering wasn't the norm. I needed to prove to my dad that this was where I belonged, that I had made the right decision.

Smitty walked up to me as I stood waiting for the boat's lines to be secured. "Always appreciate times like these that you spend with your father," he said with a serious look on his face. "My father died a couple of years ago and I truly wish I had more time to spend with him. It's always special to have your father with you, especially to share an experience like this."

It was a sobering thought. I had always thought of my parents as invincible. It never occurred to me that there would come a day when they would no longer be there. "When that day comes, I wonder if I will be able to say that I made the most of all the time we had together," I whispered under my breath as I stepped closer to the boat.

With smiles lighting up their faces, Dad and John stepped off the Ranger III and onto Isle Royale. The reunion was joyous. Moments later, we were all aboard the Pickerel, heading down the channel toward Daisy Farm. It was time for me to play the role of tour guide. We stopped and explored the historic Edisen Fishery, a great example of a turn of the century Isle Royale fishery.

"Commercial fishing was a huge part of Isle Royale's human history," I proudly stated. For the first time in my life, I felt like I truly knew my stuff. The island had become such a huge part of me that I wanted nothing more than to tell all of its stories. Deep down inside, I longed for my father's approval. "The Northwest Fur Company began commercial fishing on the island before 1800. By the mid 1800s, individual commercial fishermen began to set up fish houses and cabins all over the island. A man by the name of Pete Edisen operated this one for more than 50 years. The Park Service now operates it to show visitors an accurate example of the lifestyle of a commercial fisherman."

A short walk through dense spruce and fir trees brought us to the Rock Harbor lighthouse. "This lighthouse was built in 1855, to protect passing boats from running aground on these treacherous rocks. It was abandoned just 24 years later. Today, it's open to the public, and it houses a museum that highlights shipwrecks and lighthouses around the island."

Several hours later, after enjoying a spaghetti dinner in my little cabin, the three of us strapped on our backpacks and began hiking up toward the Ojibway Tower. Ominous clouds hung expectantly in the warm, moist air. The human history of Isle Royale is interesting, but it's the natural history that really fascinates me. Hiking on this trail, I was completely in my element. Not only had I hiked it so many times that I could do it blindfolded, but I could also identify nearly every species of plant on the route. John's encouraging questions opened a floodgate of information. I identified the plants and the birds. I told stories about how each species of mammal is said to have arrived on Isle Royale, and I explained how the isolation of the island creates a fragile balance between life and death.

We walked up the trail for about an hour, soaking in the silence and the beauty of our wild, pure surroundings. With dusk approaching, the temperature began to cool, yet we were perspiring slightly where our backpacks settled against our backs. We had finally reached the open meadows and rocky slopes which, to me, signaled that we were approaching our destination. Suddenly, from around a bend in the trail, an enormous, dark, moving shape appeared. It turned its head and displayed a massive, velvet covered rack of palmate antlers. We breathlessly watched this fearless moose, in the prime of its life, amble through the birch and fir trees.

As we crept away, I could feel that my father and brother were already in awe of this place that I called home.

"How many moose are there on the island?" whispered John.

"This February, the researchers estimated the number to be 500. That's before the calves were born. Just two years ago, they estimated that there were about 2400 moose on the island."

"Wow!" exclaimed John. "Why the sudden drop in population?"

"Well, look around. Notice anything wrong with the trees? They basically ate themselves out of house and home. You can see a distinct browse line on all of these fir trees. That's their winter food source. When you add the fact that we've had a couple of consecutive rough winters, and that the tick population is out of control, you can understand that it makes a deadly combination. It's pretty typical that the moose population fluctuates, but this is the most dramatic change in such a short period we've seen since the wolves arrived around 1949. Typically, the wolves keep the moose numbers from fluctuating too much. I can't wait to see what happens over the next few years."

"And what about the wolf population?" asked my dad.

I was enjoying my role as the knowledgeable tour guide. "Researchers say there are 24 wolves on the island, divided into three packs, and a few loners. The wolf population varies, according to the moose cycle. Typically there is a lag time between population rises and drops among both the wolves and moose. The moose population rises as a result of small wolf numbers. With a high moose count, the wolves begin to thrive for a period of time, up to several years, until they ultimately bring the moose population back down. At that point, the wolves begin to die due to a lack of available food. The number of wolves has been increasing recently, because of a high moose mortality rate. In fact, the last couple of winters, the wolf packs have hardly needed to make any kills because the young and the sick moose were dying left and right. It's hard to say what will happen to the wolves now that the population of moose is quite low. The moose that survived the hardships the last couple of winters are strong. They are the healthy ones, the cream of the crop. Rolf Peterson, the lead wolf/moose researcher on Isle Royale, told me that he thinks the number of moose will probably increase during the next couple of years and the wolf numbers will decrease. These natural cycles are so fascinating!"

The sun was nearly below the tree line by the time we reached the tower. We climbed the four flights of metal stairs and arranged our gear inside the small room. To the west, a dramatic show was just unfolding; the entire northwestern sky had erupted in a fiery explosion of crimson. A soft, warm breeze seemed to blow from the sun itself. We looked down on the lonely ridge top, already beginning to show the first hints of the coming change in seasons. The silence was deep and pure. Each of us stood in quiet contemplation along the railing of the tower, looking down on a storybook scene of utter wildness and perfection.

"You fit in here very nicely," said my dad. My heart skipped a beat. "It would be great if you could do this for a living. Is it possible to make a career out of it?"

Somehow he knew exactly what was on my mind. My destiny was being shaped even as I spoke. "It is possible. From what I hear, it's rather difficult to get a paid job, but it's my biggest goal to return next year as a paid National Park Service ranger."

A gentle smile crossed my dad's face and the creases around his eyes spoke a thousand words. My dream was taking shape with the support of one of the most important and influential people in my life.

A New Goal

As the small Park Service boat disappeared from the Siskiwit Bay dock, Smitty, Shawn and I crossed the adjacent meadow and entered the dense northern forest. The shadows grew long as we hiked along the Feldtmann Ridge trail, which led us away from Lake Superior and toward the heart of the island. Marshy wetlands gradually gave way to forested slopes. Five and a half miles later, a ridgeline covered with meadows greeted us, with a stately tower guarding the top.

We had arrived at the Feldtmann fire tower, a tall metal building with an inspiring view of the entire western half of the island. The last rays of sunlight were warming the earth and the first bright stars were glistening in the dark sky overhead. It was time to celebrate, and what better way to celebrate a long hike than with food! Dinner consisted of a gigantic meal of burritos and tortilla chips. We talked and laughed long into the night, underneath a sky full of stars hanging so close that I almost imagined we could touch them.

The summer was waning, and a disturbing feeling was beginning to gnaw at my stomach. It was August 22nd and I had less than two weeks left on the island. A summer that at times seemed to stretch on forever was slowly coming to an end. The thought of returning to my mainland lifestyle was suddenly terrifying. What did I have to return to? I no longer had a girlfriend, a job or even a place to live. And more importantly, could I even return to the society I had left behind? Most of my friends were still living in the area, but would I even be able to relate to them anymore? They were completely content rushing to work, going to the same restaurants, the same bars and the same places they had been frequenting for years. How could I even begin to explain how I had changed?

Over the next three days, we backpacked over 52 miles under a warm sun and a brilliant blue sky. On our last day, as we neared McCargoe Cove and the end of the rugged Minong Ridge trail, Smitty stopped with a smile on his face. "I have an idea," he said. "Next year, let's hike the Minong in a day!"

"Is that possible?" I asked, already knowing the answer.

"As far as I know," continued Smitty in that same confident voice, "we would be the first to ever try it. It would be far more difficult than the Greenstone. In fact, it's about 48 miles from end to end via the Minong

Ridge trail, and far more rugged than the Greenstone. You've seen that the trail isn't maintained, and it doesn't even have boardwalks across some of the swamps. It would definitely be a challenge, both mentally and physically."

"Count me in!" I exclaimed. Any mention of being back on the island the next year was music to my ears. Looking forward to an adventure of that caliber was enough to propel me past the harsh realities that would confront me on the mainland over the winter.

The Sunset of Summer

As dawn broke on September 1st, I lay quietly in my tent listening to the loons in the nearby harbor. An hour or so later, I had packed up my belongings and was backpacking away from Threemile campground, toward the ridge. It was time to begin my goodbyes. It didn't take long to reach the familiar Greenstone ridge. As I approached Mount Franklin, I slowed my pace.

"I don't want it to end," I said to the trees. I clambered up the large rock on top of the mountain. A cliff dropped steeply below me revealing a tremendous view of secluded lakes, islands and meadows. I thought about how nervous I was the first time I set foot on Isle Royale. With a smile, I realized how much I had grown. I was beginning to know my inner self like few people do. I would never be the same.

In the far off distance, beyond an immense wilderness of frigid water, lay Canada. I closed my eyes and let the wind caress my face. I tried to memorize every sight, sound, feeling and smell, so that when times got rough in the outside world I could close my eyes and return to this moment in time. As the moments passed, a deep sense of sadness welled up from my soul. How does one say goodbye to such a pure and perfect place? With tears streaming down my face, I turned from the mountain top and headed back toward Daisy Farm. I didn't want to leave Isle Royale because I knew that I would never feel this free again.

The big day arrived on September 3rd. A knot formed in my stomach as I said my goodbyes to Smitty and Shawn and reluctantly boarded the giant blue boat tied up at the dock on Mott Island. Moments later, the Ranger III was coasting down the channel, gliding through Middle Islands Passage and turning away from the island of dreams. As I looked back toward the gradually disappearing wilderness, a strange peace came over me. In the depths of my soul, I knew I would return.

The Wrong Side of Michigan

Houghton, Michigan, was an absolute shock to my system. The noise that I had been separated from for months now filled my ears and vibrated through my very being. Cars seemed to zip by in every direction. I had just started my car for the first time in over three months and I sat frozen behind the wheel.

Deliberately, I eased out into the roaring traffic and soon realized I was barreling down the highway at a terrifying speed. Buildings became a blur out my window as I gripped the steering wheel, willing myself to go on. Suddenly, out of nowhere, a car flashed past me, followed by another on its bumper. My first thought was that one of those two cars was going to get somebody killed. I risked a glance at my speedometer and realized I was only going 20 miles per hour! After a summer of traveling no faster than a boat powered by a 30 horse power engine, everything felt as if it were moving in fast forward. "What's the big hurry?!?" I yelled at the next car that whizzed by.

A strange thought entered my mind. "Does Isle Royale really exist?" I wondered. While on the island, everything else ceases to exist, but once off the island, I was left wondering if all that just happened was only a dream, an unbelievably realistic dream.

The following day, as I neared the great Mackinaw Bridge, which connects the upper and lower peninsulas of Michigan, I heaved a deep sigh and leaned my head against the window. The bridge was only a couple of hundred yards in front of me when, on impulse, I veered off onto an exit.

"I can't do this!" I cried. "It's all wrong. This is not where I'm meant to be!" I tried to cross the bridge three more times, swerving onto the exit at the last minute each time. To me, this giant bridge represented the last gateway separating civilization from the wilds of the Northwoods. By crossing, I was forced to admit that I was leaving the wilderness and entering civilization. Just then it occurred to me that I was no longer going home. I had left my home behind.

Chapter 2:

1998: Return to Paradise

A blanket of white covered the ground as the first rays of glorious sunshine poured over the fields and forests near Grant, Michigan. It was January 2nd, 1998, and I wanted nothing more than to escape into the backcountry.

Randy and I jumped into my red Chevy Corsica and turned north onto M37. Scattered throughout the car was an assortment of gear, from cross country skis and snow shovels to full backpacks and a tent. Our goal, however, was to survive without the tent for the next two nights. On several occasions in the past, we had built a quin-zhee, or snow shelter, to sleep in. We had piled snow high into a dome, let it settle and harden for an hour and then methodically dug a tunnel inward. From there, we rounded out a sleeping area inside, complete with shelves and air holes scattered around the dome. One night at a time was the most we had stayed underneath the snow, but this trip would be different.

The farther north we drove, the greater the number of trees that surrounded us and the more my heart relaxed. The sun was shining bright and warm in the cloudless sky.

"I read this really strange story the other day," I said. "It was told by a missionary from the jungles of Africa when he returned to his support church back in the states a month or so after the incident. He was living in a small village in the jungle and would travel once a week to a city nearby to get money and medical supplies. The only way to get to the city was to hike through a wild stretch of jungle. It was such a long journey that he was in the habit of camping in the jungle on the way back. The missionary loved his time alone in the jungle and often used that time to pray and meditate. He said that he often feels close to God in a wild place."

"One day, while in the city, he was unknowingly followed by a rather shady character. The stranger had seen the missionary before and figured that he must be from the village in the jungle. Hatred welled in his heart and he decided to grab a couple of his friends and follow the missionary into the jungle that evening so they could rob and kill him."

"The missionary left the city in the late afternoon and set up camp just before dark. He lit a fire and began his prayer time. As usual, he felt the close presence of God. The night passed without incident and he returned to his village the next morning."

"The following week, while back in the city, the same shady stranger approached him and said he had a confession to make. He told the missionary that he and several of his friends had followed him into the jungle the week before. They watched him set up camp and were going to rob and kill him after dark. Just as darkness fell, they were startled to see that the missionary was not alone. Surrounding him were 18 armed guards with huge swords. Wide-eyed, the missionary didn't know what to say. He knew he had been alone in the jungle."

"The missionary finished this story while at his support church back in the states. Suddenly, a man from the congregation stood up and asked when that incident had occurred. The missionary narrowed it down to the exact night and said it was probably the early morning here in America. The man from the congregation then said that he was out golfing that morning and suddenly had a deep feeling that he needed to pray for his missionary friend so many miles away. The feeling was so intense, that he left the golf course and got some members of the congregation together to pray."

"A silence fell over the congregation. Then suddenly the missionary asked those who had gotten together to pray that morning to stand up. Eighteen people stood up."

There was silence in the car as both Randy and I soaked in the meaning of the story. We turned off the highway and onto a small road, our trailhead nearly in sight.

"Do you believe it?" asked Randy.

"I don't know," I said. "If it is true, it's pretty powerful."

"I wish I had some obvious sign like that from God," replied Randy. "I want to believe He's here, but how can you be sure when He doesn't seem to make Himself known to the average person? What if the missionary made up that story?"

"I don't know any more than you do Randy, but what if he didn't?" I countered. "That would mean there is an incredibly powerful being up there who does listen to prayer."

"Maybe we should start praying for the snow to last!" said Randy, with a smile. "The sun is downright hot today!"

With that, we slipped into another conversation. But deep down inside, we both had a nagging feeling about something. If there is a God, why doesn't He show Himself to us? Little did we know the full implications of that thought.

It was late morning by the time we pulled up to Red Bridge on Coates road and began hiking down the Manistee River trail. There was still a fair amount of snow, but it was melting before our eyes. Randy had rigged up a sled that he would drag behind himself to carry his skis, shovel and a few other necessities. My skis were strapped to my pack, the tips 10 feet above the ground. We hiked along a ridge above the river enjoying some sweeping views of rolling hills covered with skeleton trees. Babbling brooks meandered along hidden glens full of silent trees.

By mid afternoon, it was apparent that we would not be building a quin-zhee. The snow was practically a memory. We decided to set up camp on a high ridge with awesome views of the river far below. Clouds were creeping in from the west and a light breeze was whispering through the adjacent white pines. All of a sudden, we realized we had left the tent in the car, assuming we would not need it. We rested our packs against a tree and raced the three miles back to the car. Darkness was upon us and the weather had begun to change by the time we arrived back at our campsite.

We sat down to cook dinner just outside the tent door. The ridge dropped down a steep slope beyond our feet to the river below. Gusts of wind soon began pummeling the tree tops around us. It was still too early to turn in, so we decided to take a walk.

Deeply engrossed in conversation, we walked down a dark, lonely two-track road. The wind howled eerily through the forest, like a ghost on patrol. Soon, the conversation steered back towards the missionary story I had told earlier. Minutes turned into hours as we strolled through the darkness talking about the spiritual world. For no reason I knew, the hairs on the back of my neck began to rise. A sense of foreboding crept into my consciousness. We had come to an open field, well away from our camp, with several old, abandoned cabins along our path. Our conversation became choppy as we walked by the empty windows and into a black evergreen forest beyond. Just in front of us, a metal sign hung from a wire and was rattling in the wind.

"This place creeps me out," whispered Randy.

"I agree one hundred percent," I answered quickly. Maybe our spirituality conversation was getting to me. "This place seems evil. Let's get back to the tent."

We retraced our steps through the dark, evergreen forest, past the deserted houses and back into familiar territory. I couldn't shake the eerie feeling that someone or something was watching us, but we still couldn't stop talking about angels, demons and spirits.

I breathed a sigh of relief when we arrived back at the tent. Within minutes, we were enveloped safely in our warm sleeping bags, as the winds roared up and down the nearby ravines. Still, we couldn't sleep and in no time at all we returned to our previous conversation. I lit a candle lantern and hung it from the tent ceiling. A warm glow illuminated the tent.

The conversation grew quite animated and finally Randy exclaimed, "God, if you are up there, show us a sign!"

It came with a roar. A blast of wind raced up the ravine, rocking the tent and sending the candle lantern spinning out of control.

"Okay, Okay!" Randy gasped. "We get the picture!" The roar quieted to a purr, leaving the lantern spinning slowly above us. We looked at each other with matching expressions of disbelief and shock.

"Do you think that was a sign?" I asked breathlessly.

"I don't know," replied Randy, "but something powerful is going on around us. Maybe we should take the candle lantern down before it lights this tent like a torch."

It was after midnight and fatigue was setting in. We began to nod off when an ominous sound began in the depths of a nearby ravine. It was a roar unlike anything we had ever heard. It grew by the second until the ground began to shake. A blast of wind pummeled the tent, flattening it in an instant. It picked me up and tossed me against Randy. The top of the tent pushed down on me so hard I had to push back with all my might just to open enough space so that I could breathe. The howling roar reached a deafening level, and we were suspended in a moment of awe.

As quickly as the wind came upon us, it left. We cautiously stepped outside of the tent, still listening to nearby wind gusts roar up hidden ravines. Strangely, it was so calm where we stood that we could have dropped a feather and it would have fallen straight down to the soggy earth. My tent had been secured with eight stakes. All eight had vanished. One of the poles was bent at a sickening angle.

"That was a close one," I said, as I looked down the steep embankment towards the river, which was bathed in darkness. "Maybe that's a sign that we need to move the tent away from the edge."

We moved the tent and fell, exhausted, into our sleeping bags. Not a breath of wind ruffled the tent the rest of the night despite the continued dreaded howling up the adjacent ravines. We awoke the next morning to the sound of gentle rain pattering against the nylon tent fly. The day seemed to pass by as if we were in a dream. Dense mist hung in the air all day and periodic cold showers fell from the sodden sky. We eagerly explored up and down the ravines, finding hidden glens filled with lush ferns and peaceful babbling brooks. A sense of tranquility permeated our conversation, as if somehow we knew that we were in good hands.

That evening, we looked at all of our winter gear scattered around on the snowless ground. Randy broached the question we had both been avoiding. "How are we going to get all of this gear back to the car with no snow to slide it on?"

"Maybe we should leave this one up to God," I said with a chuckle. "You never know. We might get a massive snow storm tonight."

That night, we repeated our previous night's route through the forest, but instead of sensing something evil, we continued to feel a deep sense of peace and happiness. The next morning, my mouth dropped open when I stepped out of the tent. A thin layer of ice covered everything. It was thin enough that our boots could break through but thick enough to slide a sled full of gear with ease. An answered prayer!

I walked over to the edge of the ravine and said a silent "Thank you." Just then, something caught my attention above the river at eye level.

"Randy- look!" I exclaimed. "A bald eagle!" The eagle flew by and landed in a tree just across the river. For countless minutes, the eagle seemed to be looking right at us.

"Maybe that's our guardian angel?" whispered Randy. "Or maybe it's God Himself coming to us in the form of an eagle."

"Whatever it is," I said, "it's a good sign. There is hope after all."

For the weeks and months that followed, I desperately held onto that symbol of hope. The next time Randy and I got together, he showed me a picture he had taken the day after the wind storm. It showed our tent, sitting where we had hastily set it up in the middle of the night. On the right side of the picture was the edge of the ravine, where the tent had been when it was bowled over. Perhaps it was from a drop of water that got in the camera or perhaps an error in the developing, but whatever the reason, the image next to the ravine was spine-tingling. Right where the tent had been was a ghostly image in the shape of an angel.

No Ordinary Life

As the days of winter grew longer, I couldn't keep the image of that eagle out of my mind. It continued to be my symbol of hope that helped me weather a difficult time in my life. Without Isle Royale, I felt lost. I had transferred from one meaningless job to the next, anxiously awaiting confirmation that I would return to the only place that I felt completely at peace. Many of my friends couldn't understand me anymore and decided to keep their distance. I lived at home with my parents who remained encouraging, but I couldn't shake the feeling that I had somehow regressed in life.

A warm spell in late March only intensified my feeling of discomfort. I was now working for an environmental company at the edge of the city. It sounded good on paper, but the reality of it was that I was an indoor salesman. I was selling environmental wastewater equipment via computer and phone. My office was a small room filled with computers, printers and a fax machine. At the far end of the room was a tiny window that looked out onto a manicured lawn.

One day, as I was staring out the window dreaming of life anywhere but there, my boss walked into the room and said, "Can I see you in my office, Mike?" It sounded like a question, but it really wasn't. I slowly pulled my eyes away from the window and walked out of my depressing office into a large, spacious office with two massive windows looking out over a parking lot.

"I have an offer for you," began my boss. "How would you like to work for us full time? I could give you a good salary, benefits and the guarantee of a year-round job. How does that sound?" He looked at me with the calm assurance of someone who knew exactly what his employee would say next. What came out of my mouth was a bit of a surprise.

"I'm sorry," I began, "I'm just not interested."

He looked at me as if I was suddenly a hideous alien from another planet. "Why on earth not?" he exclaimed after an awkward pause. "This is a good job and a good place to live."

A dreamy look crossed my face. "I want to see what else is out there," I said, slowly gaining confidence. "The world is a big place."

My boss sighed. "Listen," he said with one last effort, "I have lived in lots of places around the country and the world and this city is perhaps the best place I've ever lived. Grand Rapids is an excellent place to settle down!"

"Maybe this is a great place to live," I continued adamantly. "*You* know that, but *I* don't! I haven't seen what else is out there. Everyone expects me to settle down now that I'm out of college. They want me to get a high paying job, get married, have kids and live in a big house in the suburbs. How often does that *really* bring happiness?" I was on a roll now. "I'm 23 years old. Why on earth would I *want* to settle down here?"

The conversation was over. I had overstayed my welcome. Dejectedly, I wandered back to my miserable office and stared out the window at a passing jet high in the sky. "I wonder where you're going?" I said quietly.

My friend from the adjacent office poked his head in the door. "What was that all about?" he asked hesitantly.

"I just refused an ordinary life," I said with a growing smile.

"Good for you," he said. "At least one of us will get out and do something interesting. Look at me, I'm stuck here."

The very next day, like a message straight from heaven, came the call from Smitty asking if I would like a paid job as a National Park Service ranger on Isle Royale. I was returning to paradise without a backwards glance!

Guardian Eagles

May 1st arrived with startlingly blue skies and a blazing sun. I said a tearful goodbye to my mom, and then drove off into the "wild blue yonder." By the 6th of May, I was in Porcupine Mountain Wilderness State Park in the Upper Peninsula of Michigan. My body was bursting with excitement as I began a five day backpacking trip. I parked my car at Lake of the Clouds overlook and literally skipped down the Lake Superior trail, reveling in my return to the Northwoods.

A pain in the arch of my foot began gradually, but soon became severe. By the time I neared the shoreline of Lake Superior, it felt as if each end were in a vice that pulled sickeningly in opposite directions. I could barely walk as I hauled myself onto a rock overlooking the gigantic lake.

"What on earth is wrong with me?" I pleaded to my closest companion, a curious herring gull. "How am I supposed to finish this backpacking trip if I can hardly walk? And more importantly, what will I do this summer if I have troubles walking? I'm leaving for the island in one week!" It was my worst nightmare to begin a season on Isle Royale with an injured foot.

"God, if you can hear me, please help," I whispered.

I rubbed my foot, soaked it in the frigid water and pulled out my lunch. The gentle lapping of the water combined with the warm sunshine on my back was hypnotic. I forgot about my pain and lost track of time. My mind was consumed with the thought that I wanted to live my life to its fullest. Suddenly, I broke out of the trance and realized several hours had passed. Like a bolt of lightning, I was back on the trail hiking southwest toward Big Carp River. Hours passed in blissful happiness. When I reached the Big Carp River trail, I decided to take a side trip up to Shining Cloud Falls. The trail wound up from the lake and meandered right next to a deep drop-off to a rushing river below. It was then that I remembered my foot. It didn't hurt anymore!

"Thank you, God!" I said out loud. The words had barely left my mouth when something startled me. A massive bald eagle soared by, not more than six feet away. Surely my guardian angels were in the form of eagles. I was in good hands. It was going to be a summer I would never forget.

A Glimmer of Enchantment

I stood, eyes straining out the bow windows of the Ranger III, anxious to catch a glimpse. Dense fog hung in thick curtains around the boat. I knew we were close, but still it eluded my sight. Seconds ticked into minutes. Suddenly, it appeared from within the deep white mist; a ghostly image of a rocky, rugged shoreline covered with twisted balsam firs and bright orange lichen. Impressive, white capped waves crashed into the rocks and sent white water spraying high into the air. We had come to a wilderness deep in the heart of an unforgiving freshwater sea, a collection of wild and rugged islands thrown precariously amongst the deep, cold, crystal blue waters of Lake Superior. We had arrived at Isle Royale.

Within minutes, I could make out the opening to Conglomerate Bay, then Tonkin Bay. Rock Harbor lighthouse appeared as a white beacon on the hillside, welcoming me home. I looked west down the harbor, trying to catch a glimpse of my former cabin. Soon, Daisy Farm was in view. I looked up, hoping to see the mighty fortress atop the Greenstone Ridge. The Ojibway Tower was there, just as I had left it. I smiled as I looked around, trying to soak up this feeling. "It's all here, exactly as I remember it, just as if I had never left," I whispered to the wind.

It wasn't until I was off the boat and walking down the trail to my new home that I could truly comprehend the magnitude of it all. I was once again living my dream!

This summer would certainly be different than the last. I was going to live in Rock Harbor, the main portal for all visitors arriving at the east end of the island. There was a visitor center, a small store, a lodge and a restaurant. My job was to educate the public and try to connect them to this place by presenting evening programs, leading guided walks and helping to operate the visitor center. I was going to live in a cabin nearby, called the Ralph house, with two other employees, Bill Kinjorski and Otis Johnson.

I ambled slowly down the Rock Harbor trail listening to the perfect song of white throated sparrows. The sweet smell of balsam fir filled my soul with contentment and my heart soared with happiness. A narrow side trail brought me down to the water's edge and in front of me sat a beautiful, old, log cabin with a wide, screened-in porch along the front. Framed through the trees was a stunning view of Rock Harbor channel, several small, rocky islands and the pounding waves of the open lake beyond. I smiled the smile of someone who is at the very start of a grand adventure. It was day one of an exciting journey, and countless days of absolute happiness stretched out in front of me like the first day of summer vacation.

The next day, Smitty and I were sitting in his office, discussing the adventures of the previous summer and the plans for the one ahead, when suddenly he interrupted himself.

"You know, there's a girl working on our staff this summer that I think you'll really get along with very well."

"Do tell!" I said.

"Her name is Susanna. She grew up here, on the island. Her dad had my job, as Chief of Interpretation. A couple of summers ago, she lived on the Kenai Peninsula of Alaska and I just pulled her out of Puerto Rico, where she's finishing up a semester abroad."

"Sounds good so far," I said hesitantly.

"She's 20 years old and hasn't been back to the island since her family moved away, when she was 13. I think she's even more excited than you were to come back! She looks great on paper anyway."

I had to wait nearly two weeks before I met her in person. I spent the time in between hiking as much as I could. Smitty and I backpacked together on nine of those days, covering over 100 miles of rugged terrain. Over a third of the mileage was "cross country", meaning that we didn't follow the trails; instead, we used a map and compass to find our way to undiscovered places. We bushwhacked through some of the wildest land I had ever imagined. Our conversations focused on one of two things: adventures, past, present or future, and women. By the time those nine days were over, I was more anxious than ever to meet this mystery girl.

The big day arrived on the 27th of May. As the Ranger III pulled into the dock at Rock Harbor, I couldn't help but wonder if there was someone on board who would change my life. As the new staff descended the boat ramp, I instantly knew which one was Susanna. She was absolutely stunning. Her wavy, blonde hair fell gracefully to her shoulders and her strong, fit body flexed as she picked up her backpack. Deep brown eyes took in the scene around us as if she was trying to soak up every moment. It was then that she smiled. If I hadn't been holding onto one of the dock pilings, I probably would have ended up floundering in the frigid waters of Lake Superior. Her smile not only lit up her own face, but it seemed to light up everyone else's, as well. Every guy within a half mile radius was instantly under her spell.

My head was swimming as introductions were being made. Suddenly, I was aware that Susanna was taking a step toward me.

"Hi. My name is Susanna," she said with a shy smile.

"I...ah...well...ah...my name is Mike," I said, and instantly wished that I could crawl under the dock and hide. But her eyes smiled delightfully and our friendship began.

The following day, I drove the new seasonal staff around Scoville Point and into the protected water of Tobin Harbor. On the north shore of the harbor is a small dock and a trailhead. This was the exact location that Smitty and I had ended our marathon hike the year before. The current plan was that everyone was going to hike back to Rock Harbor by climbing from Hidden Lake up to the Greenstone Ridge, following the trail to Mount Franklin, descending, and taking the Tobin Harbor trail to Rock Harbor. I planned to drive the boat back to Rock Harbor and then hike up the Tobin Harbor trail to meet them at Mount Franklin.

The thought of Mount Franklin stirred in me a hidden memory from the end of last year. I desperately wanted to beat the rest of the group there so I could spend a few moments alone feeling the wind on my face and soaking in the feeling of my return to paradise.

Half an hour later, I had the boat tied up at the Rock Harbor dock and was striding confidently into the forest. "What a change from the beginning of last year!" I exclaimed out loud. Fire seemed to fly from my feet as I raced along the Tobin Harbor trail and up the Mount Franklin trail. As I approached the rocky outcropping on the top of the mountain, I slowed my pace and a strange sensation flooded my soul.

So much had happened since I had last stood here with tears flowing unchecked and a determination to one day return to this magical island. In some ways, it felt like it was just yesterday, but in other ways it felt like a lifetime ago. I closed my eyes as a gentle breeze kissed my face. "I'm back!" I said to the trees as I happily strode on down the trail.

Hooked on Adventure

It was late afternoon on May 31st and I was exploring off-trail, through the dense, green forest near the Ralph house. Low clouds hung in a gray sky and the forest was dripping from a recent rain. I was just cresting a small hill when something on the ground caught my attention. My heart skipped a beat as I looked down on a dead moose calf that couldn't have died more than a day or two before. A few flies had found him and were crawling in and out of his open mouth.

"How did you die, little fellow?" I whispered as I bent down to get a better look. Suddenly, an uneasy feeling overcame me; I felt that I was being watched. The hairs on the back of my neck stood on end as I turned to face a dark shadow walking around a dense thicket of alder. The mother moose appeared, and she was furious! As most mother animals are, she was extremely defensive of her young, dead or alive. Her ears flattened and she lowered her head in a terrifying charge.

One of the first things incoming rangers learn about Isle Royale is how to read moose. "The first two signs of aggression you often see in moose are the flattening of the ears backward and the hair on the back of the neck standing up," said Rolf Peterson, the head moose researcher on the island, during training. "This may be the precursor to a charge, so beware!"

It took me a split second to comprehend the situation and another to turn and run. I raced down the slope, the sound of thunderous footsteps pounding one step behind me. A moose can run at more than 30 mph, so I had very little time to get to safety. The adrenaline rush was so intense that my vision momentarily blurred. In a flash of clarity, I noticed a tree to my right and lunged behind it. Silence enveloped the forest. With wide eyes and a frantic heartbeat I peered out from behind the cover of the tree. Standing just 20 feet away was a gigantic moose swaying her head back and forth, in an expression of utter fury.

For the next ten minutes, a stalemate hung in the air between me and the cow moose. I didn't move a muscle, and she refused to back down. Finally, with a snort, she turned and walked back to her calf. A few more minutes filled with tension passed before I got up enough nerve to sprint to a more distant tree. My escape seemed to take forever as I ran from tree to tree, finally reaching the Tobin Harbor trail.

My heart was pounding as I entered the Ben East house, where Susanna lived with two Student Conservation Association volunteers, Shannon and Heather. Since setting foot on Isle Royale, they had been talking nonstop about their hopes of seeing a moose. After I told them about my recent encounter, both Susanna and Shannon were intrigued.

"I'd be happy to show you where it is," I said. The excitement level jumped a notch as both girls eagerly followed me outside, on our way to spotting a moose.

Soon, we entered the forest near the little hill where the dead moose calf lay. We crept along like thieves. Our plan was to make a wide circle around the area to give the cow moose plenty of space. Despite the adrenalin packed afternoon, the only thing I could concentrate on was the fact that Susanna was walking right next to me. My thoughts turned inward as I wondered if this was the girl for me. All of a sudden, a loud 'crack' broke the silence and instantly brought me back to the present. Our heads spun around just in time to see a large moose barreling toward us.

Shannon and I took off running. After a few steps, I stopped with the realization that Susanna wasn't following us. She stood, calmly watching the approaching whirlwind, as if this was the most normal thing in the world. Her soul was truly a part of the island. She was home.

"You have to run, Susanna!" I shouted. The moose thundered ever closer. To my relief, she sprinted past me with a wild smile on her face and into the safety of the dense forest. The three of us reunited along the trail, our sides heaving and our hands on our knees to prevent them from collapsing beneath us.

"That was close," I panted. "Maybe she doesn't want us hanging around there." That was the understatement of the year. I looked at my two companions and nearly burst out laughing. It was Susanna's first moose sighting in seven years and it was Shannon's first time ever to see a moose.

Both girls had smiles that stretched from ear to ear and looked like they were ready to run right back into the forest to try to see the moose again.

"That was awesome!" said Susanna with a glimmer in her eye. She was hooked. From deep down in her soul, she was a moose spotter. It wouldn't be the last time we would find ourselves in close proximity to the largest member of the deer family.

Susanna and I clicked from that moment on. She was so easy to talk to and always yearning for an adventure. We talked about anything and everything, from trivial small talk to serious, philosophical and religious beliefs. We even talked about the number of kids we wanted to have and the qualities we looked for in a future spouse. We went on numerous backcountry trips together, just the two of us in a lonely, romantic wilderness. But there was an invisible boundary between us. Much to my dismay, we always talked as if our mates would be other people. Our friendship grew deeper, but friendship was all there was. Susanna made it quite apparent without having to broach the subject that this was all she was willing to give.

At nine o'clock on the evening of June 15th, we set off in my canoe. The Northwoods summer sun dominated the sky and darkness lingered an hour and a half below the horizon. We paddled past several tiny, rocky islands, each with a few stately trees clinging to life.

"Let's go look for some moose," Susanna said, with that glimmer in her eye that meant she was ready for an adventure.

Hidden Lake is a great place to spot moose, especially at dusk. There's a natural salt lick in the wetland area on the far side of the lake. Moose frequent the area and lick the salt, especially in the early summer after surviving a long winter on a diet lacking salt. We pulled the canoe up onto the shore near the narrow piece of land that separates the harbor from the lake. Ever so quietly, we left the canoe in the bushes and crawled to the shoreline of the lake. Immediately, Susanna spotted two young moose.

"They're probably no more than a year or two old," I whispered. "It looks like they're alone, though-no mother to protect them."

We decided to walk around to the far side of the salt lick to see if there were any more moose in that area. Cautiously, we crossed a spongy bog, sinking ankle deep in wet moss. We entered a very thick spruce forest with branches that seemed to grasp at our clothes. With a feeling of unease, we followed an animal trail that led us through the trees. My pulse quickened as I looked around at hundreds of moose prints on what seemed to be a moose highway heading toward their salty hors' devours. After walking for a minute or so, we emerged from the forest and found ourselves on the edge of the marshy salt lick. A few steps across an open piece of land brought us to a twisted, sorry excuse for a spruce tree. The light was fading fast as we watched one of the young moose feeding a few hundred yards away.

Ours ears perked up as a low sound resembling thunder began to resonate from deep within the forest. Instinctively, we moved halfway around the pitiful spruce tree until only our heads were peering toward the dark entrance we had come out of just a few minutes earlier. The ominous sound grew louder and the ground began to vibrate beneath our feet as an enormous cow moose emerged from the forest. Following her were two tiny calves, perhaps one or two weeks old.

The three moose walked within five feet of us as they calmly plodded toward the lake, some 50 feet away. Much to our growing dismay, the calves sensed our presence. While the cow moose slurped noisily from the lake, the calves approached us. They inched closer, their ears standing on end with curiosity. They were absolutely fearless knowing that their powerful protector was nearby.

"Go away!" I whispered. "Shoo!" My words had no effect. They seemed determined to check us out. There were no good escape options. We were completely immersed in their territory, far from safety. Our options were to stay behind the pathetic spruce tree or make a run for it into the dark forest. We huddled down as far as we could and began to pray, heartbeats thundering in fear.

A moment later, the calm mother moose issued a loud snort. The calves instantly whirled and ran back to their defender, then wandered along the shore of the lake. In the silence of the growing night, I exhaled so loudly that I thought they might turn around and charge us, but within minutes they were out of sight.

Soon, we were creeping back through the eerie, dark forest, across the bog and to our waiting canoe. I didn't fully breathe a sigh of relief until we were well away from shore drifting through a serenade of loons. "This is what life is all about," I whispered to Susanna. "What an incredible opportunity to experience a part of nature that others will only see on the Discovery channel."

Instead of discouraging us, the close call only brought about more adventures. We began canoeing together every chance we had. One of our favorite things to do was glide in the canoe onto the glass-calm waters of Tobin Harbor in the early evening. Silently, we would watch the sun set, dusk grow, and the first crystalline stars appear in the black sky above. We'd smile as the loons called out in the darkness, their perfect voices echoing back and forth between the forested hills. Well after dark, we would slip back to shore, return the canoe to its resting spot and say goodnight.

Then there were the nights when an ancient magic awakened in the heavens. The sky danced with green ribbons of light in an intensity I've rarely seen. Susanna and I would sit on the Tobin Harbor dock, shoulder to shoulder, and watch as the northern lights pulsated for hours. I could almost imagine the world slowly spinning on its axis.

Even if I had dreamed it, I couldn't have imagined a more romantic time in my life. But the invisible barrier between us had never been breached, and I wondered if we were destined to simply be close friends who shared the wonders of the world together.

Secrets of the Minong

As the days of June melted into July, I began to think more and more about my upcoming adventure. After we hiked the Greenstone trail in a single day last year, several people had criticized us. "How can that be any fun?" they said. "How can you see anything while hiking that fast?" It was almost as if we had personally offended them by hiking the length of the island in a day.

It was because of this wave of criticism that we decided to keep the idea of hiking the Minong in one day an absolute secret. "I'm not in it to make a name for myself," said Smitty in disgust. "As far as I'm concerned, nobody has to know. I think it's an amazing challenge and an adventure of a lifetime and that's all that counts!"

"I agree!" I chimed in. "Let's keep it quiet. Rumors will probably begin to fly after the fact, but that's the stuff that makes legends!"

On the morning of July 3rd, Smitty, Shawn and I rose at three o'clock in the morning and were following the narrow beams of our headlamps out into the Isle Royale night half an hour later. A few stars strained to be seen through a thick mantle of clouds. We hiked along the Tobin Harbor trail and turned towards Mount Franklin. By five o'clock, a miserable rain had begun to fall through the darkness, soaking our clothes and seeping into our skin.

The moose didn't seem to mind the weather; by the time we had arrived at the official starting point of the Minong Ridge trail, McCargoe Cove, we had already seen eight moose! It was just after nine o'clock in the morning, and we had hiked more than 15 miles.

It was sheer determination alone that allowed me to complete those first 15 miles. We had all hiked this stretch of trail many times before, so the excitement level was low. This combined with the weather had necessitated that our willpower kick into overdrive just to keep us going. All of this changed, however, when we set foot on the Minong. Instantly, my mood changed as a burst of excitement coursed through my veins. As if in response to our increased excitement, the rain stopped and soon a warm sun began to filter through rapidly dispersing clouds. Our conversations became spirited and our bodies responded to our abrupt attitude change with a burst of unbounded energy.

At one o'clock, we stopped at Todd Harbor for lunch, already 22 miles into our journey. "Almost half way!" exclaimed Smitty. The sun broke out of the clouds and dried the last of our gear. That afternoon we passed through some of the most rugged and beautiful terrain on the island. By mid afternoon, however, the sun was becoming our enemy. On top of the sizzling, exposed ridges of the Minong, we found ourselves guzzling the last of our water. In late afternoon, Smitty and I clambered down the half mile detour to North Lake Desor to fill our water bottles. We had hiked more than 34 miles, but the last five miles had taken their toll.

As Smitty, Shawn and I relaxed in the cool shade near the trail junction to North Desor, we faced the possibility that we wouldn't be able to complete this trail in a single day. Carrying only day packs and a dwindling amount of food, the prospect of spending the night along the trail was not appealing. We analyzed the trail in our minds; the next 10 miles would make or break us, as it wound through thick forests, over ankle-turning, rocky outcrops, and around a myriad of obstacles. Wetlands and beaver ponds dotted the landscape, bringing into question how we would cross through the oppressive mud and water and still make it to the other side with dry boots. Wet boots would cause our feet to blister within a mile on a trail as rugged as this one. To compound all of these other problems we could expect a frightening army of mosquitoes to emerge with the onset of dusk.

When we set out on our hike again, I thought I was going to faint. My feet felt like they had been worn down to nubs and they clung weakly to my sore ankles. My legs ached and cramped up, causing spasms that made it difficult to continue. I limped noticeably for the first hundred feet. But something that I cannot explain happens to a person at that point of a physical challenge. The adrenaline kicks in and soon the rhythm of the trail seeps into your mind, body, and soul, cheering you on and adding a spring to your step. Your mind pushes the pain away and simply commands your body to walk. Step, two, three, four, step, two, three, four. I slipped into a dream-like sensation and motored down the trail as if I had just started out on a mile-long stroll. All three of us seemed to get in sync with this rhythm as the hours stretched on into dusk.

My mind slipped into a trance as my feet carried me along, but it was jolted back into reality when I spotted a trail junction, marked by a slender brown sign. "Just over two miles to Windigo!" Smitty cried. It was nearly dark and the thick forest around us was beginning to glow with a silver sheen as the half moon illuminated the land. My senses remained alert during that last hour of walking- even the forest seemed energized.

Finally, we passed Washington Creek Campground and less than half a mile later, we touched the sign marking our destination, "WINDIGO." We had done it!! What most people thought was either impossible or simply insane, we had accomplished. Our friends in Windigo were pretty surprised to see us. They asked a few specific questions, and we filled in the blanks. The legend had begun.

Our journey wasn't over yet. We still had to get back to Rock Harbor. After a day of rest, celebration, socializing with friends and consuming vast quantities of ice cream, we prepared mentally for another marathon. At three thirty in the morning on July fifth, we began hiking back to Rock Harbor via the Greenstone Ridge trail. Our mood was certainly lighter that day. We had nothing to prove. Stories and laughter bubbled out from within us as if it were the last time we would be able to tell them. Molly McGee from Tennessee was discussed in great detail, much to Shawn's dismay. At times, I laughed so hard that my stomach ached and tears streamed down my cheeks.

Piercing blue sky dominated all day and a light breeze kept the heat and bugs away. The open meadows along the ridge were carpeted in flowers at the height of summer. As we neared the end of the Greenstone Ridge trail, and thus the marathon, Smitty abruptly turned to us and blurted out an idea. "The only long trail that we haven't hiked in a single day is the Feldtmann Loop, which is a little over 30 miles long. Next year, we could cover all three long trails in a single, three-day weekend!"

Shawn and I responded with doubtful silence. "That may be too much for me," Shawn finally admitted.

"Hmmm….," I said hesitantly. "The Triple Crown…I like it! Count me in!"

My heart felt fulfilled as we triumphantly touched the sign announcing that we had arrived in Rock Harbor. After hiking nearly 90 miles during two of the last three days, my body was feeling the exhaustion. It was time for a long, long nap.

Late July and early August passed with mixed emotions. I was eagerly anticipating a visit from my best friends, who lived in Lower Michigan. On August seventh, Randy, his girlfriend Tracy and our long-time friend Al arrived on the Ranger III.

"Who's the cute blonde in the visitor center?" Tracy asked.

"That's the girl I've been telling you about," I said, a bit dejected. "About a week and a half ago, she told me she needed to spend some time apart, so that she could connect with the island on her own. She said that since arriving in May, she had yet to feel the magic that she had felt here when she was growing up." I paused in contemplation. "How can she break up with me when we aren't even dating?"

"I think you need a backcountry adventure with your best friends!" said Randy.

And he was right-that was exactly what I needed. The next afternoon, the four of us set out on a canoe trip across Tobin Harbor with visions of wilderness and peaceful solitude filling our minds. When we reached the other side of the bay, Al and I heaved the 80 pound, 17 foot canoe onto our shoulders and began the portage up and over the Greenstone Ridge to Duncan Bay. I was so used to doing things like this that I barely gave it a second thought. We waited anxiously for Randy and Tracy to catch up. The minutes ticked by until we decided to walk back up the trail toward the top of the ridge, to find out what was taking them so long. Their 17 foot canoe, plastered in gobs of thick green and red paint, probably weighed closer to 100 pounds. The look on Tracy's face was one of pain and anger.

I cringed as they hauled their canoe the remaining distance to Duncan Bay, dropped it loudly on the ground and proceeded to tell me it was the hardest physical activity they had ever done in their lives. Al and I began laughing until Randy and Tracy chased us into the surprisingly warm waters of the bay. For the next hour, we all lounged in the crystal blue water, a hot summer sun shining down on our little piece of paradise. Loons called in the distance and a bald eagle flew nearby. Randy and I exchanged meaningful glances as my mind cleared of the worries and doubts. Peace returned.

The next few days were some of the happiest days of the summer. The air was hot and the water of Lake Superior felt warmer than I could ever remember from the previous summer. Al, Randy and I, without a care in the world, took every opportunity to swim. After dark, we would drift silently in our canoes across the black waters of the inland bays, listening to the loons and watching millions of diamonds sparkle in the heavens above.

The third and final night of this canoe trip was spent in Duncan Bay campground. An image from that night is one I'll remember the rest of my life. Just as we were settling down in our sleeping bags, a blood red moon rose over the Greenstone Ridge. The world was absolutely silent; almost expectant. Suddenly a loon began a wail that must have echoed halfway across the island. A chill ran up and down my spine as I imagined it to be the soul of the island itself calling out in some ancient language so perfect and pristine that it was almost haunting.

Return to the Mainland

The days grew shorter and the nights crisper as August threatened to empty into September. My conversations with Susanna had remained brief and strained, until one evening, almost a month after she said she needed her space, something changed. It was already almost dark on a calm, clear evening, when she abruptly asked me if I wanted to go canoeing. Within minutes, we were talking as if the last, tense month had never even occurred. For the next week and a half, we canoed and walked together every chance we had, as if making up for wasted time. Our friendship rebounded and it almost seemed as if the friendship was moving toward something more…but not quite.

I woke up on September 5th with a heavy heart. Today was the day she would leave the island. We hugged goodbye, her arms resting for just a moment on my shoulders. I smiled, but in my heart, I wondered if I would ever see her again.

Whenever problems are weighing on my heart, I love nothing more than to escape into the backcountry on a solo trip. As my legs propel me down the trail, my mind can wander as freely as a bird flying through the sky, and sometimes I manage to find a solution to my problem. Often times I don't find any solution to my problems but come back refreshed and rejuvenated nonetheless. So it was that as soon as the Ranger III left the dock, I grabbed my backpack and disappeared into the wilderness for the next three days. Much of those three days I spent off trail, or cross country, where I could soak in the essence of the island with very little possibility of running into another human being.

It was late afternoon on the second day, and I was deep in the heart of a tangled cedar swamp somewhere between Sergeant Lake and the Ojibway Tower. While soaking in the peaceful scenery and absolute absence of manmade sounds, I stumbled upon something that made my heart begin to race. I had just climbed over a fallen tree, branches scratching my legs, when I stopped in my tracks. In front of me was a full grown, half-eaten, dead moose. The vegetation around the moose was matted down and I could see trails leading away in several directions, as if I had just interrupted something. Once again, an eerie feeling that I was being watched came over me. I experienced déjà vu, but unlike the last time, I knew it wasn't a cow moose that was watching me from deep within the forest. This was the work of a predator. Peering through the thick undergrowth, I had an overwhelming feeling that wolves were crouching in the shadows. Two years on the island and I had yet to see a wolf, but this was not the time or the place. Quietly, I kept hiking toward the tower.

September 9th dawned cool and calm. Fall was in the air. It was the day I had looked forward to with anticipation and dread. I loaded my gear on the Ranger III and took a slow stroll back towards the Ralph house. "Time is such a funny thing," I whispered to myself. "At times I feel like I've just arrived. And at times I feel like I've always been here."

It was still hard for me to imagine life off the island, but there was a current of electricity running through me that I didn't feel the year before. This time I *knew* I would return. Not only that, but I had another grand adventure waiting just around the corner. With a spring in my step and a smile on my face, I hopped onto the Ranger III, bound for Houghton.

Practical Jokes on the Pacific Crest

Smitty had a mischievous grin on his face as he turned to me and said, "Okay, here's what you're going to do. When we step off the plane, my friend John will be there and will come up to you to shake your hand. Instead of shaking his hand, you could put your hands together and bow, like a Buddhist monk. Then, say something philosophical."

"Philosophical?" I asked skeptically.

"For instance, you could say something like this." Smitty's voice went up an octave and a deep look of concentration passed over his face. What he uttered sounded almost musical. "As the moon wanes, so may our friendship wax!"

"You want me to say what?!" I exclaimed.

"It would be a great practical joke." There was an expectant pause as Smitty looked more and more satisfied with himself. "Okay, now practice. Pretend I'm John and you've just gotten off the plane."

The rest of the flight into Reno, Nevada was pretty much a practice session. We came up with other bizarre things I could say after the bit about the moon. We practiced a far-away expression in our eyes and spoke in a slow chant. "Even though the granite walls crumble into the canyon, our friendship will stand the geologic test of time."

Soon, we were stepping off the plane, and I was walking calmly, monk-like, into the terminal. Quietly, a scraggy-looking man in his fifties came up to me and asked in a jittery voice, "Hey man, you got a quarter I could use for coffee?"

My monk-like walk turned into a nervous fidget. "No. Sorry," I said, and turned to walk away.

The dirty man followed me closely and continued in a low voice. "Come on man, just a quarter. All's I need is a quarter for some *coffee!*"

He was becoming more and more adamant about it. I repeated that I didn't have any money and looked for Smitty to bail me out. Just then, Smitty burst out in loud laughter and the strange coffee man followed suit, holding his stomach as if it ached from laughing too much. I watched, disbelieving, as the two men embraced and slapped each others' backs, all the time laughing uncontrollably. "Mike," gasped Smitty, "I'd like you to meet John."

That was just the beginning. As I was about to find out, the next 19 days would be filled with non-stop practical jokes. Along with John, Smitty and I were also meeting up with Chiggers and Ralph, two long-time friends of his from Olympic National Park. Our goal was to hike for almost three weeks on the Pacific Crest Trail starting in Tuolumne Meadows, Yosemite

National Park, California. We would have to average nearly 23 miles a day in order to make it to the tiny town of Belden, 354 miles to the north. I was by far the youngest in our group. Having just turned 24, all the others were at least twice my age. I figured that I would leave them in my dust.

I could probably write an entire chapter on the hilarious personalities of my hiking partners. Chiggers lived up to his odd name through a barrage of bizarre stories and his presence on the trail was a non-stop comedy show. Ralph was a little more reserved, but an equally amazing and fascinating trail partner. John had a warm laugh and an easy-going personality. Adding Smitty to that group, I knew it would be the trip of a lifetime. And, to top it off, these men could hike, challenging me to my limits.

On the morning of September 11th, under stunning blue skies, we donned our packs and headed north from Tuolumne Meadows into the wild unknown. In the first eight days, we planned on hiking a little more than 150 miles, at which point we would reward ourselves with a two night stay at a lodge in South Lake Tahoe. The days melted into each other in glorious bliss. Having just come off a summer on Isle Royale, it was far easier to get into the rhythm of the trail than to ride in a car or a plane. Day after day, we marched north through Yosemite's backcountry and beyond into Toiyabe National Forest. Our goal for each day was simple: get up at first light, eat a few snacks, hike three or four hours, eat breakfast, hike three or four hours, eat lunch, hike three or four hours until dark, set up camp, eat dinner, sleep. The landscape was absolutely breathtaking. Mountains dominated the horizon, with ribbons of snow streaming down through their massive boulder fields. Sub-alpine lakes of crystal clear water hung like precious gems among white boulders and stately green fir trees. Mountain summer held on with hot days and cold, clear nights.

On our eighth day, we slipped out of the mountains and into the bustling town of South Lake Tahoe. It was still such a strange concept for me to be in civilization. I felt way out of my element. It really struck me how out of touch with reality I had become when I nearly peed on a tree along a city sidewalk, without giving it a second thought. Fortunately, I remembered in the nick of time that it was appropriate to use bathrooms while in civilization, not bushes. With a smile on my face, I realized how intertwined the wilderness and I had become. At that moment, I felt more closely related to the wolves, eagles and foxes than to most human beings. I was part of the wilderness and the wilderness was part of me.

On September 20th, I gladly stepped back onto the trail and strode northward, toward Belden. Our ranks were reduced by one, as John decided to bow out before the next segment. Smitty, Chiggers, Ralph and I entered the Desolation Wilderness with only one thing to do: walk. Life was so simple. Day after day, with all my possessions on my back, I felt the primal urge to walk. It was as natural and necessary as eating and drinking. Idly, I wondered if this was how our ancestors felt. Life demanded that they walk to survive. It must have been as natural to walk as it was to breathe for them. A few days later, a cold, light rain turned summer into fall and within a day, it turned to winter. Snow blanketed the mountains adding an urgency to our steps. We trudged on, and walked into Belden on September 29th, 354 miles and what seemed like a lifetime since we began, 19 days earlier.

Chiggers' tiny, dilapidated Ford was waiting for us in Belden, compliments of a car shuttle by friends Elaine and Brant. One last practical joke topped off the trip. The car was covered in tiny action figures and in the driver's seat was a large, mounted mule deer head with massive antlers protruding from it. Elaine, Brant and their kids had decorated the car and left instructions that they wanted everything back in one piece. That posed a problem. The car was barely large enough for four grown adults with full packs, much less a giant, mounted deer head. We strapped the packs onto the small, home-made, wooden roof rack, then sat back wondering what to do with the deer head. Finally, Chiggers attached it to the front of the roof rack facing forward, as if a full grown deer sat alive on the roof, its big, brown eyes staring ahead as we drove out of the mountains and down into the lights and traffic of Reno.

Chapter 3:

1999: From the Great North to the Deep South

The deep blue sky and the warmth of bright sunlight seemed to hint at the arrival of spring, although a quick glimpse at my surroundings reminded me that winter still dominated. Piles of glistening snow covered the forest floor of the Porcupine Mountains in the Upper Peninsula of Michigan. Laughter permeated the cold air as snowshoers crunched their way up the slope. It was hard to believe that I was working at that moment in time. For the last five months, I had lived in Houghton, Michigan, and worked for an outdoor retail store called Down Wind Sports. One of my duties was to lead locals on snowshoe walks in the surrounding snowy forests. The owner hoped they would get interested in snowshoeing and come to the store to buy new snowshoes. Already into the third week of March, this would be our last excursion.

Over the weeks, my customers had become my friends. To top it off, Randy, Al and our friend Renae had come up for a visit from the Lower Peninsula of Michigan. Despite not being selected to fill a winter seasonal job with the National Park Service, the past few months had been a blast. I lived with Smitty and Shawn in Houghton, worked 30-35 hours a week at Down Wind Sports and cross country skied every chance I got. The snow was unbelievable that winter. It just kept piling up. Twice, we had to shovel the roof to prevent it from caving in. By the middle of March, the official snowfall for the year stood at 210 inches, with another month of snow accumulation still possible. Locals said it was an average winter; I was in heaven.

The sun was almost hot as we climbed out of the forest and into the dazzling sunshine flooding onto the Escarpment trail. Randy, Al and I gawked at the scene in front of us. From our perch, high on the ridge top, we could see the Upper Carp River far below, twisting through massive snow banks and into an ice-covered gem called Lake of the Clouds. In the distance, the deep blue waters of Lake Superior glistened like a gem.

"I know she's the one I want to marry, but it's such a big step." Randy had been talking for quite some time about asking Tracy to marry him. "I wish I had some kind of sign from above so I would know for sure."

"I'm keeping my eyes out for eagles!" I said helpfully.

"It's weird," continued Randy, as we searched the skies for the familiar bird, "I can't imagine not being with her, but this next step is like ending a chapter in my life. What if I'm not ready for that to end?"

"So you know without a shadow of a doubt that you want to be with her?" I clarified, and Randy nodded his head 'yes'. "And you're just waiting for a sign?"

"It's just such a big step and I want it to be perfect," pleaded Randy, but his eyes were beginning to shine. "Maybe this summer I'll ask her. I'd like to be on my sailboat when I do…if I can get it fixed in time…or maybe my canoe. I just want it to be so special. It has to be perfect."

Al and I just looked at each other, shrugged and went on talking about places we wanted to explore. The idea of asking a girl to marry me was incomprehensible. I realized the importance of the decision Randy was struggling with, but I just could not imagine myself in that situation. Idly, I thought about Susanna and in the back of my mind wondered if I would ever be in a position to ask her to marry me. I almost laughed out loud at the thought. "I'm not even dating her," I mumbled under my breath. A sense of unease crept into the far reaches of my brain as my mind flooded with memories of her. Suddenly, an alarming thought popped into my brain and I knew it was true. If I married someone else, I would forever wonder what it would have been like to marry the sensitive, beautiful, adventurous blonde I had met last summer.

We spent the whole day exploring the rugged Escarpment. The late afternoon shadows were growing long as we drove back to Houghton. In the parking lot of Down Wind Sports, Randy gazed up at a startling sky. Moisture in the air had created a perfect silvery halo around the sun. He pulled out his video camera and began recording, then slowly brought it down with a look of wonder on his face.

"Mike, Al," he began hesitantly, "what does that look like to you?" Randy was pointing up at the halo which had a perfect sundog, an explosion of moisture-created light, on one side. The halo connected directly to the sundog and, in the glistening early evening light, looked exactly like an enormous diamond ring in the sky.

Al and I were utterly speechless and overcome with wonder. Randy had not only gotten his sign, he had it on video tape. That summer, he would go on to propose to Tracy in his canoe at night, while showing the footage of that moment.

A dark red sun dropped like an enormous red balloon below the distant tree-line. The evening sky turned from blue to red to pink. A light breeze crinkled the surface of Washington Harbor. Two common mergansers floated by and the spring peepers had already begun their song. I stood on the Windigo dock surveying an island paradise. It was May 4th, and life was returning to this desolate corner of Lake Superior. As I slowly walked up the trail to my new cabin, an echo reached my ears; a haunting, magical, pure sound from the island itself. It stopped me dead in my tracks and brought tears to my eyes. The mesmerizing call of the loons welcomed me home as they sang into the night.

My third year on Isle Royale landed me on the west end of the island, a region I hadn't explored very extensively. This summer, I was the lead Interpretive Ranger at Windigo. Once again, I would live alone, but this time with the modern conveniences of electricity and running water. My cabin was part of a four-plex and looked like a quaint, wooden Swiss chalet. Much to my delight, my season had been extended to five months on the island. During the coming months, I would have no phone, no e-mail, no TV, and very few worries. Mail would arrive from Minnesota twice a week, but my food would come from Michigan only once every two weeks on a small boat.

The early days of the season were dominated by cold rain pattering on the roof, the first leaves of spring peaking from small openings in the bare branches, millions of frogs singing throughout the night and scraggy moose wandering around. Twice a week, the Voyageur II, one of the passenger boats from Grand Portage, Minnesota, arrived with excited campers ready to take on the challenges of spring on Isle Royale. Apart from that, Windigo was quiet and lonely. In the evenings, I began taking silent walks around the vicinity, watching and listening as I went. Sometimes I canoed instead, with the same goal of silently observing the return of life to the island. Occasionally, I would stop and sit in a comfortable place, mesmerized by the simple purity of my surroundings, utterly content to be alone with my thoughts.

The days of May slipped by in happy solitude and contemplation. The arrival date of the seasonal interpreters was postponed because of gale force winds and massive waves. They remained in Houghton for an extra night and it wasn't until the evening of the 26th that they arrived. There she was. Walking up the hill toward the visitor center, with a big smile on her face, was Susanna. She was so beautiful I nearly ran into the large wayside sign next to the visitor center. Somehow I avoided it and we awkwardly embraced. This summer would be different for us. She was going to live once again in Rock Harbor on the east side of the island, and I would live on the west side, 42 miles of trail separating us.

The following day, we began seasonal training in the newly constructed, modern visitor center. The visitor center looked like a large log cabin with an observation tower on one end. In the observation tower was a second order Fresnel lens gazing out onto the calm water of Washington Harbor. The Fresnel lens was developed for lighthouses and was very effective at projecting light a long distance. This one had been taken from the lighthouse called Rock of Ages, which stood guarding the shoals in the far southwest corner of the island.

"Every one of us in this room is an interpreter," said Smitty in a voice that could make the most boring concept seem interesting. "Mike, explain to the rest of the group what an Interpretive Park Ranger is."

"Well," I began, "an Interpretive Park Ranger is someone who tells the story of the park to the visitors. Our job is to try to connect the resources of this park to its visitors. We try to make it meaningful for them, so that they will ultimately grow to love and protect this place."

"Why are you an interpretive park ranger?" continued Smitty, while looking at me.

I hesitated, knowing the answer was far more complex than words could possibly explain. "Many people don't know how to make a meaningful connection to a place like this because they are so far removed from true wilderness. It's very important that they make this connection. I honestly believe that wilderness runs deep in all of us. It is intertwined with our souls and keeps us alive more than we could possibly imagine. Without the realization of what it does for us, both physically and spiritually, I think people would not only miss a big part of what life has to offer, but also inadvertently destroy our clean air, pure water and earthly treasures."

There were some nods of approval around the room from those who had lived or traveled in true wilderness. The rest of the seasonals had a blank look on their faces. I smiled, remembering how I was when I first arrived on the island exactly two years earlier. If someone had said this to me back then I probably would have looked at them with the same expression of bewilderment. "Once wilderness touches your life, you will never be the same," I said quietly. "This summer will change you, forever."

A Candle in the Window

As the days of June slowly ticked by, my social life improved dramatically. The population of Windigo soared from five to 25 community members. The feeling of camaraderie is amazing in an isolated place. We began hosting potlucks and impromptu gatherings centered around fresh, homemade bread and games. By far, the most popular social event was meeting to watch the sunset from the dock in Washington Harbor. Sunsets over Washington Harbor are out of this world. In the seemingly endless days of early summer, the sun crawls ever so slowly beyond the trees on the far side of the harbor. Any clouds that happen to be floating across the sky are soon bathed in glorious pink, all of which is reflected on the mirror surface of the protected harbor. Night after night, nearly the whole community would gather down at the dock for the evening's entertainment. TV holds nothing on an Isle Royale sunset.

On the final day of June, I hopped on the Voyageur II and took it around the island to Rock Harbor. There, waiting for me on the dock, was Susanna. After dinner together, we sat back talking about all our adventures from the previous summer.

"I'm in the mood for an adventure," said Susanna with a sly grin. "Let's go canoeing in Tobin Harbor…just like old times." There was some sort of hidden magic going on that night that neither of us was aware of. Before we knew it, we were paddling effortlessly into the smooth waters of Tobin Harbor as the shadows grew long. We stopped at Hidden Lake and promptly saw a moose. Smiles crossed our faces as we remembered the close call here from last summer. Up to the Greenstone Ridge we raced, trying to catch the sunset from on top.

An hour or so later, as darkness became complete, we crept back into our canoe and paddled out onto the mirror surface of the harbor. The nearly constant call of loons echoed from trees to water, and right into our souls. A dense fog was rolling in, making it easy to imagine that we were the only people left in the world, hidden in an orb of mystery. Silently, we drifted out into the darkening water, past rocky islands with tall, proud spruce trees reaching into a misty void. Out of the dense fog appeared a faint light coming from a tiny island. As we neared, the silhouette of a small cabin came into view with a single candle burning in the window. The scene was so utterly perfect that I couldn't tear my eyes away. It brought to mind the candle in the window of my Daisy Farm cabin that stormy night in early July almost two years ago. The image of a candle in a window symbolized warmth, safety and happiness in my mind. For minutes, or possibly hours, we floated by the warm glow from the cabin, somehow suspended in time and space. In the back of my mind, I dreamed that my future was within that cabin, Susanna wrapped securely in the warmth of my embrace.

A Falling Star

That magical feeling continued the next evening. It was one of those nights where the stars looked like they were within an arm's reach. Susanna and I lay on the wooden porch of her house in Rock Harbor and gazed at the heavens above. Hour after hour, we watched the stars move slowly across the black northern sky, huddled together to keep out the chill.

"Let's make our own constellations," I said. "You choose one, then I'll choose one and we can memorize what they look like. That way, wherever we are, we can look up in the sky and see our constellations together."

My mind was racing. Was this finally our time? Was a relationship about to begin? "Okay, that one's mine," she said, as she pointed up at a group of stars that formed the shape of an 'S'.

"That's a beautiful constellation," I whispered. I couldn't help but admire her smooth face bathed in the starlight. After a moment of silence, I pointed upwards. "Just a little to the right of yours are a few stars that form the shape of an 'M'. Do you see it? That's mine! Now, memorize where our constellations are and whenever you see them, you'll know that I'm thinking of you."

"I wonder what the stars will look like in the country where I'll serve as a Peace Corps volunteer?" she said, her eyes glazing over with dreams of adventure. "I'm nervous, but I'm so filled with excitement. I can't believe that within six months, I'll be living another life."

My heart sank a notch as I glanced over at Susanna, who was lost in thought. I realized at that moment that she was light years away from wanting to form a serious relationship. I couldn't blame her. I had certainly felt that way in the past, and in many ways, I still did. Perhaps our relationship was destined to be only temporary; an amazing friendship carried out in one of the most romantic corners of the world. A shooting star shot through the darkness of the sky overhead, but we were both so lost in thought that it barely entered our consciousness.

The Triple Crown

July 10th seemed to pass by ever so slowly. I was restless all day long, wondering how Smitty was faring on his way to Windigo via the Greenstone Ridge trail. It was the first time any of us had attempted hiking the length of the island in a single day, solo. It was a new challenge, both mentally and physically, but it was necessary if we were to carry through with our plans for the 'Triple Crown.' The Triple Crown was the ultimate challenge that a person could commit to on Isle Royale; hiking 42 miles on the Greenstone Ridge trail one day, 31 miles around the Feldtmann Loop the next day, and on day three, hiking 47 miles back home on the Minong Ridge trail. Since I lived on the west side of the island and Smitty lived on the east side, we each needed to hike one section alone. The only logical choice was to walk the Greenstone solo, since the Minong was much more strenuous and therefore, risky. Shawn stuck with her instinct and said this challenge was too much for her. Idly, I wondered if it was too much for any of us.

Finally, at seven o'clock in the evening, Smitty walked in the door, exhausted after the first stretch of the hike. I remembered very clearly the feeling of hunger that overwhelms a person after such a hike, so I had fresh homemade bread and a gigantic taco dinner waiting. We laughed and chatted nervously about the miles and miles of trail that lay ahead of us the next few days. The following morning, we were on the trail by six. Clouds hung low in the sky, keeping the weather cool, and thus decreasing the amount of water we needed to drink to prevent the onset of dehydration. As we hiked around the Feldtmann Loop, I felt strong. My body was so accustomed to hiking that it felt natural to be on the trail all day. During the two months that I had been on the island so far, I had already backpacked 15 days and walked over 400 miles. Even so, it was a crazy thought to be embarking on another 120 miles over the next three days!

Stories of our long hikes had leaked out each of the first two years. Most people thought it was crazy to hike the 42 miles of the Greenstone Ridge trail in a single day. When they found out we had covered the 47 miles of the rugged Minong Ridge trail from Rock Harbor to Windigo just two days before the Greenstone, they simply thought we were insane. Some people thought it was an amazing accomplishment. They asked questions about the adventure, and it provoked self-wonder; "Could *I* hike the island in a day, too?" Other people were resentful and even angry. We certainly weren't in it for the fame and attention. We had our own reasons for attempting these strenuous feats, and it didn't matter that other people didn't understand. We knew that with careful planning we could do the hikes safely, so nobody needed to worry about bailing us out. All of the mixed feelings that had swirled around our previous hikes made us decide that once again, we would try our hardest to keep the hike a secret.

We returned to Windigo at seven o'clock, after successfully completing the 32 mile Feldtmann Loop. Washington Harbor was so inviting that we decided to jump in for a quick swim. The cool water rejuvenated us, and then we headed to my house for a huge pizza dinner. By the time dinner had ended, we were both ready for a long night's sleep. We felt good with what we had accomplished so far, but the true test would be the next day.

Three o'clock in the morning arrived four hours before my body wanted to awaken, but we forced ourselves to wake up, and were out the door 45 minutes later. Suddenly, something caught my attention. I stopped dead in my tracks and turned towards Smitty, who nearly ran into me. Breathless, I whispered, "Listen!" A clear, deep sound echoed through the black forested hills to the south. The sound was followed one after another. I had been waiting for this moment for so long, I could hardly believe that the sounds were real. Wolves were howling! We were utterly speechless. I glanced up into the sky and nearly fell over, filled with awe. Not only were there billions of crystal clear stars above, but there was also a vivid green curtain of light dancing across the northern sky. Time stood absolutely still as I wondered if I was dreaming.

We stood frozen in awe for what seemed like hours but lasted only minutes. Slowly, the wolf howls faded, along with the northern lights. This powerful scene was exactly what I needed to get me through that challenging day. The memory of that morning left me feeling stronger than I ever had in my life. I literally flew over the rocky ridges, pain non-existent with the howls of wolves still ringing in my ears. We lunched at Todd Harbor, re-supplied our water at East Chickenbone and by sunset, we were on the home stretch of the Tobin Harbor trail.

It was nearly eleven o'clock at night when we finally touched the Rock Harbor sign. Smitty had completed the Triple Crown! I had just one leg of the trail remaining, and if I continued to feel as energized, I figured it would be simple.

I awoke the next morning feeling like I had been hit by a truck. I dragged myself out of bed and stumbled out the door by five thirty in the morning. Half an hour later, I gasped at the stunning red sky that greeted me as I stumbled down the Tobin Harbor trail. The rising sun seemed to set the eastern world on fire. In the back of my mind, however, was a sense of unease. I didn't determine exactly what was causing it until an hour later, when it began to rain. Suddenly, I remembered the phrase "Red sky at night, sailors' delight, red sky in the morning, sailors take warning!"

For nearly 20 miles, a steady, soaking drizzle chilled me to the bone. My shoes slowly succumbed to the rain and soon a heavy slosh reverberated off the ground every time I took a step. My misery was compounded when I realized blisters were forming on my soggy feet. With more than 20 miles to go, I was limping through the steady rain. Pain filled my being, and I soon lost track of time and place. The only thing I was aware of was the need to continue walking. On and on I trudged, each step overwhelming my mind with pain. Subconsciously, I realized that the rain had stopped and a hot sun now filled the sky.

When I reached the South Lake Desor cutoff, I reluctantly left my route, walked down the ridge, and filtered lake water. With bottles full of cold, clean water, I hiked back up to the ridge, laid down on a flat rock and promptly fell asleep. A few minutes passed before I jolted awake and fell off the rock. I knew that rest would not come completely until I reached my destination, so I gripped my trekking poles and pushed on toward Windigo. Exhaustion took on a whole new meaning as I neared the Island Mine trail junction. I looked up and saw a moose walking through the forest. As my eyes cleared, I realized I was actually looking at a log. In the back of my mind, I began to wonder where on the island I was. I had covered so much of it in such a short time that I was having troubles remembering which direction I was traveling. I hoped the junction ahead had a sign pointing to Windigo.

The last six miles seemed to pass as if I were in a trance. My mind began concentrating once again on the wild, haunting howls of the wolves from the morning before. I began imagining that I too was a wolf, stealthily passing like a gray shadow down the spine of the island. Strangely, a clear sense of peace came over my body and I felt no pain as I hiked toward Windigo. It was nine thirty at night when I finally touched the Windigo sign and plodded up to my cabin. Filled with an incredible sense of accomplishment, I realized the full implications of what Smitty and I had just done. In three days, we had hiked 120 miles! Once again, we had done something nobody had ever done before. The Triple Crown was a success!

Mid Summer on the Island

My youthful body and extensive training prior to the marathons contributed to a quick recovery. Within a few days, I was again scampering up the hills and eagerly anticipating my next backpacking trip.

The days of July melted into the days of August. Oddly enough, my life became more and more social. In a community that is so small, everyone seems to look out for each other, plan events and play together. We celebrated the Isle Royale holiday of Christmoose on July 25 with a huge potluck meal, games and even a piñata. In early August, we began what was called the Windigo Olympics. We separated the entire community (all 20 of us!) into 3 teams. For several days, we competed in races like canoeing, kayaking and running. We competed in games like the egg toss and water balloon volleyball. To top it all off, we ended the events with a potluck suitable for royalty.

My social life continued on the 12th of August. This time, it was in the form of much anticipated visitors. The day began with a hard rainstorm and the weather deteriorated from there. I was anxious for the Wenonah, another one of the passenger boats from Grand Portage, Minnesota, to arrive. With full Park Service rain gear on and the classic felt flat hat, I greeted the passengers off the boat and happily hugged my mom, dad and brother John. They had arrived for a six day visit!

Rain continued to fall in buckets the rest of the day, but we hunkered down in my warm, dry cabin and caught up on lots of stories. That evening, I proudly presented a program inside the new, log cabin visitor center for my family and a number of campers. Somehow, my mom had already managed to bake a thimbleberry pie. How do moms do that? After the program, we gorged ourselves on one of the most delicious pies I've ever tasted.

The next morning I awoke slowly to a strange sensation. Sun poured in through the window and the smell of pancakes permeated the cabin. For a moment I wondered where I was. Out in the kitchen came the comforting sound of my mom humming and the pancakes sizzling on the frying pan. Was I a little kid again? John was waking up and within minutes we were laughing about nothing in particular. I closed my eyes and was instantly back in the little, upstairs bedroom I shared with John while growing up in rural Michigan. My whole family was there; mom, dad, John and two younger brothers, Dan and Mark. It was once again a summer morning as I jumped out of bed with unbounded energy and asked myself, "What shall I do today?" Life was so simple and pure with mom and dad there to protect and guide us.

I lingered just a moment before walking out into the kitchen. This trip would be one I would always remember, I thought to myself. I'll enjoy and live up every moment I have with my family.

The following day, all four of us started out on a three-day backpacking trip to Feldtmann Lake. Our goal was to spend two nights along the lake with a middle day to explore the shoreline of Rainbow Cove and the ridgeline where the Feldtmann Tower stood. We did all that and more during those three days. We swam in the great lake, reveled in the silent beauty of dusk on the inland lake, watched a massive bull moose walk by camp and endured a powerful lightning storm while eating lunch at the fire tower. I felt unbelievably proud to have parents who would want to go on a backpacking trip. Now, more than ever before, I knew that they not only accepted my way of life, but also had grown a deep sense of pride for the way I lived it.

The Season of Wildness

By the end of August, the island began taking on a wilder form. The leaves began to change color, the weather became far less predictable, visitation thinned out and the wildlife grew restless. Each year, the process was the same, but it would often hit me suddenly and without warning. I would then know that the season of wildness had begun. Needless to say, it was the season I longed for the most.

In 1999, it turned on the evening of August 29th. I had begun a solo backpacking trip after work with a destination of South Lake Desor in mind. It was warm and sunny and my mind had still not perceived the shift in wildness. Within two hours, I passed Island Mine junction. Shortly afterward, a thought entered my mind. It was utterly silent in the forest. Usually, even in a wild place when you are by yourself, you hear *something*.

The wind blows through the leaves, the insects buzz about, or a squirrel chatters. That evening the forest was so silent it was almost eerie. At one point I stopped and listened. The mosquitoes were gone, the people were gone, there was no wind, the wildlife had disappeared and my ears were beginning to ring. The forest was still green with summer, but with a smile, I knew the season had shifted.

My thoughts were confirmed when I arrived at South Lake Desor campground and found it empty. Quietly, I sat back to watch the sunset and the Northwoods night progress. All the heat left with the sun and as night wore on, there was an unmistakable chill of a changing season. A full moon rose and was so bright, I contemplated putting on sunglasses. Instead, I took the rain fly off of my tent and snuggled down into my sleeping bag, gazing as long as my eyes would let me at the heavens above.

The next day, I left my tent set up in the campground and set off on a day hike to Malone Bay. Dozens of loons were gathering on the lake in their pre-migratory meetings. On the higher parts of the ridge, the undergrowth had all turned yellow with the advancing season. As the day progressed, I not only saw a half dozen moose, but also an osprey and several large pileated woodpeckers. As mid afternoon slipped into late afternoon, the wildlife became even more restless. All of a sudden, a flash of white caught my eye. Elegantly, a bald eagle rose from a tree and took flight over the far end of Siskiwit Lake. Seconds later, I rounded the bend and was suddenly face to face with a cow moose and calf only 30 yards away. Was the eagle trying to warn me? The mother snorted and pranced away. Perhaps the eagle was trying to tell me that something else was about to happen.

The shadows were growing long as I neared the Ishpeming Tower. "Only about four more miles to go," I thought to myself. Suddenly, a high pitched sound broke the silence of the forest. Was it a dog? Moments later, the forest exploded with deep barks, yips and howls not more than 100 yards off the trail. It sounded as if the entire central pack of wolves was lurking in the dim light of the forest. My heart pounding, I grabbed my binoculars and crouched to the ground. Perhaps it was finally my time to see this elusive predator of the north. For nearly three years now, I had dreamed of the day I would finally gaze upon this magnificent creature. I figured that the statistics had to be on my side. I had already lived on the island for more than 11 summer months over three years and had hiked more than 2000 miles. Surely, it was my time. Earlier in the summer, I had been walking with Smitty and Shawn along Siskiwit beach when a wolf crossed the path right in front of us. Smitty and I just happened to be looking the other direction. I knew that sooner or later, a day would come when I would see a wolf. Had that day arrived? My mind was racing.

I held my breath and soaked in the sound of pure wildness. They were so close; I could almost imagine the dense undergrowth moving with their powerful bodies. As abruptly as it began, it stopped, the sounds fading among the tangled brush. Wildly, I looked back and forth trying desperately to catch a glimpse. It was not to be. Someday, I said to myself. If I had questioned it before, I did no longer. The season of wildness had begun!

Reflections in the Northern Lights

Rain fell in horizontal sheets most of the morning. I hunkered down in the visitor center trying to get a few things done at work, but anxiously looked out the window. It was September 12th, and within minutes, Susanna would be walking through the door. Her season in Rock Harbor was over and she had decided to spend two weeks on the west end of the island. She had arrived the day before and immediately headed out on the Huginnin Cove trail to spend the night along the shore of Lake Superior. Just before she left, she said something that had been on my mind for the last 24 hours. "I have some exciting news!" she had said with a huge smile on her face. My mind had been wandering all morning and I barely noticed the person walking through the door just before noon.

"Hi!" Susanna's incredible, white smile could light up the darkest night. It shone from the midst of a face dripping with raindrops. "If you don't mind, I'm going to walk up to your place and take a quick shower. When are we leaving for Feldtmann?"

We were planning our next backpacking trip to begin right after I finished work for the day. "I should be home by 4:30. How about then?" I smiled as she left, knowing the surprise which was waiting for her on my kitchen table. "Happy birthday," I whispered. For the past few days, I had been creating a card for her. On the inside of the card, I had listed all the adventures we had experienced together on Isle Royale. The moose chase, the canoe trips, swimming, northern lights, falling stars, the islands we had named after ourselves, our chosen constellations, the candle in the cabin window… It was all there to help her remember our time together. On the back, I carefully glued a picture of a canoe at sunset and the words, "May the adventure continue forever…Love, Mike."

I could hardly contain myself as I raced up the hill to my house in the late afternoon. Not only had she undoubtedly seen the card, she also had this amazing news for me. "She's probably realized I'm the man of her dreams!" I said to the squirrel intent on chattering at me from his safe perch on a tall branch. I skipped into my house and looked expectantly at her.

"Here's the big news," she said with that stunning smile illuminating the room. "I'm going to Guatemala!" I paused, a vacant smile still covering my face. "With the Peace Corps," she said to clarify.

"Right!" I said encouragingly. Of course. That was her big news. She went on to tell me all about the amazing place where she would spend the next two years of her life. I glanced at the table and saw the card still sitting untouched where I had left it. She hadn't even looked at the card! The more she talked, the more my heart sank as I began to feel like I had missed out on something. Finally, I couldn't stand it anymore. "Did you look on the table?" I whispered.

She paused, confused for a moment. Suddenly, her eyes lit up as she saw the card. "Is that for me?" I just nodded, realizing she hadn't even seen the birthday card yet. As she read it, her eyes misted over. "We have had some amazing adventures here, haven't we?" she whispered. "I'll never forget them." For a brief moment, we stared at each other, not talking. A strange sense of peace came over me as if I somehow knew this wasn't the end of our adventure.

That evening, we happily walked the eight and a half miles to Feldtmann Lake. Just as we were nearing the lake, the sun broke out of the dense, low clouds and instantly set the sky ablaze with color. We set up camp and gorged ourselves with cheesy mashed potatoes, macaroni and cheese and hot chocolate. We talked about anything and everything. We laughed and talked seriously about the world we lived in. Darkness was long since complete when the true magic began. Suddenly, there was a massive explosion of neon green to the northeast across the still water of the lake. We quickly walked to the shore as ribbons of green light danced into the black, star-choked sky. The air was absolutely still. A deep chill cut to the bone, but I hardly noticed. The entire sky erupted in pulsating, green light, but what really touched my soul was the stunning image of the lights shining off the smooth, perfect skin of the smiling face next to me. There have been few times in my life when an image has been so utterly perfect that time has no choice but to take a back seat.

That night seemed to go on forever, but the adventure of that backpacking trip had just begun. The following morning, we woke up to the sound of a heavy thunderstorm pummeling the tent. It sounded as if the sky was being ripped apart right above our heads. It stopped after an hour, but an unmistakable chill hung over the island. By mid afternoon, we had worked our way up to the Feldtmann Tower.

All of a sudden, a loud, desperate squeal pierced the air. It came from the thick forest near the tower. Susanna looked panicked, thinking the sound came from an injured hiker. When I realized what the sound was, I smiled. "Let's go moose hunting!" I said. Silently, we held hands and crept to the edge of a dense thicket of spruce. Through an opening in the green, we could see a cow moose just 20 yards below in a small clearing. She was letting out loud, sharp grunts, much to the dismay of her calf. Just then, another set of grunts came from our right. A massive bull moose with gigantic palmate antlers ambled into the clearing, spooking the calf into a run. The rut was well under way.

For the better part of the late afternoon and early evening, we watched the two moose in their ancient, desperate mating dance. The smell of fall was all around in the wet leaves and a chill hung in the air. When it was nearly dark, we noticed a slight change in the manner of the bull. He seemed alert and anxious. The cow continued with an air of indecisiveness, as if she expected another bull to show up at any moment. The bull tossed his head violently against an offending tree and then looked directly toward our tiny hiding place.

I kept thinking about the statement I had used to calm many visitors over the past three summers, "A moose can only see about as well as we can on a foggy day." I wondered if I could see the short distance to the bull if it was foggy. My heart began to pound as this irrational, 1500 pound beast shuffled its feet and stared in our direction. Ever so quietly, we turned our heads and said a silent prayer as we retreated towards the safety of the tower. A crashing of hooves came from the clearing behind us and I looked just in time to see the infuriated bull chasing the helpless calf away from its mother.

Thick clouds covered the sky and the darkness enveloped us. We ascended the steps of our fortress and finally breathed a sigh of relief and excitement. Our hearts sang and happiness permeated the tiny walls of our castle. No matter what the future held, I knew those memories would last a lifetime. No one could ever take away those precious days in a remote and hidden wilderness with the most amazing woman I had ever met. The romantic days on Isle Royale had come to an end.

Backpacking on Isle Royale's Backbone

Anxiously, I stuffed the last few items of my house into my open backpack. This was it; the day I would leave Windigo. It was a surprisingly warm, sunny day on the 22nd of September. The northern summer had not quite given in to the strengthening fall. I had already packed up most of my belongings and sent them on a small boat around the island to Mott. Now, I had less than 48 hours before I needed to be in Rock Harbor, 42 miles away, in uniform to greet the next boat from Copper Harbor.

The amount of light these days was beginning to shrink fast. I knew I had to make it to Hatchet Lake that night or I would be very hard pressed to arrive all the way in Rock Harbor in time to meet the boat a day and a half later. It was already three thirty in the afternoon and I needed to hike 19 miles before I could set up camp.

As I took the first few steps onto the trail leading east, a burst of excitement filled my soul. Life on the trail is so simple. My only objective was to hike, letting my mind slip into a blissful state of thought. My legs responded with incredible power and energy as I flew up the trail through the forest I had grown to love.

The shadows grew longer and longer until finally, the fiery red ball dropped beyond the western horizon. The autumn dusk faded fast and soon I was walking with the silvery glow of a ¾ moon. My senses were heightened and my eyes adjusted to the low light. Far below me through the trees, Siskiwit Lake lay like a glistening silvery jewel. From it came the far-off wail of a loon.

It was after nine o'clock when I finally reached the junction with Hatchet Lake trail. Here the trail descends steeply from the Greenstone Ridge through a dense stand of birch trees to the shore of the lake. Along the lake were a few scattered tent pads, my ultimate destination. My flashlight created a tunnel of light in front of me with absolute darkness beyond. I was half way down to the lake when two tiny reflections came back to me from along the trail. Instantly I froze, my mind conjuring up images of some mythological creature lying in wait for the helpless human. Just as quickly, I realized what it was and my heart leapt into my throat. It was a moose, so close I could hear it breathing as if it were nuzzling against my ear. Quickly, I scanned my flashlight to the right and let out an audible breath when I saw two more round reflections staring back at me. These gangly creatures can run 30 miles per hour and I was barely 20 feet away.

For the next five minutes, all three of us stared at each other without moving. A deep hush fell upon the forest as if we were all anticipating something colossal. Finally, the cow grunted and wandered a few steps away from the trail. The bull followed. I took that as my signal to continue. Silently, I glided like a wraith among the protective trunks of the trees until finally emerging at the shore of the lake. With a sigh of relief, I wandered the last couple hundred yards to the first tent pad and quickly set up my tent.

The following day, I stood on top of Mount Siskiwit surveying my island paradise. Far below, in the deep blue water of Lake Superior, the mighty Ranger III rocked like a tiny toy boat in a giant bathtub. I sat down on a boulder at the top of the peak and sighed. That boat was taking Susanna off the island and once again, out of my life. "Perhaps it's best that way," I whispered to myself. "She has her dreams, and I have mine." A strange but incredibly strong feeling welled up inside of me. Somehow, I knew I would see her again.

My Island Says Goodbye

The wind was howling and white caps covered a growing sea. I stared out across the vastness of Lake Superior. A massive storm was in the forecast with gale force winds and waves rising to 10 feet. Isle Royale owes its sense of wildness to this massive freshwater sea. Few places on earth can compare to this awesome wilderness when the lake is angry.

With my goodbye said, I turned to walk back to the Mott Island dock, where the Ranger III stood waiting. The big day had arrived. Leaving the island was always traumatic. After five months of simple, pure wilderness living, it was nerve-racking to think of returning to the outside world.

An hour later, I was aboard the Ranger III and heading down Rock Harbor channel towards the open, angry lake. The wind had the icy breath of winter on it. The ominous weather kept everyone inside, except me. As I surveyed my home one last time, I caught a glimpse of a large bird soaring along shore and matching the speed of the boat. I strained my eyes toward the bird trying to get a better look. Suddenly, it banked back towards the interior of the island, revealing the bright white head and tail of a bald eagle. My island had said goodbye.

The early December sun had already fallen beyond the western horizon, leaving the thick, northern Florida forest an inky black. I drove east across the panhandle of Florida on a lonely, deserted road. At the crest of a small hill, I could see the faint lights of a small town. My map said it was Blountstown.

As I got closer, the lights seemed to shimmer and rotate. With a start, I realized they were the flashing lights of dozens of emergency vehicles at what looked to be the main intersection of town. "Must be a bad accident," I said quietly.

With my car at a complete standstill near the intersection, I rolled down my window to let in the warm, moist air. "What a novelty!" I said to myself. "It's December and I'm in shorts and a t-shirt!" Palm trees decorated in glistening Christmas lights swayed in a soft breeze. I had left the cold of the north just a couple of days earlier, but it already seemed to be a distant memory. A completely new adventure was right around the corner for me. "By this time tomorrow," I said to nobody in particular, "I'll be living in the Everglades!"

As I sat in my car with a slight smile on my face, I slowly became aware that something wasn't as it seemed. The handful of people milling about didn't seem at all saddened by the accident. In fact, they seemed quite jolly. Just then, a huge spotlight illuminated something at the far end of town to my left and a faint sound reached my ears. "Is that Christmas music?" I asked myself in disbelief.

The spotlight began moving down main-street, much to the happiness of a couple sitting in the nearby park. I strained my eyes to see down the street and laughed at an enormously fat man in red standing on the back of a brightly decorated float waving happily at all six fans. "Ho, ho, ho, Merry Christmas!" came the voice from the float.

"Welcome to Florida," I said. "Unbelievable. I have front row tickets to a Christmas parade in the middle of nowhere." As the evening progressed, it just got stranger and stranger.

About an hour later, I was thoroughly exhausted and ready to find a campground. Fortunately, I was along Apalachicola National Forest, which has numerous camping possibilities. According to my map, there was a campground just a few miles south off the main road on Forest Road 360. "Buckhorn Camp," I murmured absentmindedly.

A dark, lonely, gravel road disappeared into the darkness beyond. Thick pine trees hugged the roadside expectantly. My little red car with my bright white, 17 foot canoe strapped to the top bumped down the rutted road. After a few miles, I could see a distinct glow ahead of me. My eyes widened a notch as the scene came into focus. A campfire at least 10-feet high threatened to ignite the forest. Behind the fire was a filthy, light blue trailer that looked like something out of a cheap horror movie. Around the blaze sat three men dressed identically in orange hats, orange coats and camouflage pants, each with a matching rifle leaning against their seats. It was then that I noticed the sign, "Buckhorn Hunting Camp." With a groan, I realized that this was my campground.

Desperately, I poured over my map. "Surely, there's another campground nearby," I mumbled. Upon closer inspection, I realized the nearest forest service campgrounds were probably an hour away down more washboard, gravel roads. The only campgrounds farther on were the expensive state parks, which often close their gates after dark. I was stuck.

By now, the grizzled old hunters were all staring in my direction like hungry predators. I pulled into the campground and was just about ready to set up camp next to my pyromaniac neighbors, when I spotted a narrow, two-track road which disappeared into the pineland on the far side of camp. Cautiously, I motored ahead, scraping the sides of my car on the sharp palmettos which covered the ground. The two-track was little more than a trail, but it was my escape. My heart lifted a bit as I drove on, until I couldn't hear or see the hunters behind me. I stopped the car and stepped out into a world bathed in soft moonlight. Crickets sang from the trees and a warm wind whispered in from the sea to the south. Quickly, I set up my tent on the path in front of my car and was soon nodding off to sleep in my first solo experience in the Deep South.

The rising sun was just peeking through the pines when I reversed back down the two-track. The hunters were long gone, but smoke still billowed out of their fire pit. Soon, I was back on the highway heading east and finally south towards my new home. All day long I continued to drive, through the seemingly endless state of Florida.

It was late afternoon when I finally drove off the expressway and on to Tamiami Trail, the highway that would take me east to the outskirts of Miami and finally to the park housing area outside of Homestead. In front of me was a prairie of waving grass that stretched as far as the eye could see. I had reached the edge of the Everglades! On and on I drove. The sun fell behind the horizon to the west and soon the darkness was complete. At last, I drove through the entrance gate of Everglades National Park and found my temporary home in Pine Island housing area.

Two months earlier, I had gotten a phone call from Matt Fagan, the Hidden Lake Environmental Education supervisor, asking me to work for him in the Everglades. A seasonal Park Service job in the winter is hard to come by. Despite being thrilled to work as a ranger in the winter, I wasn't thrilled about the prospect of working in Florida. I love the cold, snowy winters of the north. That's where I feel at home. The Deep South had creepy, crawly critters that I had no idea how to deal with. To me, it felt as foreign as the moon. Stories filled my mind of snakes slithering about in shadowy corners of stagnant lakes and massive, scaly alligators lurking in the black depths of hidden swamps. I read stories about alligators grabbing unsuspecting prey with a vice-like grip at the surface and spinning down into the gloomy depths. How on earth was I supposed to teach others to love and appreciate an alien land for which I felt nothing?

Despite all my misgivings, deep down in my mind, I was as excited as a little kid on Christmas Eve. Surprisingly, the sense of wildness abounded in this mysterious corner of the world and I was ready to explore it.

My job also sounded amazing. I would be presenting day-long programs to fourth graders at a place called Shark Valley and I'd lead three day camping programs for fifth and sixth graders at the Loop Road Environmental Education Camp. "Many of these kids," said Matt back in October, "have never been in the natural world and have no idea what it can do for them."

Flood waters from a hurricane which had hit in October had left my future home at Trail Center along Tamiami Trail in a massive puddle. I wouldn't be able to move in until early January. Pine Island, the main housing area near headquarters, was to be my home for the first couple of weeks.

Before going to bed that first night in the Everglades, I couldn't resist taking a short walk. My paranoia set in with the first strange sound and immediately I remembered all the crazy stories of alligators and snakes. My flashlight swung wildly from side to side and my heart was racing, wondering which shadow would turn into a living, slithering creature. The longer I walked, the more comfortable I became until finally I looked up. To the northeast, the sky was bright yellow from the lights of the nearby mega-city of Miami. To the southwest, the sky was black with brilliant stars hanging all the way to the horizon. I've never seen a more striking contrast between wild and civilized. I stood mesmerized at the edge of the wilderness. A shiver of anticipation ran up my spine and the lure of the unknown pulled me into the beginning of a grand adventure.

Creepy Critters in the Dark Water

"You have got to be kidding me!" I said to the inside of my car. My car sat at a small parking area in the southern reaches of Everglades National Park at Coot Bay Pond. It was late morning, December 11th, and I was ready to begin my first backcountry trip in this new wilderness. My plan was to paddle my canoe to South Joe River chickee, a backcountry campsite in the form of an elevated platform sitting above the dark water in the middle of an isolated bay surrounded by dense mangroves.

Coot Bay Pond is a tiny body of water with thick mangroves leaning into the shallow, stagnant water. According to some reputable sources, there was a narrow channel on the far side of the pond which led to Coot Bay, a much larger, open bay. This was to be my entrance into the backcountry of the Everglades and I would do it alone.

From inside the safety of my car, I could hardly believe my eyes. At the very edge of Coot Bay Pond, in the only opening I could see, sat three alligators. The black head and beady eyes of a fourth one slowly sunk beneath the murky water perhaps ten feet from shore. Not only that, but I could see no opening on the far side of the pond that might lead to Coot Bay. "What on earth do I do now?" I mumbled to myself. After a couple of hesitant moments, I said loudly, perhaps to give myself confidence, "I guess it's time to jump right in…"

Slowly, I ambled over towards the shoreline. The alligators eyed me warily, but held their ground. "There's got to be another way to get into the water." On the far side, nearly hidden in a tangle of mangroves, was another entrance into the pond. I hurried back to my car and grabbed my gear. This entire time, a thin, middle-aged man with long black hair was staring at me. He had been sitting inconspicuously on a picnic table at the side of the clearing. As I was unloading my gear, I kept one eye on the alligators and one eye on this man.

"Want some help with your canoe?" the man asked.

With two people, it's fairly easy to get the 17 foot canoe down from the roof of my car; getting it off by myself is a completely different story. To do so gracefully is practically impossible. "That would be great," I said, relieved.

As we unloaded the canoe, the man kept looking at me, all my gear, my huge canoe and the tiny pond where I was bringing it all. I knew what he was thinking. "Um…" he said finally, "how long are you going to be out?"

"It's just going to be a quick overnight trip," I replied.

His face crinkled deep in thought. An odd silence fell between us as we looked out on the tiny pond with seemingly impenetrable mangroves in every direction. Finally, he could stand it no longer. "Where exactly are you going?" he asked with a touch of awe.

"Well," I began, "apparently there's a small tunnel through the mangroves which leads to Coot Bay." Another silence fell between us as the mosquitoes hovered in closer. "If not, I'll be back in about five minutes. If that's the case, maybe you could help me reload my canoe!" I said with a nervous smile on my face.

He pondered the idea, shaking his head. "Better you than me. If you're ready, I'll give you a push. Good luck."

As I slipped into the murky water, I noticed that all four alligators were nowhere to be seen. With every shaky stroke, I imagined the massive jaws of these pre-historic reptiles closing with a snap on the fragile wood of my paddle, splintering it into a thousand pieces. Quietly, I drifted for a moment, listening to countless mosquitoes buzzing in the shadows. Then, directly in front of my canoe, I noticed a tiny opening in the mangroves. A narrow tunnel opened up between the twisted trees and I paddled into the void... swallowed by a pure and awesome wilderness.

My first paddle stroke inside the narrow tunnel hit something hard beneath the surface of the murky water. Instinctively I yanked the paddle up so fast that I nearly flipped over the opposite side of my boat. With a sense of horror, I peered into the dark gloom of the rusty water expecting to see the mighty jaws of a gigantic reptile. Instead, I saw mangrove branches.

It took just ten minutes to weave my way through the tunnel and into the open space of Coot Bay. Slowly, my nerves settled and the strokes of my paddle became a thoughtless meditation. The warm sun and rhythmic sound of my paddle in the water put me at ease. Coot Bay ended in Tarpon Creek, a wide passage into the largest inland bay, named Whitewater. The minutes turned into hours and the hours slipped into late afternoon. The sun was getting low in the sky when I turned around the last corner toward my campsite. Just then, a thought crossed my mind and sent anxious chills up and down my spine. Frantically, I searched my canoe for an item I already knew was back in my car. For the first and only time in my entire life, I had forgotten to bring my tent on a backcountry trip.

It was too late to turn back. The thought of paddling through that narrow tunnel and over the alligator infested swamp in the pitch black was more than I was willing to consider. The alternative, however, was sleeping under the stars on an exposed platform with enough nighttime mosquitoes to pick me up and carry me away to a miserable and lonely death.

Feeling like a failure, I offered up a desperate prayer as South Joe River chickee opened into view. Three tents were already set up on the platforms. A hopeful thought crept into the back of my mind and deep down inside an indescribable peace came over me. Somehow, I knew it would be all right.

The three tents were occupied by a group of six people from Wisconsin. There were two adults my age and four Native American teenagers. The teenagers had gotten into trouble at some point in their past and were working towards becoming better people. As soon as they heard my plight, they opened up their overnight homes in an act of true generosity. That evening, we laughed together and told stories of where we had come from and where we hoped to go. At sunset, the mosquitoes came out in armies so ferocious it was like the height of summer in the Northwoods…and this was their winter! I cannot even imagine what they're like in the wild stretches of the Everglades during the calm heat of summer.

The next morning I said goodbye to my new friends and paddled off onto a mirror-like surface. I looked down into the reflection and saw the sky, a few wispy clouds and on the edges of my vision, a tangle of small mangroves. I navigated north through some channels until I reached the open water of Whitewater Bay. My paddle stroke felt powerful as I turned back east toward Coot Bay. The sun was warm, the breeze tropical, the water vast and my heart was incredibly happy. There was no evidence of humans anywhere. "There's more to this place than meets the eye," I said dreamily to myself.

As if on queue, a disturbance occurred in the water perhaps 50 feet in front of me. A sharp "whoosh" met my ears. A lone dolphin cut the surface of the mirror and swam off into the radiant crystals of the rising sun, leading me into a winter full of incredible adventures. Welcome to the Everglades.

Chapter 4:

2000: One Final Royale Summer

"Ranger Mike, Ranger Mike! I have something to show you!" A wide-eyed fifth grader came running up to me, weaving through the maze of thick, jungle-like vegetation. We stood in a classic southern Florida hammock, an island of deep green trees surrounded by a sea of waving sawgrass. He quickly grabbed me by the hand and led me back the way he had come, to a smooth-barked lysiloma tree near the edge of the hammock. The little boy could hardly contain his excitement. "Look!"

He pointed at the perfect, spiraled shell of a tree snail glued tightly to the trunk of the tree. Its shell was a stunning combination of orange, white and black. "What is it?" the little boy asked with a deep sense of awe in his voice.

"That's a tree snail," I said in a whisper, just in case the tree snail could hear. "That little fella glues himself to anything that has a smooth surface during the dry months of the winter. It's the only way he can survive. If we pulled him off, it would be very difficult for him to live because he would dry up. Tree snails are only found in the hammocks of southern Florida and the islands of Cuba. There have been 58 named varieties but some have vanished forever. Those that are still here are very rare because so many people have collected them in the past." I paused as the information soaked into the mind of the little boy. "Good eye," I winked at the awe-struck face beside me. "They need protection from people like us."

"I'll always protect the tree snails," replied a determined little voice. The overnight camps at Loop Road Environmental Education Center had begun. Students from all over south Florida, many of whom had never set foot outside of the city, were being inducted into a completely different world. Just after their morning arrival, a ranger would show them around camp. The students would quickly set up their sleeping bags inside one of the five spacious, yellow, canvas tents. Over the next three days and two nights, they would be immersed in the Everglades. This experience never failed to instill a sense of stewardship in the land. By the time the students left camp, they had become warriors for a wild and beautiful land.

Pondering the Future

The days of January were sunny and warm. Even in this coolest month of the year, it felt like pure summer to me. For the first time in years, I felt like I was experiencing a true summer. How strange that it was actually in the middle of winter! I went along blissfully detached from the rest of the world until the second to last day of the month. On a warm, Sunday night I heard something that would make me wonder for years.

There was a sense of urgency in her voice. What did it mean? In the dim light of the growing night, I could barely make out those beautiful, brown eyes looking up at me expectantly. The rhythmic sound of waves lapping against a sandy shore filled my ears. In one direction was the massive blur of lights from the mega-city called Miami, in the other direction were stars dropping to a black horizon.

"When I return from the Peace Corps, will you be married?" she repeated.

"I don't think so," I managed to say while thoughts shot through my confused brain. Why was she asking me this? My mind wandered backwards through the previous weeks as I struggled to make sense of her question.

In the first week of January, I received an e-mail message from Susanna. Her flight to Guatemala was going to leave from Miami, an easy one-hour drive from my home in the Everglades. She would have one evening in Miami before leaving the country for more than two years. I met her at the airport and brought her to a completely foreign world: South Beach, a collection of restaurants, night clubs, bars, and beaches at the edge of the city. We had spent the evening exploring the streets, dining under the stars outside of a fancy restaurant, and wandering along the edge of the ocean. The evening was ending too quickly.

I realized what had triggered Susanna's question. Earlier in the evening, I told her that I was dating someone. She hadn't really shown any type of reaction until that moment. Was she concerned? And if so, why? Perhaps there *was* more to our relationship than simply friendship.

The moment passed and the rest of the evening flew by until I said a half-hearted and confused goodbye at the doorstep of her hotel. With a slight turn of her head, she glanced back at me one last time, a tiny tear glistening at the edge of her eye before she disappeared down a quiet hallway.

"Maybe you need to stay here and hang out with us," Jessica said as I took a step toward my car. "Stephanie's here and Pete will be back any minute. That's perfect for a game of UNO."

I glanced beyond Jessica toward the pond in the back yard, glistening in the morning light. My eyes went from the pond to a stand of thick cypress trees which lined the far side of the housing area. A wild land of silently swaying sawgrass began just past the trees and stretched to the horizon. Beyond that lay a labyrinth of mangrove channels, brackish water and forgotten islands. "I need to get into the backcountry," I said quietly.

"You seem so sad and lonely," pleaded Jessica. "You need your friends at a time like this."

Ever so slowly, my mind was beginning to clear. "It's when I'm around people that I feel sad and lonely," I countered. "I've never felt lonely in the backcountry. That's where I feel at peace and that's where I go when I need to think."

Jessica continued to try to comfort me. "Things don't always turn out the way we had envisioned, but the way they do turn out is usually better than our initial hopes." She paused, and then smiled. "We'll have a game of UNO waiting for you when you come back tomorrow."

My heart was still heavy an hour later when I slipped away from the visitor center at Everglades City and paddled out across the calm water of Chokoloskee Bay in the far northwestern side of Everglades National Park. It was the end of February and the short cool season was already transitioning into hot, muggy weather. Brown pelicans whirled in the gentle, salty breeze and came crashing into the water, gulping down fish after fish. My mind barely registered their comedic plight for food as I concentrated on a vague color change in the mangroves more than a mile away across the open water. That color change represented a break in the mangroves, a tiny portal into a primeval world of utter wildness. The channels between mangroves were too narrow for powerboats, but wide and deep enough for my canoe and many types of marine creatures.

At last, I slipped through the gap in the mangroves and took a deep breath of clean air. It was time to think. Relationships had usually taken a back burner for me. If an adventure came up, I had no problem leaving a girlfriend. So, it didn't come as too big a surprise when Jennifer, the woman I had been dating long-distance, said she didn't see our relationship going anywhere. But for some reason, this break-up was difficult. Two nights earlier, I had been on my way to the airport in Miami to pick her up when I found out she wasn't coming. When living in remote places far from home, it's always a big highlight when someone plans to visit. I had spent hours pouring over the maps and finding the perfect canoe adventure for us to embark upon together. Instead, I was doing that trip by myself.

I thought about my life and where it was going. For some reason, my thoughts kept returning to Susanna. "I wonder how you are…" I whispered. Perhaps it was the memory of her that kept me from truly giving myself to any other relationship. My heart prickled with the sensation that perhaps I had somehow missed out on something. The one woman that continued to pop up in my mind was the one woman I couldn't have. Susanna was gone and no other woman would ever take her place. It all left me feeling utterly and hopelessly lonely.

With my mind reeling, I paddled deeper and deeper into a maze of mangrove channels and calm bays. Somewhere in this tangled web of trees and water, I paddled out of the complexities of civilization and into the wilderness. I was soon so deep in the labyrinth that I knew I wouldn't encounter another human.

A tiny bay was just opening up when suddenly something broke the surface of the water only a stone's throw away from me, then disappeared. My thoughts returned to the present as a tiny dorsal fin broke the surface of the calm water for the second time. Silently, I drifted closer until the water parted right in front of my canoe revealing a small dolphin with a smooth, dark gray body. Slowly, I turned away to not disturb him, but a slight noise made me turn around. The dolphin was following me! Hesitantly, I turned the canoe back around, only to watch with dismay as the dolphin turned and swam away.

An idea crept into my mind and I decided to follow my new friend. For several minutes, I paddled toward the wake of the dolphin, but surprisingly, the dolphin swam only fast enough to stay a couple of canoe lengths ahead of me. So, once again, I turned around and headed back toward the open bay. A slight gap in the mangrove walls revealed the end of the labyrinth and the beginning of the open ocean. A quick glance behind told me that the dolphin had also turned and was swimming toward me once again!

For several minutes, this game went on. When I would paddle towards the dolphin, he would swim away, but as soon as I turned to leave, he would follow me again. This mysterious creature of the sea was playing with me. Finally, the dolphin disappeared under the water and silence returned to the tiny bay. I smiled and paddled toward the open ocean. I wondered if he was lonely, like I was. Where were his friends?

Suddenly, right next to my canoe, the water erupted in a foamy froth. I turned and looked directly down into the dark, intelligent eye of my dolphin. He was so close that I could have reached down and patted his head. The dolphin's eye reflected my loneliness and sorrow for an instant, and then abruptly changed to a look of laughter and joy. It was almost as if I was looking down into the soul of this dolphin and he was looking back at mine. We would be forever connected in the wilderness we shared.

That evening, I sat back and relaxed on the deserted, white sand and shell beach of Tiger Key. A blazing sun kissed the horizon, transforming the colors of the sky from light blue to orange to purple. My mind was filled with the gentle lapping of tiny waves. Peace and happiness surged through me, the shadow of loneliness a distant memory. As I drifted off to sleep under a brilliant star-filled southern Florida sky, I dreamed of a gigantic, dark eye full of wisdom and love watching over me.

The Forgotten Lands of Big Cypress

The land north of Highway 41 in Big Cypress National Preserve is as wild as the land south of it within Everglades National Park. Between the two National Park sites, there are more than two million acres of protected land, the largest swath of protected land east of the Rockies. The slightly more elevated land of Big Cypress is home to most of the remaining Florida panthers. Research from the winter of 2000 put the number of panthers at 35, with an estimated 90% living within the preserve.

For certain people, wild lands have an uncontrollable allure to them. I was lured to this area by tales I had heard about wild lands north of the highway where the panthers roam and no human being would dare enter.

It was early March when I first set foot on the Florida National Scenic Trail and began a three day trip into the wilds of Big Cypress. The temperature was already creeping into the 80s and a blistering sun beat down on me as I walked north.

Southern Florida has only two easily recognizable seasons: wet and dry. The wet season runs roughly from May through November, while the dry season makes up the rest of the year. We were now deep in the heart of the dry season. It hadn't rained in months and the wildlife was beginning to grow restless. It was dry as could be just north of the highway, but finding water didn't concern me much because I had gotten some information about reliable sources farther north. My plan was to hike about 17 miles north on the trail, then retrace my steps to mile 14 where I could catch a different trail south to the visitor center and Highway 41.

The land was a mixture of saw palmettos, pinelands, thick jungle-like hammocks and cypress stands just beginning to burst forth in their brilliant green spring foliage. Within minutes of beginning the hike, I was already immersed in a silent, forgotten world. After about four miles, I came across a couple of stagnant mud puddles with hundreds of animal tracks around them, including several that looked disturbingly like alligator tracks. As the shadows of evening began to stretch to the east, I set up camp in a beautiful pineland. Barred owls called back and forth as dusk became complete and the first few crystals of light appeared in the darkening sky overhead. It was then that I first began to wonder about water. I still had enough to last me through breakfast and at least half the morning. However, if the next day was a scorcher, I would be in trouble if I didn't find water by mid day.

The temptation to explore this area was too strong to deny, so the next morning I continued north. I had been walking just a few minutes when I heard a sharp hissing sound. Breathlessly, I listened, not knowing what I could possibly be hearing. A soft breeze blew through the thick palmettos and rustled the pine needles above. A few minutes passed and I was just about to chalk it up to my imagination, when I heard it again. Ever so slowly, I crept around a bend in the trail and found myself looking into the open jaws of an eight foot alligator. Another loud hiss and I nearly fell backward as I hastily retreated behind the safety of a large pine tree.

"You have got to be kidding me!" I mouthed to the rough, reddish bark by my head. After a few silent minutes, I cautiously peered around the side of the tree. The alligator was still there, looking with reptilian eyes at the tree I hid behind. We seemed to be in some sort of stalemate. Whenever I ventured out from the side of the tree, I was greeted with an unhappy hiss. When I remained hidden behind the tree, there was silence. As the minutes crept by, my world seemed to cross eons of time to the dinosaur age. A hot, sultry breath of air blew by my face and I almost smiled with the realization that I was living out a childhood fantasy. Fossil evidence of alligators and crocodiles has been found as far back as the Cretaceous Period, during what scientists call *The Age of Reptiles*. It was a time when dinosaurs roamed the land. I had just read an interesting article about a huge crocodile that lived during that time period. It was called Deinosuchus (meaning "terrible crocodile") and grew to be 50 feet long! My mind imagined the hissing of some terrible reptile. I was back in the age of the dinosaurs!

Finally, I heard the palmettos rustling and the alligator moving on. With surprising quickness, the long, black tail disappeared into the undergrowth. Each of us continued our own journey in search of water. As I hiked north, the trail began to fade. The only indication that it was indeed a trail was the periodic orange blazes on the trees. It became a cross country trek through thick palmettos on the ground and endless, flat tangles of trees in every direction. My eyes darted back and forth and my ears were primed for that terrifying sound of a hissing alligator. My hope for water lay in the cypress slough, a depression in the land that held water longer in the dry season. Each cypress slough I came to held the same problem: dry, cracked soil. Instead of slipping back to the reality of the 21st century, my mind and senses stayed back in the age of reptiles.

I was about to give up my search for the westward trail and the much needed water, when suddenly I crossed an old two-track road. Directly in front of me in the soft mud was a massive cat track. My eyes widened as I realized that rivulets of water were seeping down the sides of the track. A panther had just been there! An eerie sensation that I wasn't alone came over me.

I continued on, hoping to find my trail to the west or water to relieve my growing thirst. An unforgiving sun beat down on my scorched body. Finally, in the early afternoon, I remembered the puddles back at mile four and made a hasty retreat for the only water I had seen in at least 17 miles. It was late afternoon when I arrived at the brown, muddy puddles. They were full of wriggling fish and frogs hoping to live a little while longer. I didn't care. I was so thirsty, I would have slurped up any type of water.

That night, I lay on my back and stared at the opening in the jungle-like vegetation of a sub-tropical hammock. The stars were as ancient and untouched as life was back in the dinosaur age. With a smile, I realized that all the stories were true of the wild, forgotten lands of Big Cypress.

The Star that Points Home

A hush fell over the group of 24 kids as they lay back in the soft, grassy meadow and stared at a black sky filled with thousands of glistening stars. I recalled the story Matt had told me when I first arrived in the Everglades nearly four months earlier about a little boy's first experience with stars. Apparently, the boy had asked the ranger what the holes in the sky were. Having lived lives completely in inner city Miami, I knew that many of the students who come to Loop Road Environmental Education Center have *never* seen stars.

"There are *so* many!" came a whisper from one corner.

"I've never seen so many stars in my life," whispered another student.

I let the silence continue for another minute, and then said, "Choose one star up there. The star you are looking at is so far away that the light you see left that star thousands, perhaps millions of years ago. Imagine what life was like back then."

Twenty four students were in such absolute awe that it made me smile. "Now, look at the big area above us that looks milky white. That's our galaxy, the Milky Way. It contains a hundred million stars! Our galaxy is so gigantic, it's hard to imagine its size. We are just a tiny speck here on earth, dwarfed by a swirling mass of countless stars, planets and other galaxies." A barred owl hooted from the depths of the hammock, its call echoing out into the timeless reaches of space. The air was thick with magic.

"For thousands of years, people have looked at the night sky just like you are doing tonight. Why was it advantageous for people to know the night sky?"

"Wouldn't that help them to know where to go?" said a little girl from the other side of the circle.

"That's right," I said. "Travelers of all sorts used the night sky to navigate. All of these stars spin across the sky except one. Anybody know which one?"

"The North Star!" a little boy shouted out with excitement.

"Very good!" I said with a laugh. "Everyone look through the gap in the trees over there." I pointed across the gravel road to a break in the trees just to the left of the dark hammock. "Do you see that bright star? That is the North Star. It always points to the north." A sudden wave of homesickness hit me with such force, I nearly gasped for breath.

Somewhere, far to the north, was my island, waiting for me to come home. That star pointed the way home. Instantly, my mind was floating in the midst of a northern forest listening to the music of loons.

"That was the star I picked," came a little voice next to me, jarring me out of my fantasy.

"That's a good star to pick," I answered a bit wistfully. "Anyway, many early explorers used that star to help them navigate. They also used the stars to determine when to grow their crops or when to harvest them. They even used the stars to gain a familiarity and comfort with the night."

"Nighttime can be very frightening. Early explorers and even the Indians of long ago were scared just like you are. In order for them to grow to know the night sky, they would draw lines between the stars and then fill in the rest with their own imagination. Today, we call these constellations." I paused to let this sink in. "Now, what I want all of you to do is find the star you picked out before. Don't tell anyone where it is. Look around that star and connect it to several others. Make your own personal constellation. Memorize where it is in the sky. In the days and weeks to come, I want you to remember this moment. Remember your constellation. When things get tough back at home or at school, I want you to be able to close your eyes, see your constellation and feel the same peaceful feeling as you feel right now."

With a deep sigh, I laid back amongst the tall grass and looked longingly at the ancient scene above me. It was so perfect, so untouched. In the heart of it all, glistening ever so strong was a giant "S" peering back down at me.

The Wilderness Waterway

One of the ultimate adventures in south Florida is to canoe the Wilderness Waterway. This 99 mile canoe route begins at Everglades City in the northeast part of Everglades National Park to Flamingo and ends in the southern part of the park. The route takes you through hidden bays, lonely rivers and tiny waterways with names like "The Labyrinth" and "The Nightmare." I was so intrigued by the Wilderness Waterway that I purchased all the detailed nautical charts for the route and had been studying them every night for weeks.

The evening of March 31st couldn't come quickly enough. When work was over that day, Jessica brought Pete and me to Everglades City and wished us luck on our journey. We had enough food and water for seven days, but hoped to do the journey in six because we had to be back to work on the seventh day.

The sun set gloriously over Chokoloskee Bay and we looked back at the last few beach houses before turning up the Lopez River. The next sign of civilization we'd see would be 99 miles and six days later. One by one, the stars blinked on for their nightly duty. The darker it got, the more I began to notice an unusual greenish light emanating from within the water. Pete noticed it too. "Maybe it's a reflection from the lights in Chokoloskee," I reasoned.

Soon it became apparent that we weren't looking at a reflection at all. We were looking at the phosphorescence, a phenomenon in the ocean where microscopic, single celled algae, called Dinoflagellates, emit a brilliant green light when disturbed. With each passing moment, the green grew more and more intense. It looked like a radiant, neon green flame was erupting from our paddles every time we dipped them into the water. After a few moments, we began to notice the same green flame streaking out alongside the canoe. We were spooking fish, which in turn stirred up the algae as they shot away from us.

We paddled in silent awe for hours. "Maybe we should paddle all night," said Pete.

"It's awfully tempting," I said. "I've never seen anything like it." We continued in silence for a long time, until I said, "I've always felt like there are a certain few places in the world that hold magic. They are few and far between, but this place is one of them. I completely underestimated South Florida. You always hear about the hordes of people, the high rises, the overpopulated and expensive beaches and hotels. This area is a hidden secret. South Florida is one of the few places on earth that's magical." Even as I said this, I was having a hard time realizing what I had learned. Who would have thought a northern boy who loves the snow could fall in love with what some people call a southern swamp?

The hot days of early April melted into one another as we paddled onward. We saw dolphins and sharks, a sea turtle and a manatee. Above us flew powerful osprey and eagles, graceful swallow-tail kites and bright pink roseate spoonbills.

On our fourth day out, we rounded a tight corner and slipped into a narrow mangrove tunnel that the maps called "The Nightmare." We had been warned about The Nightmare by several experienced paddlers over the last few months. "Whatever you do," one of them had said, "*don't* enter The Nightmare during a lowering tide! You'll get stuck in the low tide mud for hours and believe you me, you do *not* want that to happen. The mosquitoes will tear you to shreds!"

The inside of The Nightmare grew narrower and narrower. We maneuvered around countless obstacles in the brown, chocolaty water. I imagined I was deep in the heart of the Amazon and at any moment would encounter a bare-backed, deeply tanned man poling along in a dugout canoe.

Instead, we were met with solitude. The Nightmare took almost half a day to complete, but we made it through.

Some days we talked about life, our jobs and our future dreams. Other days we paddled in contented silence for hours at a time, happily soaking in the sense of wildness. The only sounds were those of lapping waves, light winds and crying birds.

On the last evening of the Wilderness Waterway, we camped at Roberts River Chickee, a small platform camping area way up Roberts River. It was late afternoon when I jumped into the water to cool off. As I floated around, it occurred to me how much I had grown. Almost four months earlier I had nervously begun my first canoe trip in a foreign world, scared to death that an alligator would grab my paddle and pull me in. It took several months of intensive backcountry study to begin to feel at home. I had grown to know the Everglades. I had heard its heartbeat, felt its sorrow and experienced its joy. Somewhere in the course of the winter, I had become one with the Everglades. I was simply an extension of the sawgrass prairie, the hush of the pinelands and the tangle of mangroves.

As I climbed back up onto the chickee, I looked down into the murky water and saw a shadow rising. In horror, I watched as an alligator that easily matched my height rose to the surface of the water where I had been swimming just seconds before. As much as you think you know a place, there's always more to learn!

The Call of the Northwoods

Despite falling in love with the Everglades, the image of the North Star pointing the way home filled my heart with an intense longing to return to the north. In mid April, I drove from Florida through Georgia, Tennessee,

Kentucky, Indiana, the lower peninsula of Michigan and finally the upper peninsula of Michigan.

In just two weeks, I was on my way to the Island. May 2nd dawned clear and cold. By mid morning, the Ranger III was humming across the calm surface of a giant fresh-water sea. A biting north wind rose off the icy water. Like a dream, Isle Royale rose before us out of the depths of Lake Superior. The closer we got, the more excited I became. The mighty Ojibway Tower, a lone lookout on the rugged, exposed Greenstone Ridge, beckoned us. Finally, we cruised through Middle Islands Passage, marking the season's beginning, the awakening of a wilderness island from a long winter nap.

We stopped at Mott Island to unload and refuel. Four hours later, we cruised into Washington Harbor and pulled up to the dock in Windigo, my home once again this season. The loons were already there to greet me, their calls echoing back and forth across one of wildest places in America.

Ever so slowly, the island cleared the cobwebs of civilization from my mind. The problems and worries of only a few days earlier seemed like a different lifetime. When the Ranger III returned to the mainland two days later, it left just three people in Windigo: Larry, Scott and me. Larry and Scott were anything but social. I found myself going for long periods of time without seeing another human being.

On the 7th of May, I grabbed my backpack, slipped out of the visitor center and onto the Feldtmann Lake trail. Little by little I became part of the island once again. The crisp sound of white throated sparrows, the smell of cedar and the sight of Grace Creek overlook were like a reunion with old friends. With a deep, contented sigh, I surrendered to the magic of the island and became one with its wildness.

I hiked the eight and a half miles to Feldtmann Lake campground and set up my tent along the edge of the pristine lake. It was obvious that I was the first person to have walked the trail this spring. The entire route was nothing but moose tracks. That evening, I sat for a long time at the edge of the lake thinking about life. It was impossible to forget the woman of my dreams as I looked out across the mirror surface of this lake that had held the perfect reflection of dancing northern lights and Susanna's silhouette last September.

Just then, a splashing sound broke me out of my trance. A large bull moose with velvety antler stubs ambled by, no more than ten feet away. Idly, I wondered if he was the same giant from last fall that we had encountered near the tower. Suddenly, he stopped and looked startled, as if I had broken *him* out of a trance. I could almost see the wheels turning in his head. More than likely, I was the first human being he had seen in over six months.

The next morning, I woke up to driving rain and howling wind battering my tent. I went back to sleep, hoping it would blow itself through. No such luck. By mid morning, I was hurriedly packing up my tent in a downpour and racing toward the Feldtmann Tower. The wind on the ridgeline was nothing short of brutal. Bullets of sleet and rain pummeled me from the west, their stings apparent even through three layers of clothing. Despite good rain gear, everything was soaked after a couple of hours and I was chilled to the bone.

It was late afternoon by the time I walked into the Island Mine campground, guarded by an army of thick trees. The storm had eased to a steady drizzle, but the temps still hovered in the low 40s. Amazingly, my sleeping bag and extra clothes had stayed dry. A few minutes later, I was huddled in my warm sleeping bag after a hot meal, listening to the drip, drip, drip on the tent.

When I awoke the next morning, it wasn't raining. Cautiously, I poked my head out the tent and was amazed to see a pure blue sky! I had survived the storm. By mid day I was back in the deserted community of Windigo. It wasn't until the middle of the next day that I saw my first human being in nearly five days. When Scott walked into the visitor center, I had to clear my throat twice in order to speak. I probably looked at him with the same startled look that I had gotten several days earlier from the moose.

On May 13th, I finally had some people to talk to. I woke up excited because this was the first day the Voyageur II would arrive with passengers from Grand Portage, Minnesota. Shortly after breakfast, I walked out my cabin door and turned onto the trail that led to the visitor center. The sky was dark and ominous with impending rain. Just around the corner of my cabin was a cow moose with a very large belly. She seemed edgy. Quietly, I slipped back into my house and grabbed my camera. After the first click of the shutter, she looked at me with angry eyes and took a few steps in my direction. Not wanting to be trampled, I backed up a few paces and peered out from behind a corner of my cabin.

After a couple of minutes, I decided to prod her along. I figured that if I took a few steps toward her, I might be able to spook her off of the trail and I'd be able to reach my path. Besides, she had turned away now and was busy stripping the tiny, light green leaves off of any bush she could find. With a deep breath, I stepped out from the safety of my cabin and took a few steps toward her. Immediately, she wheeled toward me, as fast as lightning, and took a few steps in my direction. Hastily, I retreated back around the corner and leaned against the cool, damp wood.

I contemplated my options. She was completely blocking the trail that led to the visitor center. That option was out unless I could sneak through the dripping forest full of dense, green undergrowth. I could go all the way around on the narrow, gravel road used to bring supplies up from the dock. But that would take some time. I laughed at the thought of telling Smitty I was late for work because a moose blocked my path. How many places on earth is that not only a possible excuse, but a legitimate one?

Gradually, I became aware of the sound of crunching through the forest. I peered around the corner and was almost disappointed to see the moose ambling away. Little did I know that the adventure was far from over. With a smile, I walked confidently toward the trail and was nearly there when the tables turned again. With an infuriated snort, the cow moose lunged toward me. There was no time to retreat to my cabin. Out of desperation, I did a nose-dive behind the nearest tree I could find, which fortunately was a good sized balsam fir. My freshly cleaned gray and green uniform skidded along the sodden earth and my face pressed against the tattered bark of the fir tree. A silence fell over the forest; the only sound was the pounding of my heart. I felt gripped me with fear when I noticed the sound of breathing no more than a foot away from me on the other side of the tree. From my position against the bark, I couldn't see the head of the furious moose, but I could see most of her body.

We sat there for what seemed like hours, but was probably only a minute or two. With a sigh of relief, I heard her wander off again. After a few minutes, I got up my courage and began jogging down the trail. The cow moose was so enraged that she pinned me behind two more trees over the next 20 minutes en route to the visitor center. Finally, I lunged into the visitor center and slammed the door.

Several hours later, I was at the dock as 26 passengers stepped off of the Voyageur II. I gathered them together for an orientation talk to the island. "Welcome to Isle Royale National Park," I said. "You have now entered the wilderness. In a few minutes, I'll go over some of the rules and regulations of the park as well as what to look for while you are on your adventure. But first, let me just say this." I paused as I surveyed 26 excited faces, faces that just hours ago were leaving civilization and a world of organization and ease. Most had no idea how truly wild this place was. "Congratulations for making it here. This island has a huge sense of wildness to it. You are all about to have the adventure of a lifetime."

A Summer of Magic

Spring slowly turned to summer and with it the pale lime leaves turned to a deep, dark green. The adventures piled up one after another. The late June wildflowers were more intense than I had ever seen. Orange and yellow hawkweed, mixed with the dazzling white oxeye daisies covered the meadows in an incredible burst of colors.

In the middle of June, I left the island for a couple of days for Randy and Tracy's wedding in the Porcupine Mountains. To get to the wedding site, I had to take four boat rides, hike 16 miles and drive two hours, a trip which ended up taking four days!

A week later, during the heart of wildflower season on Isle Royale, Smitty and I hiked yet another marathon. This time, we called it the Yo-Yo. It was an abbreviated version of the previous year's masochistic walk. I had done some research and discovered that the average American walks less than 200 yards a day (according to *Backpacker Magazine*). Based on that fact, I determined that the average American must walk about 88 miles a year. Conveniently, that was the distance to walk from Rock Harbor to Windigo and back again using the Greenstone Ridge trail and the Minong Ridge trail. We decided to do that in two days. After the accomplishment, we made ourselves t-shirts which read, "A year in two days."

The days of July began with a four day backpacking trip with Smitty and Shawn along the windswept and wave battered southern coast of Isle Royale, south of the Feldtmann Ridge. The days were beautifully sunny and warm. July ended with another sensational four day backpacking trip along the Greenstone and Minong with my brother John. Summer was in full swing and I wished with all of my might that it would never end.

On August 3rd, less than 24 hours after John left, Randy and Tracy arrived. "I have a request," Tracy said, soon after setting foot on the Windigo dock. "I want to see a moose."

"I'll see if I can arrange that," I replied with mock confidence. Two years earlier, when Randy, Tracy and Al had visited, I had seen moose right before they arrived and the day after they left. For some reason, despite wandering amongst the highest concentration of moose on the planet, we had not seen any during their visit. In fact, Tracy had never seen a moose in her life and very much wanted to change that. Little did she realize just how much of a moose encounter she would have.

The morning of August 6th was gray and rainy. We holed up in my cabin and poured over maps, dreaming of adventures. In the early afternoon, we paddled in a light rain to the end of Washington Harbor, around Card Point and into Grace Harbor. The rain stopped as we portaged a short distance into the network of waterways at the mouth of Grace Creek.

"This is really prime moose habitat," I said with a smile as we wound our way around nearly hidden obstacles in the dark water beneath the canoes. Surrounding us was a vast wetland of tall grass, thick bushes and water-loving trees.

After exploring the wetland for more than an hour, we found a hidden nook at the end of a narrow waterway. It was a perfect spot to relax in our canoes and eat a snack. Somewhere in the dense foliage beyond the water's edge, we heard the snap of a breaking branch. Some of the bushes were shaking like leaves in a stiff breeze.

"That's got to be a moose!" I whispered.

"I see it!" exclaimed Tracy. "Actually, I think there are two in there!"

Ever so slowly, we retreated as the rustling sound came closer and closer to the water's edge. Randy peered very intently at the waving bushes. "Actually, I think it's just one, very large moose," he said in an awed voice.

Sure enough. A gap in the bushes revealed an incredibly large, bull moose with a gigantic set of velvety antlers.

"Back up! Back up!" I said in a hoarse whisper. The moose came into view briefly, looked at us suspiciously, and then continued crashing just out of view among the dense bushes along the edge of the channel. We took a few paddle strokes forward, then watched as the moose stepped out from the bushes directly into our path, successfully blocking our escape back to the open water of Lake Superior.

Immediately, the moose began feeding on the soft underwater vegetation. He seemed to completely forget about us. He was so close we could see his powerful shoulder muscles flex as he dunked his head under the water again and again. The seconds turned into minutes and the minutes crept by until almost an hour had passed. The entire time, we sat in our canoes and marveled at this magnificent creature. "Welcome to my Discovery Channel," I joked. Finally, he moved a little bit to the right of the waterway. "Let's go for it!" I decided quickly.

"Let's go for *what?*" asked Randy in a sharp whisper.

"Here's our chance to get around him!" I replied. "The next time he dunks his head, follow me." The looks on my friends' faces made me wonder if they would indeed follow.

As we watched the moose chewing reeds above water, our adrenaline began to flow. The instant his massive head disappeared under the water we made a break for it. Time stopped as we paddled quickly near the left bank of trees and bushes. When we were exactly even with the body of the moose, a confused head erupted from the water. Our eyes locked and his eyes seemed to widen in surprise. We had no other option but to continue paddling at this point. Fortunately, the giant was a gentleman and let us pass.

"That...was...awesome!" Randy said, pronouncing each word slowly.

"That was the most amazing moose encounter I've ever had," I replied with a loud exhale. Tracy gave a little laugh knowing I say things like that all the time. "I'm serious this time," I said, a little defensively.

As we paddled home to Windigo, a mysterious fog came and went until it finally lifted to reveal a startling sunset of red, pink and purple. "Any other wildlife requests, Tracy?" I asked.

She smiled and thought about it for a moment. "How about a wolf?" she answered. "Can you handle that?"

A New Dream Takes Hold

As the days of summer grew shorter and cooler, an odd sense of urgency came over me. Perhaps it began the day I went over to my neighbor's house and picked up his map of Glacier Bay National Park in Southeast Alaska. A tiny settlement called Gustavus was indicated on the bottom right corner of the map and beyond that lay an enormous area of pure wilderness. There were countless mountains, rivers, bays and islands with intriguing names like Mount Fairweather, Beartrack River, Torch Bay and Puffin Island. I've always been drawn to maps, but this one captivated me like no other map ever has. The surrounding world disappeared as I was drawn farther and farther into its contour lines. I almost imagined I was tumbling head over heals into the heart of this new world. Alaska held a spell on me. There was no other land like it. I made up my mind right there that, if given the opportunity, I would go to Glacier Bay in a heartbeat.

Somewhere deep inside of me I knew that this summer on Isle Royale would be my last for awhile. With that realization came an intense urgency to live up every moment. In late August, I backpacked along the Greenstone Ridge trail to Hatchet Lake in the center of the island and had a wonderful reunion with my dad and my brother Mark. We spent several more days on the trail soaking up the late summer heat, swimming happily in every lake we came upon in the wilderness.

The next week, I again backpacked up the Greenstone to South Lake Desor. Cautiously, I looked around to make sure nobody was looking, and then slipped into the lake with full snorkeling gear. I attached a dry bag to my fin with a short line and spent the afternoon snorkeling around several very intriguing islands. Several times, I was surrounded by loons, who eyed me curiously. My mind raced with the thought of how loons kill certain waterfowl that venture into their territory. They come up from the depths like a torpedo with blinding speed and spear the unsuspecting intruder with their dagger-like bill. Fortunately, in late August they seemed to be more curious than aggressive.

The days grew wilder as September arrived. Periodic storms hammered the rocky shoreline and twisted the exposed balsam fir trees. Brilliant orange and yellow began to dominate the deciduous trees of the interior and the smell of fall hung in the air. The ground cover turned red, then brown and curled up. The moose lost the velvet on their antlers and became irritable and unpredictable. The wolves seemed to be on the move, their howls often ringing out under the star-filled nights.

One Final Backpacking Trip

On September 21st, with just eight days left on the island, I turned my back on Windigo for the last time, heading out on an unforgettable seven day backpacking trip across the wildest parts of the island. I needed time to think, time to soak it all in, time to reminisce.

I began by hiking around the Feldtmann Loop, camping one last time in the tower. At Siskiwit Bay, I headed off trail along the slippery, rocky shoreline and camped in a small, forested, cross country site at Finn Point along Hay Bay. The following day I continued along the shoreline until Malone Bay, then walked up to the ridge and stayed the night in Ishpeming Tower. At sunset that evening, I climbed the crow's nest which was shaking like a blade of grass in a strong wind. The entire island seemed to stretch out below me, all bathed in the golden light from an autumn sunset. The view was so untouched and so perfect, it had the feel of something eternal.

On day four, I saw a kaleidoscope of colors on the Greenstone Ridge before descending into McCargoe Cove. The next day, I grabbed the Park Service canoe at Lake Richie and proceeded to paddle and portage my way to Wood Lake. That night, I sat back in my tent listening to the grunts of numerous moose nearby. The sense of wildness was stronger than I had ever felt before. It seemed almost as if I was suspended in a timeless world. On day six, I paddled and portaged my way back to Lake Richie via Lake Whittlesey and Chippewa Harbor. A cold rain began to fall, testing my determination and willpower.

It was nearly dark by the time I made it to my old cabin at Daisy Farm. As I stepped inside the cabin, I felt as if I were back in 1997. Everything was the same as when I moved in way back in the spring of that year. The smells, the sights, the sounds, all took me back in an instant to the summer that changed my life. It was almost as if I had never left.

On my final day of backpacking, I stepped out of the cabin before dawn, the temperature well below freezing. As I scooted along the trail toward the Daisy Farm campground, a blinding sun rose over Middle Islands Passage. With a deep breath, I turned and hiked up the trail that started it all four years ago. I could almost hear the echo of my foot-falls from that May evening long ago.

At the tower, I ate breakfast, then glided across the ridge to Mount Franklin. I was nearly at the rocky outcropping on the top of the mountain, when suddenly I slowed. A cold, northerly wind caressed my face. It smelled pure and clean. I closed my eyes, as I had done my first summer on the island, trying desperately to memorize that feeling. It was hard to imagine, but I felt a part of the island like never before. The wildness of the island coursed through my veins.

At Threemile campground, I had a happy reunion with Smitty. That night I stayed with Smitty and Shawn at Mott. We talked and laughed about life on the island, but a knot in my stomach had already formed. It was time to say goodbye.

Total blackness enveloped Smitty and me as we stepped out the door at six o'clock the next morning. A few stars twinkled in an inky black sky. We walked around the Mott trail, constantly hearing the grunts of a bull moose. It was a bit eerie to not know where he was.

Several hours later, I stepped onto the Ranger III with a heavy heart. A chapter in my life was closing before my eyes. Somehow, over the last four summers, I had tapped into the soul of this wilderness and part of my soul would forever remain. I stood by myself along the railing of the boat, staring out at my island. Suddenly, a brilliant white spot caught my eye along the shore. Tears began to flow unchecked as I looked at the bald eagle hopping along shore. My guardian had once again come to say goodbye. Ever so slowly, the island disappeared behind me, swallowed up in the vastness of Lake Superior. "Goodbye my island, my home, my forever love…"

Battling My Demon

"What on earth is wrong with me?" I said to the sign at the trailhead. "Maybe I've been alone too much recently. It's just another backpacking trip. I've done tons of solo trips in my life." Deep down inside of me, a war was waging between my pride and an unsettling premonition. I stood by a sign which read, "Great Gulf Trail." Between the dripping trees I could just make out some of the high country on the flanks of Mount Washington in northern New Hampshire. I had been standing now for 20 minutes in a steady downpour at the trailhead trying to decide whether to take a step forward or back. A chilling wind crept up my spine and the temperature felt every bit like the 37 degrees it read on the bank sign back in the town of Gorham.

It was October 16th and I had planned on spending four days in the White Mountains of New Hampshire. My ultimate goal was to climb Mount Washington, a 6,288 foot mountain in the midst of a sea of exposed alpine tundra. The mountain has some of the worst weather in the world. Three major weather patterns converge on top of the mountain creating insane winds and weather so brutal that people have died in every month of the year while attempting to climb it. Most deaths were related to hypothermia from exposure. During an April, 1934 storm, a wind speed was clocked at 231 miles per hour. It may have even been faster than that, since at 231 mph, the wind gauge broke! For comparison, hurricane force winds begin at 75 mph.

The trails going up the mountain are almost as outlandish as the weather. In places, the trails are nearly vertical with staggering drop-offs.

Earlier in the day, I had been trying to wait out the storm by hanging out in a small, local bookstore in Gorham. Nearly every book I picked up had to do with death on Mount Washington. One book listed the names and recounted the stories of more than 120 people who had died while climbing the mountain.

The US Forest Service ranger at the visitor center only added to my concern. On average, she had happily informed me, hurricane force winds pummel the summit on 40% of all days. By October, hurricane force winds are the norm in the alpine zone and high temperatures at the summit average only 36 degrees. It's the combination of wind and temperature that is the real killer, any time of the year, she said. In January of 1934, a state record of -47 degrees was recorded with a wind speed of 100 miles per hour. The wind chill that resulted from those two extremes cannot even be recorded on most wind chill charts because they don't go that low. Any exposed skin, she had said with a smile, would freeze instantly.

Normally, statistics like those only get me excited. I love brutal conditions. I had just spent six days in the wilds of the Adirondacks of New York climbing eight of the highest peaks in the state, half of which happened to be winter-like ascents. Despite the dangerous conditions in the Adirondacks, I never had a premonition like this one.

"Maybe I should call my parents," I said to the water-logged sign as an icy trickle of water crept into a seam of my rain jacket. I knew I couldn't do that though, because there would be no way to hide the fear in my voice. They would certainly hear it and undoubtedly begin to worry.

Finally, I decided to hike in to the base of the mountain and have a look around. No one said I *had* to climb it. My pride was beginning to win out and my heart was feeling lighter. "I've already told so many people that I was going to climb Mount Washington," I mumbled to myself. "What would they think if I said I didn't even dare enter the forest surrounding it?" As I crossed the Peabody River, a bitter wind ripped through the skeleton branches of the nearby birch trees taking the last few golden leaves to an early grave in the frozen earth. Like a tightening vice, the premonition returned, stronger than ever. If I climbed that mountain, I would not return alive.

The next day, I woke up without the sound of rain on my tent. A light breeze hummed through the trees and I could see bits of blue sky above. The alpine zone was tantalizingly close. I had made up my mind the night before that I would spend this first day cautiously checking out the lower peaks near the giant. That way, I could get a feel for the alpine zone and be able to escape with less difficulty. That would still leave me with two other days and maybe a third, if I wanted to ration my food, to attempt the ultimate goal.

Soon, I was climbing the incredibly steep Six Husbands trail, a daypack of survival gear strapped to my back. A few windblown, twisted trees gave way to low, hardy bushes. These, in turn, gave way to exposed, lichen covered rocks which were copper, orange and even green in color. I had reached the alpine zone. Mount Jefferson, at 5,716 feet, loomed above me. The lure of a mountain peak is tough to overcome. Fog and sun played hide and seek as I cautiously scrambled higher and higher until suddenly, I found myself looking down on the world. Clouds hung way below in the valleys and the tundra seemed to stretch on forever. I was smiling from ear to ear until I turned around and looked at Mount Washington. The mountain looked evil. Dark clouds raced by a snow covered summit. The hairs on the back of my neck stood on end as the premonition returned.

I turned my back on the giant and strode off toward the second highest peak in the region, Mount Adams. An hour later, I stood at 5,799 feet, the rocky summit of Adams. Looking down from the top, I could see Star Lake nestled like a sapphire between massive peaks. Beyond that, deep in the valley, I could see tiny houses and moving cars. I imagined I was in a plane looking down on a world where I didn't belong. The lure of the next mountain proved too great to overcome. I hiked down from Adams, past the lake and up Mount Madison on the other side.

That evening, I sat in front of my tent sipping hot chocolate as a soft glow from sunset filled the valley. "Maybe this mountain isn't so dangerous after all," I chuckled to myself. "Tomorrow, I will try to climb you," I whispered as I looked up towards the summit of Washington, which somehow still looked ominous and frightening even in the sunset's glory.

That night, I dreamed of scaling peaks. I could hike up any I wanted, except one. This one seemed impossible to climb, no matter what I tried. A bitter, gray light was just seeping into my tent when I began to wake. Immediately, I knew something was wrong. A soft pattering noise came from the rain fly and a distant roar filled my ears. When I stepped out from the safety of my tent, my face felt the stinging sensation of light rain. That solved the mystery of the pattering noise, but what about the roar?

The premonition returned stronger than ever and waged a war against my stubborn pride. I was like a machine though, unwilling and unable to accept defeat. By mid morning, I had packed my survival gear and was once again ascending to the high peaks. I decided to scramble up the

Sphinx trail and at least get to the Sphinx Col, a saddle between two mountain peaks, where I would have a better idea of what the weather was like in the alpine zone. From there, I could climb over Mount Clay and begin the ascent of Washington. Little did I know just how brutal the war was on top.

With my jaw set, I scrambled higher and higher into a frightening, alien world. Periodically, gusts of wind rocketed by, leaving me to wonder what the ridgeline was like. The light rain turned to a heavy mix of rain and sleet as I ascended into the foggy edge of the clouds. A sound, like the screeching of a banshee, grew as I neared the Sphinx Col.

Within minutes, I reached the col and was nearly flattened by hurricane-force winds. Tiny pieces of ice rattled against my rain gear. As I continued to walk I imagined I was a car driving through a cloud of insects at 75 miles per hour down the expressway. The roar was deafening. Somehow, I managed to open up my pack and put on my ski goggles. Stubbornly, I continued up toward Mount Clay.

Less than half an hour later, I stood atop Mount Clay at 5,533 feet. I had about 750 feet of elevation to gain and just over a mile to walk in order to hit the summit of Washington. I had walked just a few feet down the other side, when a roar like a freight train hit my ears, followed by a blast of wind that knocked me completely over. Rain and sleet pummeled my fallen body. From my vantage point, I looked down a stair stepping 1,000 foot drop to the valley below. I looked up toward Washington. A few rock cairns disappeared into a blanket of thick clouds. The premonition was like an angry beast with open claws and an evil smile ready to devour me at any moment. It was so strong that I could see my gravestone and the sad, lonely cries of my family and friends. My demon had found me.

"Is it worth it?" came a soft, soothing voice from a long way away. "You have more life to live. It's not your time."

I closed my eyes and imagined an eagle flying over me. "I'm going back down!" I screamed at the raging storm. Gentle arms helped me to my feet, but when I looked around, nobody was there. The image of a black, knowing eye slipping under calm, warm water flashed across my consciousness. An incredible peace came over me as I turned and headed back toward the col and the safety of my tent.

Days later I was with my brother John at his home in Delaware recounting the adventures of the White Mountains.

"That's a really wild story," he said, a cup of hot chocolate steaming in his hands.

"I learned a lot up there," I said. "You have to know when to turn back. Each backpacking trip I do, I grow to know myself a little bit better. My guardian angel stayed with me, but I almost lost due to my stubborn pride. I won't let my angel down again."

Transition Complete

Heat enveloped me as I stepped from my car into a dripping sub-tropical forest. A warm breeze blew off of Lake Delancy as I quickly set up my tent in hopes of beating the next rain storm. I had been driving all day since South Carolina and hadn't fully realized the immensity of it all. All of a sudden, I felt a stinging sensation in my arm. Without thinking, I slapped it and quickly brushed off a mosquito. With a smile, it hit me. I was back in the land of perpetual summer.

Three days earlier, on November 21st, I had left winter in Michigan. Slowly, I drove south into fall and now I found myself in summer. It was an incredibly weird and awesome transition which took me through barren, snow dusted fields in Michigan and Ohio, snow capped peaks in West Virginia, light blue and green hills in Virginia, cotton fields in South Carolina, brackish, coastal waters in Georgia and finally the sub-tropical heat and dripping palm forests of Florida.

Another year of adventure was about to begin.

Chapter 5:

2001: A New Dream Unfolds

"Ah-Ha!!!" screeched the Inspector as he picked up a tiny piece of trash with a small pair of tweezers. A collective groan came from the fifth graders surrounding him. He inspected it closely with his huge magnifying glass, and then peered at the anxious students through his dark sunglasses. "Who left this here?!?" he bellowed.

The students just looked at each other with surprise. The Inspector, wearing a long, white lab coat and bright yellow hard hat, continued his search around the tents. To an untrained eye, he seemed quite old. He walked with a slight limp and an obvious hunched back. His hair was very curly, brown and gray and it erupted out of the side of his yellow hard hat like an afro. His long, gray beard wiggled as he walked and blew in the light breeze of a warm, early January morning.

The Inspector made a few notes on his clipboard, and then moved on slowly to the next tent. "Ah-Ha!!!" he screeched as he picked up a candy bar wrapper.

"I told you to pick that up!" came a frustrated whisper from a little boy.

"I did!" replied another little boy as he looked desperately at the Inspector. "I think we were sabotaged!"

"Silence!" boomed the Inspector. "If I find out there was sabotage, the guilty tent group will be disqualified!" A hush fell over the crowd as 24 sets of bulging eyes looked at the old, odd fellow in front of them.

The silence was broken by a young girl. "Where's Ranger Mike?" she asked innocently.

"Ranger Mike is here?!?" growled the Inspector.

"Shhhhh…" someone whispered to the young girl. "Remember, Ranger Mike said not to mention that he is here. He doesn't get along with his uncle, the Inspector!"

The Inspector looked at the anxious students in front of him, a barely discernable smile cracking his lips. "I've made my decision for today," he said sternly. The air was so still and quiet, you could have heard a pin drop. "Remember, this is only the first tent inspection during your stay here. There will be a final one tomorrow, and the overall winner will be determined then. Today's winner is…tent number three!" A jubilant cheer rose up from the five girls who called tent number three their home. At the same time, groans could be heard from the other 19 students. With that, the Inspector limped off and within moments, Ranger Mike appeared, ready to continue day two of the Loop Road Environmental Education Camp.

Melting into the Forest

Adjacent to the education camp was a large, densely vegetated hammock of thick, green sub-tropical vegetation. A narrow loop trail passed through the hammock. It was used by the rangers for night walks with the students on their second night of camp. Another trail led off from the loop and meandered through the western edge of the hammock to the far end where it emptied out into sawgrass prairie. To the east lay a huge, unexplored tangle of jungle-like land.

On January 23rd, Sandy, our boss at the education center, decided to take us on a tour to show us what a true South Florida hammock looks like. Sandy was an interesting character. She had grown up in the wilds of South Florida. For a portion of her childhood, she lived with the Miccosukee Indians in the wilderness. She was as tough as anyone in the area and knew more about the region than most could dare to dream about. Now in her mid 50s, she seemed hobbled with the pains of Multiple Sclerosis and age. But as I found out on a cool, clear afternoon in late January, looks can be deceiving.

The day program was done and there were no camps that week, so Sandy said to Pete, Jessica, Stephanie and me that she wanted to take us exploring. She grabbed her cane and we all walked across the dusty, gravel road to the hammock.

As the afternoon shadows lengthened, we explored farther and farther into the wild eastern section of the hammock. We followed a faint path to an old whiskey still, leftover evidence of the lawless days of the early part of the 1900's. At the far edge of the hammock, we found a muddy, water-filled depression in the soft ground. "A gator hole," whispered Sandy. During the dry season, an alligator must have come and wallowed out a hole, where water ended up collecting. These holes can be found dotting the Everglades. In late winter and spring, hundreds of animals can be seen using the water collected in these holes. Despite there being dry, parched land elsewhere, life-giving water is usually found year-round in the gator holes. It is an essential ingredient to this South Florida ecosystem.

Along the far edge of the gator hole was a mound with cracked eggs on top of it. An alligator nest. A shiver went up my spine as we stood, silently watching. With the sun nearing the horizon and a light breeze muting any approaching sounds, I felt like we were sneaking around a dragon's lair. Any minute, he or she might return.

On the walk back out, we went through such thick sections of vegetation that I found myself floundering in the twisted vines and branches of a snarled section of the hammock. Oddly, Sandy moved ahead unimpeded as if she didn't even notice. When we returned to the gravel road, we all looked and felt scratched and beaten up, except Sandy. She looked fresh and strong, as if it hadn't affected her at all. She had a gleam in her eyes, a hint of the wilds hidden in the Everglades.

Later on that evening, Pete seemed a little spooked. I asked him what was wrong.

He looked around slowly and spoke hesitantly. "The way Sandy moved through that hammock was eerie. I was having a tough time keeping up with her on our way back, but managed to stay just behind her. She seemed to melt through the forest. As she walked, that tangle of vegetation seemed to move aside for her."

There are certain people that you meet in life that are so in tune with the natural world, that they have become part of the wilderness itself. Sandy was one of those. She had become one with the Everglades. Her entire life, she had lived and breathed it and now it was as if she was the human personification of that wilderness.

The Dinosaur by My Tent

Sandy was an inspiration. As the winter progressed, I thought more and more about that afternoon in the hammock. I wanted more than ever to immerse myself in the natural world so that I, too, would become one with it. "Most people are so far disassociated with the natural world," Sandy said to me one day, "that they forget we rely on it for our clean air, clean water, food, shelter…even our spiritual connections."

It made me think about my adventure in Big Cypress last March. It was time I returned to that forgotten wilderness north of Highway 41. On February 10th, with a full pack on my back and plenty of water, I once again walked north into the wilds of Big Cypress. With each step away from the road, I felt more and more in tune with the land. My senses heightened until I began to catch the slightest change in the wind or the slightest snap of a branch from an unseen animal. The temperature soared into the upper 80s.

I set up camp in a dry cypress dome. As the shadows grew longer, I walked among the silent trees. I found a huge population of ants moving from one cypress tree to another about 20 feet away. They walked with determination in a straight line, carrying their babies and supplies to a new home. I stood for a long time watching, listening and feeling the heartbeat of the earth. I imagined the Indians roaming the wilderness long ago. "I wonder if they saw these same sights, felt these same feelings?" I whispered.

A blazing sun dipped through the bare cypress trees and slipped below the horizon. One by one, the crickets began to sing their nightly song. Soon, barred owls were calling back and forth as the heavens opened up, pouring forth thousands of stars that looked like glistening diamonds in a midnight black sky. A sense of peace enveloped me as I sank into my sleeping bag.

At first I wasn't sure what had awoken me in the wee hours of the night. For some reason, I was suddenly wide awake, looking at the dark ceiling of my tent. At the edge of my senses, I heard a rustling in the palmettos nearby. The seconds ticked by slowly and my heart began to beat faster. An ancient, primeval sound ripped through the darkness. Instantly, I was back in the dinosaur age with some fearsome carnivore right outside my tent. That wasn't far from the truth. Another bellow split through the tense air, followed by the sound of large, clawed feet scuffling around.

I held my breath as an alligator walked right by my tent, in search of nearby water. Gradually, the sound of bellowing disappeared into the night and was replaced once again by the music of the crickets.

Escape from Carl Ross Key

When I saw the eagle peering at me intently at East Clubhouse Beach, I should have known to take caution. The water was so calm, though, and the air was so still that it was easy to let the late February, southern Florida weather lull me into complacency. I spent the first night at Clubhouse Beach, and then began paddling across the glass-like surface of Florida Bay to Carl Ross Key.

Carl Ross Key is a classic example of a remote tropical island. Palm trees sway in the soft Caribbean-like breeze, white sand and shell beaches cover the shorelines and pelicans swirl in the deep blue sky. The tiny island is surrounded by a wide expanse of shallow Florida Bay water. With the exception of Sandy Key, an uninhabited bird-filled island right next to Carl Ross Key, the closest piece of land is more than five miles away. If you paddled straight south from there, the next piece of land you would encounter would be somewhere near Grassy Key in the midst of the Florida Keys, some 20 miles distant. If you paddled straight west from the island, the next land you would encounter would be Mexico, well over 1,000 miles away. In order to get to and from the island, you have to time it with the tide. If you happen to arrive or depart at low tide, you have a long slog through thick, sucking, sandal-losing mud in order to get onto the island.

The year before, I had paddled to Carl Ross Key with several friends and spent a stunning, full moon night on this remote and enchanting island. It is definitely one of Everglades National Park's most intriguing backcountry campsites.

As I paddled across the warm, mirror smooth water of the bay in late February, wind was the last thing on my mind. Dozens of small sharks fed in the shallow water, their triangular dorsal fins splitting the surface. A gasp of air came from a small sea turtle as it floated briefly on the surface and then disappeared below. Pelicans whirled about in the still air.

It took a couple of hours to cross the open water. When I arrived at the island, I was disappointed to see a small motorboat and a tent along the shoreline. I found a spot to set up my tent on the open beach at the opposite end of the island. The air was full of the calls of white pelicans, cormorants and gulls. I went swimming and lounged in the blazing sun. Idly, I watched as huge cumulous clouds began to build over the mainland and creep out over the bay.

As the birds settled down on Sandy Key, an eerie silence settled over the islands. The storm hit from the north with a furious, frightening violence. My tent was nearly flattened by the wind and pounding rain came in sheets. I jumped into my floundering tent and propped some of my gear onto the wind battered side. Within half an hour, the rain stopped, but the wind continued to rage.

By ten thirty in the evening, six hours of crushing wind had taken its toll. I decided to take the tent down and sleep underneath my canoe. By then, the stars were twinkling above, but the angry winds continued to howl.

I slept surprisingly well and awoke to a beautiful, blazing sunrise. Immediately, I heard the roaring wind. The tide was low and the waves were curling in the distance with frothing white tops. Even worse, the raging wind was from the northeast, the exact direction I needed to go to get back to Flamingo, the tiny community where I had left my car. All morning, I lounged around waiting for the tide to rise and the wind to shift. Shortly after noon, I had the more predictable of my wishes granted. The tide had risen so the water was high enough to attempt the crossing. The wind, however, still screamed directly from the northeast.

"God, be with me," I wrote in my journal just before pushing my 17 foot canoe into the crashing waves. With lightning speed, I moved to the center of the canoe and began paddling hard. From experience, I knew that if I stayed low and in the center of the canoe, I would have a much better chance of paddling directly into a strong wind. It didn't take long to realize, however, that I wouldn't be able to paddle directly into the wind. So I tried paddling more toward the west, leaving about 45 degrees to the wind. The thought of being swept out toward the depths of the Gulf of Mexico made me think twice about this idea. So I tried paddling 45 degrees to the east of the route I needed to go. After 20 minutes, I was still barely off shore and already exhausted from the exertion. With a sinking heart, I realized I was stuck.

As I retreated to shore, I noticed the little motorboat on the other end of the island. There were five people quickly packing up to leave. Casually, as if I find myself in this situation all the time, I moseyed over to their camp.

"Quite a wind, huh?" said an older man, looking in my direction.

"Yeah," I said dejectedly. "I tried to paddle into it, but it's too strong." In the back of my mind I was wondering if they might be able to pull me back to Flamingo.

As if reading my mind, he said, "I'd offer to help you back, but we're going in the other direction. We're going to the Keys."

"Oh, that's okay," I replied with fake happiness. "I wanted an adventure!"

"We do have some food and water we could leave with you if you would like," said a woman. "Also, if you need to call someone, I have a cell phone."

"Thank you very much," I said. "Hopefully, I'll be out of here soon though. Do you have any idea how long this will last?"

"Well," said the man, "they were saying it may die down a little overnight, but the three days beyond that look very windy." The group was starting to get into the boat.

"Maybe I will take you up on that offer," I said. They generously offered me a couple days worth of food and water. I called Pete and Jessica and explained my situation and that I might not be in to work the next day. Within a few minutes, the boat had pushed out into the choppy waves and had disappeared around the corner. My heart sank and for the first time in a long time, I felt totally alone.

The rest of the afternoon crept by. The wind continued to batter the shore. I sat for a long time, just watching the world go by. Fortunately, the sun was hot. "I guess if I'm going to be stranded, I might as well be on a deserted tropical island!" I said to the birds that were once again circling me.

By dinner time, the tide was low again, leaving me no choice but to wait. My next two chances to leave the island would be in the middle of the night or the middle of the next day. As the sun dropped below the angry sea, I thought about the forecast of a slight drop in the wind tonight and then very heavy winds again for several days to come. I looked through my supplies, wondering how long they would last. It was then that an idea popped into my head. "I wonder…" I said to myself.

I went to sleep under my canoe again but this time for just a couple of hours. At ten thirty that evening, I woke up and listened. It was hard to tell, but I convinced myself that the wind had died down a bit. The water level was high. "I'm going for it!" I screamed.

With a quick prayer, I pushed off into the black, stormy sea half expecting to be pushed right back onto the island. Once again, I sat directly in the center of the canoe and aimed my boat toward the distant blinking lights of a tower in Flamingo, more than five miles away. Surprisingly, I began to make some progress, even though I knew the wind was pushing me toward the open Gulf of Mexico. If the wind proved too strong and I had to turn around, I could be in a lot of trouble. If I missed the island on my return I better be prepared to canoe all the way to Mexico.

I paddled hard, non-stop. My senses heightened. There was no moon, so I relied entirely on my sense of hearing. After a while, I was able to hear the different wave heights. Each time a large wave came my way, I was able to steer into it at the last second to keep from tipping. The black seas shook my boat for hours, but it held firm. I didn't dare stop paddling, even for a second, out of fear that I would be pushed broad-side to the waves and flip over.

Gradually, a strange sense of peace enveloped me. I kept looking up at a sky full of sparkling diamonds. Several falling stars burned across the heavens and the water glowed at times with the phosphorescence. The distant lights played tricks on me. At times they would appear close, but then drift away again.

Eventually, I noticed the waves were diminishing in size and the paddling became easier. Within a few minutes, mangroves popped up in front of me. I was almost back! I was in the lee of a small island called Bradley Key, perhaps half an hour from the Flamingo marina. It was after three in the morning when I finally pulled into the calm, deserted marina and gave a prayer of thanks to the sparkling heavens above.

The Trust Walk

"Ranger Mike," a little girl whispered, "what's that?"

We were in the heart of the hammock at Loop Road Environmental Education Center. A stunning half moon penetrated the jungle-like vegetation with a silvery glow. I was standing perfectly still waiting for the rest of the students to catch up. The little girl was pointing up in the tree next to me. Casually, I looked in the direction she was pointing and saw the silhouette of a tiny owl with pointed ears less than an arm's length away.

"That's a Screech Owl!" I whispered as quietly as I could in a very excited voice. Silently, I tip-toed on. Each of the students, in turn, crept past the owl and down the silvery trail. It was as if we were walking in a fairy tale.

In a few minutes, we got to the last hundred yards of the trail. I gathered the boys and girls together. "We have spent the last two days exploring the Everglades," I began in a soft voice. "We've explored *this* hammock on *this* very trail. You know the area well." I paused to let the information sink in. "I have a challenge for you. It's called a trust walk. I challenge each of you to walk the rest of the trail by yourself. I'll send you one by one down the trail. Use this rope fence as a guide. It will take you back to the little gravel road next to the education center and your tents. You will find your teacher waiting for you there."

There were frightened gasps rippling through the crowd. These were kids from the inner city. Most had never spent any time in a natural place until the day before, much less walked in a scary forest by themselves at night. But they had also learned to trust Ranger Mike over the last two days. I had led them into a water-filled cypress slough. We had walked past dozens of dozing alligators, scampered through waving fields of sawgrass and explored into the far reaches of the hammock. In just two days, an amazing confidence had spread around the students and they were already starting to love and trust the Everglades.

"Who would like to go first?" I whispered.

"I will, Ranger Mike," said a dark haired boy, confidently.

I smiled inside and a tear came to my eye. I knew this little boy came from a rough life back home. He had started the camp with a far-off, dejected look and a sad demeanor. By the end of the first day, he was smiling and I knew that the wonder of the natural world had touched his soul.

His confidence seemed to encourage the others. One by one, I sent them down the dark trail. I was the last to go. "This job is truly amazing," I thought to myself as I strolled back to the road where two dozen fifth graders were chatting happily among themselves. It was a moment none of them would ever forget for the rest of their lives.

North to Alaska!

On the morning of March 26th, I received a phone call that would change my life forever. I was offered a summer job as a park ranger in Glacier Bay National Park, Alaska. My job would involve a wide variety of duties, everything from leading guided walks and staffing a quiet visitor center, to presenting programs aboard a 2,000 passenger cruise ship.

The days of March slipped into the days of April and my mind left Florida and began wandering up to Alaska. I dreamed of the map I had seen last summer and all it represented. My mind swam with images of wild mountains, untouched rivers and pristine lakes. I wanted to go to Alaska more than anything I had ever wanted in my life. Surely, the sense of wildness in Alaska would be like no other place on earth.

A pink alpenglow sprinkled the craggy tops of massive, snow-covered peaks. Alaska loomed bigger and bigger in front of me, until it surrounded me. The Alaska Airlines jet dropped between towering peaks into a fjord-like opening where the bustling, coastal town of Ketchikan sat in the glow of sunset.

Minutes later, I burst out the doors of the airport in a full sprint, a maniacal smile on my face and my hair blowing wildly in the wind. I wanted to roll on the ground and sing at the top of my lungs. I had arrived in Alaska! I raced down to the shoreline and plunged my hands into the frigid North Pacific water. I was the happiest person on the planet.

It was April 21st, and I was on my way to Glacier Bay. By the time I woke up the next morning, I was in downtown Juneau. When I looked out the window, the view nearly took my breath away. Impossibly steep, towering, mountains seemed to reach to the heavens. They were completely snow covered and seemed to glow from within.

"A place like this really exists," I whispered.

By midday, I was in a tiny, twin engine plane rising above Juneau, only half an hour from Gustavus, a community of 400 people right outside of Glacier Bay. Swirling clouds twisted around the mountains. In some places, sheets of rain fell to the earth, and in other places the sun pricked holes in the blanket of clouds, sending rays of heavenly light to the world below.

I was in the co-pilot's seat, shoulder to shoulder with the pilot. A massive, blue and white river of ice spilled out of the mountains into a small lake choked with icebergs.

"That's Mendenhall Glacier," shouted the pilot over the roar of the engine. I just nodded, too excited and dumbstruck to utter a word. "Is this your first time in a little plane like this?"

I continued staring out the window, but managed to shout back, "Second time in a little plane like this…first time in Alaska!" The year before, I had taken a small float plane to Isle Royale from Houghton one calm, clear, summer morning.

"You want to drive?" shouted the pilot. That got my attention. With a nervous look, I glanced at the controls within an arm's length, and then at the pilot. "Just kidding!" he yelled back with a big grin on his face. "Just seeing if you were listening to me!" We continued in silence for a few more minutes, and then he said, "We're gonna hit a bit of turbulence as we go by these mountains."

Sure enough, the plane began to shake like a rag doll in the jaws of a playful black lab. My heart jumped into my throat. I didn't want to seem nervous, so out of the very corner of my eye I glanced at the pilot to see if he was tense. He seemed to bounce with the plane, eyes half closed, in his own personal meditation. Slowly, I began to relax and marvel at the white, undeveloped countryside below. The ride became smoother as we glided over Excursion Inlet. With one last bank, we turned toward a flat, tree-filled area and onto a tiny airstrip.

"Welcome to Gustavus!" said the pilot, after a smooth landing. We pulled up next to a couple of deserted metal shacks.

After a few minutes, a ranger by the name of Dave arrived to take me to my new home in Bartlett Cove, ten miles away. As we drove toward the town of Gustavus, he looked at me with a serious expression and said, "This is *the* best job in the National Park Service." This was his second year and I took it as a good sign that he was as excited as someone just getting there for the first time. "We spend much of our work time aboard huge cruise ships and small tour boats. You're going to have an amazing summer!"

"This is the town of Gustavus," he said as we passed a small post office, library and school nestled among thick spruce trees. We came to a dilapidated gas station and a cross road. "Sometimes, you'll hear people talk about 'The Road' and 'The Other Road.' We're on 'The Road', and this," he pointed to the cross road, "is 'The Other Road'." We crossed a swift flowing river and then a volunteer fire department. "There're no police here, but people rarely speed. Most of the cars and trucks you'll encounter are lucky to make it past 35 miles an hour without shaking like a leaf. It's a nice change of pace from the other world out there."

The road turned and the trees seemed to lean in a bit closer. After a few more minutes, we turned again and the pavement emptied onto a narrow gravel road. A brown sign on the right said 'Glacier Bay National Park and Preserve.' Surrounding the sign was a large wetland dotted with spruce and hemlock trees and a row of jagged, white mountains on the horizon. The image was so untouched, so perfect, that I was speechless. The trees huddled closer to the road again and the image was lost in a blur of green needles. The road itself was a spectacle. As we bumped and rattled through the dense trees, I was so excited I could barely sit still. "So, this is what an Alaskan National Park is like," I thought to myself while adrenaline pulsed through my veins.

We climbed a small hill, and then descended down a curvy stretch of the road. An inner lagoon of the ocean materialized in front of us. Within minutes, we were parked in front of my new home, a cabin with brown siding and a green painted porch. The cabin was separated into two housing units, each built to sleep two people. There were several of these nestled among the spongy moss and deep green spruce trees.

As I began exploring around the area that afternoon, a light rain started to fall. This would become the norm. I was now living in a rain forest. I found out later that the area received an average of more than 80 inches of rain a year. Most of that would come in the form of light rain or drizzle.

At dusk, I wandered down to the shoreline of Bartlett Cove, a small, deep cove that branched off of the main bay. It was surrounded by dripping, dark trees. The tide was low and tiny mussels spurted water high into the air. I crept forward and listened as the shadows grew. The faint sound of running water met my ears along with the quiet breath of a marine animal in the bay. I looked across the bay beyond the forest, to snowy mountains disappearing into a blanket of clouds. A sense of wildness penetrated my mind. The adventure of a lifetime was about to begin.

Even Wilder than the Stories

Seasonal training lasted three weeks. During that time, I was like a little boy being shown the world for the first time. Everything was brand new. I learned about bears and whales, sea otters and glaciers. I hiked in the rain forest and learned how to read my surroundings for evidence of wild creatures. There were 14 other interpretive park rangers, each one with a lifetime of stories. Many of the other rangers were just like me. They had the wilderness itself running through their veins and wanted nothing more than to capture that sense of wildness found in only a few regions of the planet. We shared the goal of protecting the park and bringing information and inspiration to our visitors.

One evening, my supervisor sent me to the airport in Gustavus and I boarded another tiny plane for a two hour sight-seeing flight over the park. Glacier Bay is by far the most stunning land I've ever seen in my life. To see the glaciers from above as they poured out of the mountains and emptied thousands of icebergs into the calm, turquoise water was more than words could describe. It was going to be easy to be passionate about this park.

Near the end of training, I boarded a research boat called the Nunatak with the other new rangers and headed "up bay" for a three-day trip. Glacier Bay looks kind of like a giant slingshot. There is a wide, long base in the south and two arms, East Arm and West Arm, jutting out to the northwest and northeast. The distance from the southernmost point in the bay to the northernmost point is 65 miles. Following the shoreline, it's much farther. Our goal was to motor up both arms, following the shoreline and camping along the way, trying to see as much of the bay as we could in three days.

Within a couple of hours, we had already identified two species of porpoise, sea lions, sea otters, harbor seals and numerous species of ocean-going birds like tufted puffins and pacific loons. I was standing on the bow of the boat, rocking gently in the waves with a light rain falling on my jacket, when suddenly a huge spout of water blasted from the sea. My eyes bulged as I watched a gigantic black back break the surface of the water, followed by an enormous tail. A humpback whale disappeared back into depths.

"The humpback whales live here just part of the year," said our supervisor, Rose. "In the fall, they migrate nearly 2,400 miles to their wintering grounds in Hawaii."

Amazingly, they eat nothing while on the move (the quickest recorded journey took 39 days to complete) and nothing while in Hawaii during the winter. In other words, a humpback whale often goes five to seven months without eating! Researchers don't know why they migrate when their food source, tiny fish and krill, is in the north. One hypothesis is that their calves, born in Hawaii during the winter, would not be able to survive in the cold, northern waters of Alaska. Or maybe they tend to be more like me and love the idea of an adventure!

That day we explored the upper reaches of the East Arm, discovering several stunning glaciers which emptied out into the sea. In the evening, we set up our tents along a remote shoreline in a place called Sebree Cove, near the junction of the two arms of the bay. As dusk began to settle, somebody uttered a word that was both terrifying and exhilarating: "Bear!"

I didn't have much experience with bears, especially not the massive brown bears found on the coast of Alaska. Biologically, the Alaskan brown bear is the same as the grizzly bear. This species has a large hump around the shoulders, a dish shaped snout and long, flat claws. They can be brown, black, cinnamon or even white in color. They differ from grizzly bears only in their size. "It is not uncommon to find Alaskan brown bears that stand more than ten feet tall and weigh more than 1,000 pounds," said one of the park's bear biologists earlier in the week. "They are often twice the size of the inland grizzly bear. They gorge themselves on salmon during the latter half of summer and fall until their bellies hang so low they drag on the ground. You would think that a creature that big would be slow. Actually, brown bears can run up to 35 miles per hour over uneven terrain."

There are few creatures on the planet that can compare to the awesome power of an angry brown bear. Stories abound of unfortunate people who have found themselves face to snout with an angry brown bear. These stories have been written up in books, told around campfires and passed on from generation to generation until most people find it exceptionally difficult to even set foot in the same terrain as these giants. The idea of camping in their territory frightened me half to death.

All seven of us huddled close and looked in the direction that Rose was pointing. Across a narrow finger of water, a large, golden brown bear was ambling out of the trees and heading down to the shoreline to feed. We watched as the bear overturned rocks, looking for clams and other inter-tidal zone creatures. The bear looked incredibly powerful, yet peaceful. I was transfixed. We were watching a wild bear in incredibly wild surroundings. It seemed to be the ultimate image of what is pure and right in Alaska. Just then, a second, darker colored brown bear walked out of the forest and looked down the shoreline. Immediately, he spotted the larger, golden bear and its presence didn't seem to sit well with him. He took a few steps toward the golden bear and snapped his jaw. Nothing happened. He continued doing this for several minutes, the irritation mounting, inching closer to the giant.

The tension soared. Suddenly, the golden bear turned and took a few quick, powerful steps toward the intruder, swinging his massive head from side to side. You could almost see the eyes of the dark bear bulge for a second before he turned and fled back into the trees. Glacier Bay was even wilder than the stories I had heard!

The next day, we continued our exploration of the bay, this time up the West Arm. In the upper reaches of the bay we encountered our first really big ice flow. Small icebergs floated on the calm water amidst reflections of jagged, snow-covered peaks. For hours, we weaved our way around the ice flows until we came within half a mile of Margerie Glacier, a dazzling, white and blue giant. The face of the glacier was a mile wide. The height at the waterline was 250 feet. That's similar to a mile wide, 25 story building! The glacier twisted and turned back into the mountains for 21 miles beginning at an elevation of 9,000 feet. Next to Margerie Glacier sat an even larger glacier, Grand Pacific. This glacier was two miles wide, 150 feet tall and 35 miles long. Both glaciers emptied into the sea. The result was one of the most powerful, awe-inspiring phenomena that nature has to offer: calving glaciers.

With a thunderous roar, an enormous slab of ice fell from the face of the glacier, sending a hundred foot splash into the air and a colossal wave barreling toward the boat. Gulls whirled about in the chilly air, their cries filling the silence between the thunder. I was spellbound. The native Tlingit Indians, who have a long history of living and traveling in the bay, call this "White Thunder." This is as close as words can come to describing the sound of ice crashing into the sea.

That night, we camped in a secluded corner of Blue Mouse Cove. Sunlight streamed through a tiny break in the blanket of clouds to the west. I fell asleep, my mind swirling with images of calving glaciers, floating ice and gigantic mountains.

At two o'clock in the morning I awoke, regretting the amount of water I had consumed the night before. I stepped out of my tent into a heavenly show. Green ribbons of light cut across the northwestern sky, dancing in the still air. The northern lights were so intense that the surrounding mountains radiated a green glow. They continued until the sky grew too light with the coming dawn. This must be God's home, heaven itself.

The New Celebrity

"Hey," boomed a jolly voice. I was in full ranger uniform on the bridge of a 14 story-cruise ship and looking into the happy face of the cruise director. His hand was outstretched and he proceeded to give me a bone-crushing hand shake. It was mid May and my first day aboard a cruise ship. "Are you the one doing the program in the theater?"

"Yes, I am," I said, suddenly feeling self-conscious.

"Well then, follow me!" he said a bit too cheerfully. "Just five minutes until it begins!" Suddenly, I was incredibly nervous; my mind had completely forgotten what I planned to say to hundreds of people. A few minutes earlier, I had been shrouded in fog, riding on a 26 foot, Park Service power boat on the choppy water of the lower bay. We had been watching sea otters, sea lions and a humpback whale frolic in the waves, free as could be. A bald eagle had flown by, soaring on the stiff breeze. Slowly, a massive ship had materialized out of the fog. Everything happened incredibly fast after that. The captain of our little Park Service boat matched the eight knots of the cruise ship and pulled right up alongside it, like an invading pirate ship. A rope ladder was lowered from a side door. I proceeded to climb up that ladder with a fellow park ranger into a completely foreign world.

The cruise director led me and two of his associates followed, maybe to prevent me from getting lost. We descended several flights of stairs, walked down hidden hallways, descended a couple more, then rose one level and suddenly we were at the auditorium. Multitudes of people wandered around, shoving their way into an obviously packed theater.

"Here," said the cruise director as he stuck his large hand toward me, "I'll take your slides and get them set up. Be sure to stand near the podium during your program, so that the TV camera crew has an easier job." He was about to walk away when he turned to me and said, "Oh, do you want me to introduce you?"

"Ah…sure, I guess," I managed to say, while still thinking about being on TV for the first time.

"Real good!" he said. I noticed that he studied my name tag for a moment with one eyebrow raised and an uncertain look on his face then said, "How about I just introduce you as Mike?" Before I could say anything, he slapped my shoulder, gave me a wink, and was gone.

I had barely made my way through the throng of people when I heard the cruise director on the stage. "GOOD MORNING EVERYONE!" he said into a microphone in a booming, energized voice. "I trust you all had a *fantastic* breakfast!" The theater was packed with more than six hundred people eagerly anticipating his every word. Out of the blue, I remembered the advice I had gotten about not letting cruise directors introduce you before your program. "We have a *very* special treat for you today." My heart flipped as the audience began to clap. Any minute, I would undoubtedly pass out. The cruise director went on slowly and loudly enunciating every syllable. "I would like to introduce to you a Glacier Bay *PARK RANGER,* here to *ENTERTAIN* us! Ladies and gentlemen, put your hands together for…Mike!"

The audience exploded in a raucous cheer that must have been heard in Juneau. My head was swimming and my knees were weak as I stumbled onto the stage. I grabbed the microphone and had absolutely no idea what to say. I stood there for what seemed like an eternity. Slowly, the crowd quieted. Instead of beginning my talk, the microphone let out a high-pitched whine that reverberated through the glamorous room. For good or for bad, I had entered the world of the Alaskan cruise ship.

An incredibly weird and strangely fun day ensued. I found myself talking to hundreds of people over the course of the day. Most were thrilled that they were in Alaska. I was thrilled that I was not only in Alaska, I was getting paid to go on an Alaskan cruise ship. It was the oddest thing in the world to be wolfing down cheesecake from the buffet line while looking up at a massive glacier, calving off chunks of ice the size of buildings.

As the day progressed, I was on the receiving end of an odd assortment of questions. Most people wanted to know the name of a particular glacier or mountain; others wanted to know how to get back to the buffet line. I was happy when a visitor asked about birds, a subject about which I felt quite knowledgeable and confident.

"Howdy Ranger!" came a voice with a strong southern accent. "Name's Ned, from Dallas, Texas. Glad to meet ya!" Ned wore cowboy boots, a button down shirt and a cowboy hat. Even without the hat, he would have towered over me. Somehow I knew this conversation would be memorable. "I saw a bird the other day and was wondering if you could tell me what it was."

"Sure," I said cautiously. An odd silence fell between us and we looked at each other with strange expressions on our faces.

"Any idea what it was?" he asked finally.

I continued to stare at him with a blank expression and then asked, "Do you remember its color or shape or size?"

The Texan looked thoughtful. "Hmmm," he said with a bushy eyebrow pointing upwards. "Let's see…he was flying by the ship…" He went on like this for a few moments then turned his eyebrow back on me. "No ideas, huh?"

"Well," I said slowly, "that doesn't narrow it down a whole lot."

"Fair enough!" he boomed without missing a beat. "I got to get me back inside and get another one of them peanut butter chocolate pies." Ned disappeared in the throng of people and was replaced by someone else.

"Excuse me, Ranger?" said a sweet, elderly woman.

"Yes?" I replied, with a kind smile on my face.

"What elevation are we at?" she asked.

I paused for a moment then glanced over the side of the ship at the ocean below. "I'd say probably about eighty feet."

"Thank you very much," she said and disappeared just like the rest.

I barely had time to breathe before a high-pitched voice erupted from behind me. "Ooohh! The *ranger*! Honey, come quick! It's the *ranger*!" I suddenly had visions of running as fast as I could down the stairs nearby and jumping onto the nearest iceberg.

"This is going to be an odd summer," I mumbled quietly. When I returned to my little home in the rain forest that evening, I took a slow walk among the dripping trees. A light rain was falling, as it had at least once a day for almost a month now, but it was music to my ears. The call of a varied thrush pierced the silence of the peaceful forest. Tranquility returned to one of the wildest corners in America.

Solo, in the Land of the Giant Brown Bears

I discovered early on that the way to explore Glacier Bay is by kayak. In early May, I bought a 15 and a half foot, bright yellow sea kayak. My first few outings felt tipsy and awkward. Each time I attempted to enter the kayak I felt as if I were seconds away from rolling into the frigid north Pacific water. Once I finally did get in the kayak, I kept trying to paddle like I was in a canoe. The result was far from glamorous. At first, I was content to paddle in the lagoon. The shore was never far away and I didn't have to worry about tides or wind or waves. It didn't take long, though, for my sense of adventure to lure me on. Soon, I edged out into the main part of Bartlett Cove, and even began riding the tide into the nearby Beardslee Islands.

A sense of freedom pulsed through my veins every time I took a paddle stroke. It was addictive. It didn't take long before I was paddling every chance I got. In the latter half of May and early June I took several overnight trips into the Beardslee Islands. The wildlife back in the islands and secluded bays was unbelievable. Seals followed my kayak with an inquisitive eye. Harbor porpoises popped up to the surface, the sound of their breathing echoing back and forth among the forested hills. Dozens or even hundreds of sea otters rafted together, bobbing along in the waves and current. Pacific and common loons inhabited every little niche and cove, while bald eagles glided overhead. It was almost guaranteed that I would see more black bears than humans.

Gradually, I became more and more a part of the land and water. I felt much more at ease in the lower bay because the brown bears lived in the upper regions of the bay. Many people said I should be more concerned about black bears because they were more daring and curious and could be predatory, but the idea of fending off a 200 pound black bear was much easier to live with than the idea of defending myself against a 1,000 pound brown bear. I became accustomed to the black bears near shore and they got used to me. I grew to accept them, and they seemed to accept me. The Beardslee Islands not only became my getaway, they became my sanctuary.

One sunny afternoon in early June, I realized just how comfortable I was becoming in the backcountry. In mid afternoon, I set up camp on the northern point of Young Island, next to the entrance to Secret Bay. I sat down in a flower filled meadow and began looking around. In nearly every direction were snow-covered mountains, stately evergreen trees and sun crystals sparkling off of turquoise water. A light, refreshing breeze blew off of the water and the sun warmed me to my core.

I was so mesmerized by my surroundings that I slipped into a sort of trance. Time stood utterly still. There were no phones, no computers, no cars, no people. Life's worries and pains blew away in the soft breeze. My mind could think, unimpeded. I came back to my senses in what seemed like minutes, but actually more than three hours had passed.

I spent numerous days in early summer just like that. The blue sky and warm sun had replaced the cold and rain of spring. Darkness would never fully come during the night and the sunsets seemed endless. I explored every nook and cranny in the Beardslee Islands and soon began to know it like my own backyard.

But a slight gnawing in the deep recesses of my mind began to grow. The upper bay, the land of the brown bear, had a spell on me. I was still nervous around the giants, but I desperately wanted to explore the land north of the Beardslee Islands. I wanted to know it and feel comfortable in it. My first exploration "up bay" finally came in the end of June.

A thick mantle of clouds hung in the still air. Ever so slowly, I looked around at the rubble-filled beach and the dense forest just beyond that. The diesel engine of the Crystal Fjord, a 40-foot, deep hulled boat used to drop people off in the backcountry of Glacier Bay, was fading off in the distance. In front of me was the turquoise water of Geikie Inlet, on the west side of Glacier Bay. Its water was almost Caribbean in appearance, and snow-covered mountains surrounded it. An odd ringing filled my ears as I looked up and down the rocky beach. "Just me and the bears," I whispered. I was completely and utterly alone in the wildest, most remote place I had ever been in my life.

Little by little, I packed my gear into my bright yellow kayak and pushed off into the calm water. For the next three days I would be completely immersed in this Alaskan wilderness before being picked up again by the Crystal Fjord.

By the middle of the next day, I was really starting to get my rhythm. The sun broke through the clouds and the temperature soared to 70 degrees. I paddled to the far end of the inlet and nearly flipped my kayak while gawking at a scene so magnificent it's hard to even describe. Jagged, snow-covered mountains had glaciers pouring down their sides. A rushing, glacier-fed river the same color as the inlet tumbled over the rocky, rugged landscape.

I stashed my kayak and bushwhacked through a dense stand of alder. About halfway through the alder, I began to think very long and hard about the giant brown bears. I was so accustomed to walking silently in the wilderness that it took most of my willpower to begin to talk loudly to the bears. The last thing I wanted to do was find myself face to face with one of the giants.

It didn't take long to walk through the alder. In front of me was a wide expanse of rugged terrain in a recently de-glaciated valley. I followed the tumbling river higher and higher into the mountains. Soon, I rounded a bend and could see the glistening white of the glacier itself not far away. I sat in the warm sunshine for a long time, overlooking this beautiful valley, slowly slipping into my wilderness trance.

It was late afternoon by the time I returned to my kayak. The shadows crept along slowly in an everlasting Alaskan summer evening. It was just a few days after the summer solstice and would not get fully dark that night.

Marble Mountain was bathed in pink and orange when I finally set up my tent on a tiny island guarding the entrance to Shag Cove. Way above me on the top meadows of the mountain, mountain goats roamed about, their bright white coats glistening in the late day sun. A river otter dove repeatedly just off shore, fishing for its dinner. It was well after ten o'clock when a loud "whoosh" broke the silence. For the next hour, I watched three humpback whales feeding near the mouth of Geikie Inlet, their powerful spouts shooting ten feet into the air and their giant tails slipping beneath the surface with each dive. A fingernail moon hung in the dark blue sky. As I fell asleep that night, I could barely believe that a place like this truly existed.

I left early the next morning under a sparkling blue sky and paddled north toward Sundew Cove. The air was absolutely still and the water held a perfect reflection of the mountains and forests. It was the type of weather that could lull a person into complacency. In fact, I was so warm and the paddling was so easy, that I almost missed the bear. I looked up and there he was, walking along the edge of the water. I was no more than a short stone's throw away from shore. As if in slow motion, we crossed paths; I was on the water and he was on land. His powerful leg muscles flexed every time he took a step but he was not at all interested in me. He continued along the shoreline as if I didn't exist. The moment was frozen in time. To this day I'm not sure if it lasted a few seconds or a few lifetimes. I am sure, though, that I glimpsed the wild spirit of Alaska.

The Breaching Whale

Near the end of June, I found myself spending the day studying whales with Janet, one of the whale biologists. It was my job to learn as much as I could from Janet, so that I could pass on the information to visitors. It was cool and cloudy with barely a ripple on the mirror surface of the bay.

"Our goal," said Janet, as she steered the small boat out into the open water, "is to identify as many different whales as possible. First thing to look for is the spout of water when they come up to the surface to breathe. This typically sprays a good ten feet into the air. We'll then motor over as quickly as we can so I can get a picture of the back of the tail when it dives."

I had heard stories of being able to identify humpback whales from the back of their tails. Janet went on to tell me that the back of each whale tail is like their fingerprint; each one is unique. Janet continued, "Through our pictures, we have been able to determine that some whales have been returning to Glacier Bay for as many as 27 years in a row!"

There were no whales in the lower bay, so we continued out into Icy Strait, a large inlet from the open Pacific just south of Glacier Bay. "When it's calm, I like to come into Icy Strait," said Janet. "Keep an eye out to the west though, because the weather can change in a heartbeat. If you see a white line on the horizon, let me know immediately. That's a squall line and means major wind and waves are coming very fast. I call it the *white wall of death*."

I looked apprehensively to the west, then at our pitifully small boat. Just then, a spout rocketed into the sky not more than a couple of hundred yards away. We zipped over in that direction. The whale was enormous. Humpback whales can be up to 50 feet long and weigh 40 tons. It looked to be the size of a bus! With remarkable grace, the whale arched its back and dove back into the depths. I grabbed the steering wheel as Janet began taking pictures. She quickly identified the whale with a number and said this particular one was probably around 20 years old. There have been reports of humpback whales living to age 90.

We went on like this throughout the morning. There were dozens of whales in the area, most feeding like there would be no tomorrow. "These whales consume up to a ton of food each day," said Janet. "That's about a million calories! They will feed roughly 22 hours a day."

The wind began to pick up as the afternoon progressed. As we turned to go back home, my mouth flew open as a giant humpback suddenly catapulted itself out of the water and came crashing down with a gargantuan splash. This is called breaching. The whale breached time and again. No one knows exactly why they do this. It may be because they are happy, sad, frustrated or just trying to get barnacles off of their bodies. Perhaps it is just an exclamation point to accentuate whatever they are doing. What is certain is that it is one of the most awe inspiring actions in the wildlife kingdom.

Paddling among the Glaciers

The days of summer marched on. At times the sun would shine for days without a cloud in the sky. Other times, a cold, light rain would fall for days on end. In early July, I spent three, rain-soaked, chilly and windy days in Scidmore Bay and Charpentier Inlet. But even on days like those, I couldn't help but be amazed. The wildlife was like no place I had ever been. Whales, sea lions, harbor seals and porpoises popped up throughout the water, bear and moose covered the land and eagles were ever-present in the sky. On rainy days, unnamed waterfalls crashed thousands of feet down unnamed mountains.

For each rainy trip, a dry one followed. My most memorable dry trip came in early August. I paddled off from Queen Inlet in totally calm seas. Like magic, the fog and clouds lifted to reveal a brilliant blue sky. Along the steep cliffs of Composite Island, I happened to look straight above into the curious eyes of a bald eagle. It was so close that I could see the yellow part of its eyes. As we stared at each other, I couldn't help but wonder what the eagle was thinking about. A bald eagle can see the silver flash of a tiny fish from well over a quarter of a mile away. What did that eagle see in my eyes, which were no more than 30 feet away? In the eyes of that eagle, I saw power and honor and wisdom, all those things we strive for as human beings. Perhaps the eagle just shakes his head in pity at us. We are the only creature on the planet that thoughtlessly destroys the home where we live. Perhaps the eagles are trying to tell us that we are a part of the wilderness we occasionally glimpse and that the wilderness is a part of us. Without the wilderness, not only would the eagles not survive, but neither would we. Every living creature on the planet relies on the wilderness for clean air, pure water and sustenance.

As I paddled farther and farther up the West Arm of the bay, an unusual, thundering sound began to echo back and forth across the water. The glaciers were talking. Massive chunks of ice were dropping from the vertical walls of giant glaciers that emptied into the sea. That evening, I paddled up to the 150 foot face of Lamplugh Glacier. I found a campsite nestled in the rocks and fell asleep that night to the thunderous roar of calving glaciers.

I spent three glorious days that trip exploring the upper reaches of Glacier Bay. I walked on the glacier and felt the ground shake when it shed its weight. With the exception of the floating city that cruised by me on day two, I didn't see another human being the entire time.

The final morning, as I paddled along Gilbert Peninsula, I saw more bald eagles than I could count. Each one seemed to give me a quizzical look and a few seemed to give me a knowing look. As the miles slipped by, my kayak slowly became a part of me, the paddle an extension of my arms.

The Eyes of the Wolf

By mid August, the upper parts of Glacier Bay and the Beardslee Islands were feeling more and more like home. I had explored many areas of the bay in my kayak already. But there were still big sections of land that I knew nothing about. There was a safety net while on the water. If I encountered a bear, I could simply paddle off in the opposite direction. Without the safety of my kayak nearby, I felt vulnerable.

On August 11th, I decided it was time to immerse myself in the land. I had done a couple of short backpacking trips with friends and even a couple of solo overnights, but none of them were truly off trail where the sense of wildness permeates everything. On that Saturday, under a cloudless sky, I walked off by myself into the Alaskan wilderness.

I ambled south along a narrow, shoreline path, and then cut into the forest at Coopers Notch. When we had visited this area during training, I had been told that if I ever wanted to see wildlife, I should go to Coopers Notch, find a comfortable place nearby in the moss and wait. The Notch is a break in the surrounding hills and is used by bears, moose, wolves and others.

As I walked through the Notch in mid afternoon, I heard something large rustling in the dense undergrowth. Fresh wolf tracks dotted the muddy trail. Soon, I came to a string of meadows and was lured on by the soft sunshine. The ground was dotted with Alaska Cotton, a soft, white, cotton-like plant. There was so much moose evidence that I forgot all about bears. At one point, I spooked a huge cow moose and her calf. She dwarfed the trees in the meadow as she sauntered off.

As the afternoon progressed, I walked from meadow to meadow. A warm, summer sun brightened the world in a contented glow. Finally, I stopped at a bigger patch of trees and found a dry, moss-covered campsite. After setting up camp, I sat down in the soft moss and was soon lost in thought. Gradually, I slipped into the now familiar wilderness trance. I thought about how much I had grown since that first solo backpacking trip on Isle Royale four years earlier. Back then, sitting and thinking with nothing else to do was an impossible feat for me. As I slipped deeper and deeper into the trance, the wildness of Alaska grasped me with its perfect hold.

Twice during the night, I woke up to the sound of something large using its claws to climb a nearby tree. Somehow I put the thought of bears out of my mind and was able to fall back asleep.

It was early morning when I stepped out of my tent and looked from the trees onto the flower-filled meadow next to my campsite. Piercing blue sky dominated above and the sun was just rising above the tall, straight spruce trees across the meadow. All of a sudden, something caught the corner of my eye to the left. What looked like a large German Shepherd was loping along the tall grasses of the meadow. My heart skipped a beat as I realized I was looking at a wild wolf for the first time in my life.

The wolf continued sauntering along until he was no more than 50 feet away. He stopped in mid stride, as if he had just noticed something that didn't belong. Slowly, he turned his head in my direction. Our eyes locked for what seemed like an eternity. The eyes of the wolf were proud, powerful and utterly wild. It was as if I was looking directly into the eyes of the wilderness. Satisfied that I wasn't a threat or prey, he turned his head back and continued on as if I was not there. Within moments, he disappeared into the bush, leaving me to wonder if it was only a dream.

The Bonfire

In the late summer, I found myself feeling more and more confident not only in Glacier Bay's backcountry, but also in my ranger duties. Unfortunately, I didn't always think about what was coming out of my mouth when I was speaking to the visitors. I had repeated certain phrases and talks so many times that my mind would sometimes not register what my mouth was saying.

A classic example was when I was aboard a small tour boat in the upper bay, just shy of a stunning place called Jaw Point. It is called Jaw Point because when you arrive at the point, you get a sudden, jaw-dropping view of Johns Hopkins Glacier and all the towering cliffs and mountains around it. I had a particularly lively group of visitors that day, most of which were hanging on my every word. The captain had told me earlier that the 70 or so passengers on board averaged 70 years old.

We were nearly to Jaw Point, when I turned on the microphone and said, "Ladies and gentlemen, you are not going to want to miss this. We are coming up to a place called Jaw Point and believe me, it's worth seeing!"

"Ranger Mike, why is it called Jaw Point?" asked an elderly woman.

I had answered this question hundreds of times before. I didn't think twice as I quickly turned on the microphone so the whole boat could hear my reply. "It's called Jaw Point because when we go around it, you are going to be so impressed with the view that you will *drop* your *drawers*."

Immediately, I realized something was wrong. The words didn't seem quite right. Not only that, but the entire boat was shaking with laughter.

"Has anybody dropped their drawers yet?!?" asked a breathless, old man clutching his stomach in convulsive laughter.

"Drop your…jaw, I mean," I said slowly, then began laughing with the rest of them.

Despite my word mix-ups, I was a celebrity. Everyone wanted to talk to me or invite me to sit with them. After an amazing dinner aboard the tour boat, one of the deck hands came up to my table and whispered to me, "Your chariot awaits." We had arrived back in Bartlett Cove and a zodiac was all fired up to zip me to shore. When I stood to leave, the applause was deafening.

"Hip, hip hooray! Hip, hip hooray!" cried the passengers as I waved and hopped into my chariot with a big smile. The entire boat was rocking with cheers, the sounds echoing across the calm bay.

"Just another day at the office," I whispered. "I can't believe they *pay* me to do this!"

My confidence in Glacier Bay soared throughout the summer until the end of the year when something unexpected began eating away the peace and tranquility of one of the wildest places on earth.

I looked in horror as an ugly crane began devouring the hillside near my home. Tall, stately spruce trees were snapped in half like match sticks and stacked in half-hazard piles. For the last month, the talk of the town had been the construction on the park road. The decision had been made to widen the road and pave it. Not only that, but the plan also called for a new section of road to be put in near my house as a cut-off to the lodge.

Progress is sometimes tough to swallow. There were definitely some benefits to a paved road but I couldn't help but feel that we were somehow altering the sense of wildness. Wistfully, I thought back to the first day I had arrived in the park. When we turned that last corner of pavement and the road became gravel and narrowed, a tingle of excitement had gone up and down my spine. The feeling was exactly what I had imagined it would be. Glacier Bay was truly an Alaskan park. Progress said that if we pave the road, the access will be easier and safer. We would be able to get into town faster and wouldn't have to worry about rain turning the road into a quagmire. It was also making it more like a lower 48 park and threatening that *feeling* that the place is wild. At what point does easier and safer become a downgrade instead of an upgrade?

As if sensing an ominous trend, the weather began to turn. The brief summer was fading like a beautiful dream and was being replaced by a cold, rainy autumn. The end of August dripped into the beginning of September. The rain began to fall nearly every day again and the winds were beginning to increase.

It took just a couple of days to mow through the forest in my back yard. Then, the fires began. All those worthless trees that were hacked down and placed in numerous piles needed to be destroyed. Huge bonfires were lit and slowly, the fallen giants began to burn.

I was in the middle of Beartrack Cove, a wild, rarely visited inlet about a day's paddle from Bartlett Cove, when Indian summer hit. I spent the day of September 9th, basking in a hot sun under a cloudless sky. My mind slipped back into the wilderness trance and I forgot about the world's problems. It was so warm, I actually went swimming in the 45 degree water! The next day's weather was almost identical. The world seemed happy and alive once again.

All that changed on September 11th. When I woke up that morning, something seemed wrong. Low clouds had moved in from the southwest and a light rain was beginning to fall. Summer was certainly over now, giving way to a soggy, cold fall.

We were on our way to the cruise ship that rainy morning when we heard on a radio with scratchy reception that a plane had run into the World Trade Center. The shock of the terrorist attack was felt even in remote Alaska.

I spent that day on a ghost ship in one of the most beautiful places in the world. I was on the Ryndam, a huge Holland America cruise ship packed with people who had waited perhaps a lifetime to see such beauty. Many people never left their rooms or if they did, they walked the halls talking in hushed, sad voices. I didn't blame them in the least. I felt sick to my stomach and wanted nothing more than to go back to my little home in the rain forest and sit under a dripping tree.

That night, I felt even more let down. The sense of peace did not return. It was already getting dark when I walked to my cabin after returning from the ship. A heavy rain fell from a miserable, cloud cast sky. Out of the corner of my eye, I saw the flames. Despite the downpour, the bonfires were burning higher than ever.

Tears streamed down my face as I walked to the edge of my destroyed forest. "Will life ever be the same?" I asked, my heart breaking. "What have we done to our world?"

The next day I was scheduled to be the ranger aboard a small tour boat for the day. Despite my word mix-ups from the previous month, this duty was always my favorite. I could spend the entire day on the deck of a small boat pointing out the incredible wildlife of the park and talking to very interested visitors about the stories behind the scenery. We would get paid to look at and talk about some of the most stunning sights on the planet. At six in the morning, I found out the boat was cancelled. My depression soared as I was stuck in an office for ten hours that day. Rain continued to pour down and darkness came way too quickly.

In places like Glacier Bay though, the sense of wildness is hard to contain. Man is not the ruler of this wilderness. It does heal and it does return. On September 15th, I spent the whole day kayaking in the Beardslee Islands and Secret Bay. Harbor seals followed and looked inquisitively at me. They stared at me until I looked at them, then quickly turned away and looked somewhere else as if to say, "I'm not looking at *you!*"

The air sung with the sound of Canada geese and sandhill cranes. A sea otter swam up close to me and a humpback whale spouted even closer.

The healing began that day but was given an extra boost that night. It was well after dark and I was writing in my journal when suddenly a sound pierced the night air. Silently, I crept out my door as the hair on the back of my neck prickled and a chill ran up and down my spine. A pack of wolves were howling, the soul of the wilderness crying out in the cold Alaskan night.

Migrating South

I left Glacier Bay that year with mixed emotions. For much of the next two months, I explored the desert country of Texas, New Mexico and Arizona, soaking in the warm sun and enjoying rainless days.

In the end of November, I made yet another migration south, deep into the land of endless summer. Once again, I was going to work in environmental education at Everglades National Park. This year, I was going to live at Pine Island and work out of Hidden Lake Environmental Education Center. This was farther south in the Everglades and closer to the ever-growing city of Miami. I was ready for the change of location, but the sights in the last couple hours of my drive made my skin crawl.

Instead of approaching the Everglades from the center or west of the peninsula, as I had done each of the past two years, I approached it from the east. This is the Miami side. Never before had I seen such development. Identical new houses and condominiums covered the land. There were places that sawgrass prairie stretched to the horizon on my right and houses stretched to the horizon on my left. A thin layer of brown smog hung in the air. The traffic was hideous. As I wove in and out of traffic snarls, beeping my horn like a mad-man, I recalled the statistic that on average, 900 people move to south Florida every day! Their arrival was as sure and unstoppable as the rising tide.

It was dark by the time I arrived in the sanctuary of the Everglades. The crickets were calling and I sighed as I breathed in the warm, moist air. That evening I took a walk in shorts and a t-shirt under a full moon. A silvery glow fell on the outstretched palm fronds. The lights of Miami were ominously close to the northeast. For the first time, I saw how fragile and small the Everglades really was and it filled me with an overwhelming sadness.

Chapter 6:

2002: Whispers in Quiet Corners

"Hey Ranger Mike, there's a big snake over here," came a shaky voice from a scared little boy.

Twenty-five sixth graders had just stepped off the bus for their first day of camp at Hidden Lake Environmental Education Center on a warm, sunny February morning.

"Okay," I said with my confident ranger voice, "everyone just take a step back and I'll look at him." It was not at all unusual to see snakes. In fact, there are 26 species within the Everglades. Some, like the brown water snake, we saw quite often. They were harmless and often provided a great educational experience. Despite stories to the contrary, I rarely saw venomous snakes.

As I peered into the thick tangle of bushes where the little boy was pointing, all 25 students excitedly crowded in around me. I was not at all prepared for what I saw. My eyes widened as I spotted a tube-shaped body nearly the circumference of my leg. A chill ran up and down my spine when I noticed the distinct shape of diamonds on the snake's back. We were looking at the largest and arguably the most dangerous venomous snake species in the United States: the eastern diamondback rattlesnake.

The underbrush began to move as the snake grew agitated. "Okay," I said, a bit flustered, "let's all take three giant steps backwards. Then follow me."

At the end of the day, I returned by myself to see if the snake was still there. It was long gone; swallowed up in the wilds of the Everglades.

Another tropical winter was progressing in the sawgrass prairies of Everglades National Park. For some reason, I felt far more claustrophobic than I had the previous two years. The city seemed to be leaning ever-closer into an endangered land. As the season advanced, the night lights of Miami seemed to spread like a horrible virus, ever nearer the wilderness. More and more, I heard stories about the development in south Florida. Every day the ominous prediction I had heard during training rang through my head. "If the development doesn't slow or people don't stop needlessly wasting water, the Everglades will cease to function as a wetland in 15 to 20 years. The Everglades is half the size it used to be. The number of wading birds has already decreased by as much as 90% over the last century and the pinelands have been reduced by more than 95%. If we don't change something, during our lifetime we will see the final extinction of life in the Everglades."

In late March, the season's last group of campers arrived. As I looked out at the happy, energetic kids from inner-city Miami, I knew that the future of the Everglades rested in their hands and hearts. That evening, we all sat around the campfire circle, flames licking the dry wood, a crescent moon hanging like a question mark in the evening sky. Crickets sang softly in the night and fireflies danced in the shadows. For the first time all day, the students were quiet. I sat among them, lost in thought.

"What's the matter, Ranger Mike?" asked a little girl. "You seem sad."

I scanned the faces of the students. "I am sad," I confirmed. "I'm sad because the Everglades is dying. Too many people are choosing not to protect wild places like the Everglades. If we don't start to care, places like this will no longer exist." An apprehensive silence hung in the air. I continued. "Earlier today, we talked about endangered species. What do we mean when we say that something is endangered?"

A little boy raised his hand and said, "That means it may not always be here."

"That's right," I said gently. "An endangered species or place may not always be here. It is in immediate danger to becoming extinct. What does extinct mean?"

"It means that it's not here at all anymore," said another little boy with a dejected voice.

"Yes," I continued, "not here anymore. Gone forever. The Everglades is in immediate danger to becoming extinct." I let the words soak in for a minute then said, "Can you imagine coming to the Everglades and seeing no wildlife? No alligators, no otters, not even birds."

"The story I am about to tell you is a make believe story, but is based on the idea that this area is endangered and that species are going extinct. It's a story I wrote about what might happen if we don't care for and protect places like this. It's called, 'Always Remember.'"

I stood as still as a statue, peering into a thicket of tangled bushes. There it goes again! What is that? I wondered.

It was hot and humid, and a light rain was falling. I was standing at the edge of the great parking lot next to the great shopping mall in the greatest city on earth. A revolving, flashing sign urged me to look the other way. Still, I stared into the bushes. Suddenly, without any warning, it was right in front of me. It had wings, a small body and a beak. A bird! I was thrilled beyond belief as I recalled reading stories of such creatures that actually flew. They still exist, I thought.

In the days that followed, I went back every day to try to see it again. Day after day, there was nothing. Finally, one bright sunny morning, I stepped into the bushes. At first, a faint trail lured me on. A strange feeling overcame me as I proceeded into this foreign territory. I had to find what was beckoning me.

Finally, I came to a clearing with a fast flowing river. No birds. As I was about to turn and go, I spotted a small figure across the river. It was a very old man. He stood facing me; long white beard, old tattered clothes and a straw hat. But it was his eyes that caught my attention. They were as clear as diamonds, as piercing as lightning, strong and steady.

'Good morning,' I said. I figured he would laugh, but I said it anyway. 'I'm looking for a bird.'

He nodded with understanding, as if he knew. 'I can show you birds,' he said in a clear, strong voice.

'Birds?' I asked. 'As in more than one?'

'More birds than you could possibly count,' he answered. 'Follow me!'

With that, he disappeared into the bushes behind him. I crossed the river and plunged deep into the thicket. Everything was new. I had no idea this many trees existed anywhere in the world anymore.

For being an old man, he could really move. At last, I caught up to him. For an hour or more, we moved like deer, stealthily, through the forest. The forest ended at a massive expanse of sawgrass, waving in the gentle breeze.

Nearby, a canoe leaned against a tree. With one swift motion, he overturned the canoe, slid it into the water and away we went. Three more hours of paddling revealed the same expanse of waving sawgrass.

The shadows were growing longer when we finally stopped. As I opened my mouth to talk, he quickly put his finger to his lips. 'Silence,' he said. His voice was urgent and demanding. We listened. Nothing...Nothing...Wait. What was that? A simple, pure, magical sound came from the grass. There it goes again! Like a flute, yet crisper. Like a laugh, yet happier. Like a cymbal, yet more dramatic.

Suddenly, the sound was duplicated across the river. I was in the middle of two bird songs! I was about to cry out with delight when I looked next to me at the old man. He was looking in the opposite direction of the birds, listening very intently, as if he heard something I didn't.

What happened next will forever remain in my memory. As if on cue, the songs of a million birds began. The songs grew louder and louder until my ears echoed with delight. Across this sea of grass I heard another distinct sound. As it approached, I turned my head and the sky turned white. The earth began to tremble. Right over our heads they flew. Millions, perhaps billions, of white ibis, egrets, herons and storks. The noise thundered from the steady beating of their wings.

The songs of billions of birds around us escalated higher as the sun dropped like an enormous ball of fire beyond the horizon. One by one, the songs grew softer, then stopped, until the only sounds came from the countless crickets hiding in the grass.

A tear rolled down my face as I turned toward the old man. 'This is it,' he said. 'The very last refuge of all. Just like you and me, the birds also need a home. Their home is this secluded corner of the world called the Everglades. Without it, they could not live. You must give this place pure water and feed it clean air. It's up to you, my friend. Always remember, it's in your hands now. Always remember.'

With that, the old man turned the canoe to bring me home. We glided along the mirror surface of the water, reflecting the crystals in the sky. I took a deep, clean breath of air.

Always remember…Always remember…

As I looked around the campfire circle, the flickering flames revealed 24 more warriors for the Everglades. Some kids had determined looks on their faces. Others had tears flowing down their cheeks. Anyone can learn to care for a wild place. In some way, the wilderness runs deeply inside us all. With a smile, I knew there *was* hope.

"I want you all to hold your hands like I am," I said as I kneeled close to the fire and held my hands like a cup. An expectant hush fell over the sawgrass prairie, as if every living creature held its breath. "I leave the future of the Everglades in your hands."

With that, I stood up and walked away into the warm, star-filled night.

She Returns

In early April, I left the Everglades for the last time. Just like when I had left Isle Royale, I knew this would be my last season. As I looked into the rearview mirror at the familiar sawgrass prairie, I thought about the many students I had met and perhaps inspired over the past three years. I remembered the dolphins and alligators and all the times I had felt a sense of wildness in south Florida. Surely, the Everglades contains magic. My heart will always hold a special place for the land of endless summer. After a few minutes, the sawgrass prairie was replaced by farmland and then housing developments. "Please, God, let the Everglades weather the storm…" I whispered.

As I drove through Miami, backseat loaded to the brim and a 17-foot canoe perched on top, I became more and more anxious. A month earlier, I had gotten an e-mail from Susanna saying she was returning from Guatemala via the Miami airport. I hadn't heard her voice in over two years. Would she be the same? If she was the same, that would probably mean she still had no desire to be in a relationship. She was planning on returning to Isle Royale for the summer. I was on my way to Alaska.

My heart was filled with fluttering butterflies as I parked my car near a little café in the northern part of Miami. Her friend Mark would drop her off at the café and then pick her up the next day in Jonathon Dickinson State Park, an hour and a half to the north. I had spent much of the last two years trying to forget her; did I really want to open that wound again?

The instant I saw her, I knew my feelings were still there. She didn't see me as she walked up to the café with Mark. She was laughing, her hair golden blonde from two years spent under a hot, Guatemalan sun. She looked happy and alive and as vibrant as ever.

The reunion was wonderful. We talked and laughed on our drive to the state park. On several occasions, she stopped in the midst of a conversation, tongue-tied because she couldn't think of the right words in English. When we got to the state park, we set up camp and immediately went canoeing amongst the mangroves. We had both grown, and changed, an incredible amount over the last two years.

The spark was there as strong as ever but the ignition switch remained invisible. I left her the next day with more questions than answers. We were still on parallel paths in life, but like a cruel joke, we were living our lives in two completely different corners of the earth.

Southeast

A chill of excitement shot up and down my spine. A single word had caught my attention. Two middle aged women were whispering to each other in the corner and I strained with all my might in an attempt to hear what they were saying. Over the long winter, I had begun to believe that Glacier Bay and the entire region of Southeast Alaska couldn't possibly exist. It's never in the news and rarely in magazines, especially during the winter. Perhaps it had been a figment of my imagination. Surely, I had made up the glaciers, the mountains, the howling wolves and the feeling of utter wildness.

"Sir?" prompted a voice behind the ticket booth.

I came to my senses and walked up to the ticket window. "I'd like a ticket to Juneau, please," I said hesitantly, half expecting the ticket lady to laugh in my face and ask me if I wanted a continuing ticket to the lost city of Atlantis.

She just smiled and handed me the ticket. "You'll board in 30 minutes," she said.

Just then, the two women walked by, still whispering, deep in conversation. Once again, I made out the hushed word '*Southeast.*' The secret of Southeast Alaska is whispered quietly in certain circles. It does exist and is every bit as wild and magical as the stories suggest.

Two days later, the gentle rocking of the M.V. Kennicott in the early morning hours signaled more than just a border crossing. I had traveled north by boat from Bellingham, Washington, along the entire British Columbian shoreline and was now crossing the Dixon Entrance, an opening into the vast North Pacific waters. Surrounding the boat was the largest, wildest, and most majestic land imaginable. The early morning light revealed a rugged, rocky, windswept shoreline, ancient spruce and hemlock, and exceptionally steep mountains blending into the mist above.

That border crossing signaled the beginning of a land like no other. It was a land where dreams and possibilities were as vast and endless as the ocean. It was a land steeped in mystery and legend.

Once again, a primal instinct overtook me as I raced from the ferry terminal in Ketchikan toward the edge of the dock. With a cry of joy, I stepped upon the Alaskan soil. For the first time in months, I felt like I was home.

A light rain fell off and on all day, but it didn't matter. I had a spring in my step that couldn't be dampened. After exploring downtown Ketchikan, I found Deer Mountain trail and scampered up several thousand feet until deep snow blocked my way. Early that evening, I caught the next ferry north, the M.V. Taku, with an overnight destination of Sitka.

I spent three magnificent days in Sitka, all of which were sunny and dominated by blue sky. From there, I journeyed aboard the M.V. Le Conte to Juneau with stops in the tiny communities of Angoon and Hoonah. Dall's porpoises and white-sided dolphins played in the wake of the boat and the stunning scenery continued ever onward. There were more mountains and islands than I could count.

I found myself sitting next to a nice young Australian couple who were just beginning a year-long around-the-world tour. At one point, the man turned to me and said in a thick, Australian accent, "Ya know mate, I woulda thought for sure we woulda run out of trees and islands by now, but they just keep going on and on. Nothing manky about this land. No rubbish. No people. Makes me nackered just thinking about it…know what I mean mate?"

I hadn't a clue what he had said, but I knew it was good.

After a couple of rainy and snowy days in Juneau, I boarded a tiny, twin engine plane that bounced me over to Gustavus. As I stepped off of the plane in the direction of the familiar tin shack airport office, I breathed a huge sigh of contentment. Varied thrush and blue grouse called from the forest. The air was clean and pure and smelled of the ocean.

As the afternoon progressed, a cool spring sun pushed away all the clouds to reveal the entire Fairweather Mountain range, a collection of mountains ensconced in glaciers. Some of the mountains are as high as 15,000 feet above sea level. The clear weather was a trend that would surprisingly continue for days. In fact, I saw Mount Fairweather, the highest of the mountains in the Fairweather range, at least once every day for the first 18 days of the season. The year before, I didn't even glimpse the mountain until mid May.

As the early days of training surged by, my life in this remote wilderness became oddly social. The community at Bartlett Cove was amazing. Most of us came from similar backgrounds and had similar interests and views about wilderness. We laughed a lot, played games and looked at slides from far-away travels. We got together for potluck dinners or meals of fresh crab meat. We even started a breakfast tradition of waffles topped with pure maple syrup. But the biggest entertainment of the spring was the Lights. Night after night of clear skies meant night after night of dancing northern lights. Many of us enthusiastically agreed to be woken up at any time of night in order to see the magic; flashing white lights, dancing green lights and pulsating red, pink and purple lights. This entertainment was far better than anything a TV could provide.

Soon, we were back aboard the cruise ships exploring the upper reaches of the bay. Early that season I met a most interesting person.

"Hi," said an attractive, young blonde with her hand outstretched toward me in a brisk greeting. "My name is Jodi. I'm the Port and Shopping Guide."

It was time for lunch, and I had just piled my plate full of treasures from the buffet line. Fellow park ranger Kerry and the ship's naturalist, Amy, were with me. "Nice to meet you," I said, shaking her hand and somehow managing to avoid knocking my tray onto the spotless floor. "What does a Port and Shopping Guide do?"

She looked at me with pity in her eyes as if I had just asked the most obvious question in the world. "Basically, I get paid to shop," she replied, her voice full of condescending pride. She continued looking at me as if she expected a comment.

"Well, look on the bright side," I said, "you could be cleaning toilets!"

Anger flashed briefly on her face and for a horrifying couple of seconds I thought for sure she was going to knock the plate of food from my hands. Fortunately, the moment passed. She then tilted her head and gave me a long, sarcastic smile. "Where are you guys eating?" she asked a bit too sweetly, the sarcastic smile still firmly planted on her face.

I pointed to a table by the window. She walked that way and sat down next to Amy. I glanced around the room and considered my options. Perhaps the best idea would be to sneak outside with my food and eat somewhere else. I was about ready to make my escape, when an elderly lady near the door called out in a loud voice, "Hey *ranger*, I've been looking for you! I wanted to tell you that I have a granddaughter who is about your age. She would do really well with a sweet, young lad like you!"

I quickly turned and walked over to our table by the window. "Amy and Jodi were just telling me what life is like on a cruise ship," said Kerry with an amused grin.

"My room is so small; I can barely fit all my clothes and shoes in there," Jodi whined, a very serious look on her face. "Oh," she continued, without missing a beat, "I have to go freshen up. I'll be back in a couple of minutes."

Amy looked at Kerry and me and rolled her eyes. "The rooms aren't that small," she whispered. "She has *forty* pairs of shoes on board." She continued with a little laugh, "I've never met anyone like her. The other day, we were looking at a couple of bears on the shoreline, and she said in a shrill voice, 'I can't find them! Maybe I need to go get a magnifying lens.'"

Just then, Jodi returned. "What are you guys laughing at?" she demanded. Suddenly, her attention was elsewhere. She pointed out the window and said in a very loud voice, "Look! A submarine!"

Kerry and I looked out the window at the water. A couple hundred yards away from the ship was a bright green navigational buoy marking the shallow rocks near Rush Point. The tide was dropping so the water was flowing by the buoy. If you really used your imagination or were especially paranoid, you could almost convince yourself that the green buoy was a periscope from an unseen submarine.

"Did you *expect* to see a submarine here?" Kerry asked a little hesitantly.

Jodi cocked her head and gave us a frustrated look. By now, several of the other diners were beginning to get curious. "It's right there!" she said in a sharp voice, a confident finger pointing at the buoy.

"Jodi, sit down," said Amy with a laugh. "That's Rush Point Buoy. It's a navigational buoy that marks an area of shallow rocks."

She paused ever so briefly as she looked at Amy with a surprised expression. "I knew that," she said with a fake laugh and the roll of her eyes. "I was just *kidding*!"

Life in Glacier Bay National Park is a constant teeter-totter between two worlds. One is wild, one civilized; one ancient, one modern; one free, one expensive; one silent, one loud; one endangered, one becoming all too common.

June 13th was a stunning day of total sunshine and barely a ripple on the water. I spent the day on the Star Princess, the largest cruise ship to ever journey through Alaskan waters. It held 2,600 passengers and stood 16 stories high. It dwarfed most coastal Alaskan towns. Despite the exceptional beauty all around me, I was very distracted. As I looked at the throngs of people pushing and shoving to get a good railing view of Margerie Glacier, I couldn't help but feel out of place. My body was in one world, but my mind had already teetered over to another.

Just over an hour after I left the cruise ship, I was paddling silently into the Beardslee Islands with Beth and Marylou, two fellow rangers. As we rounded the corner, my mind and body began to relax. We paddled slowly, the sounds of breathing porpoises all around us. Ahead, on either side of a narrow channel, stood two prominent rock pinnacles. "I call these the Beardslee Portals," said Marylou.

"Oh, I like the name," I said. "Why do you call them that?"

She thought about it for a few seconds then said, "Maybe because this seems to be where the adventure really begins. Every time I paddle between these pinnacles, I feel like I've slipped from civilization into wilderness." With that said, we paddled between the portals and the transition into the other world was complete.

The sun was hot and the water, glass calm. I felt totally energized as we sliced through perfect reflections. By sunset, we found ourselves at the northern tip of Link Island. In front of us, bathed in pink, was the towering bulk of Beartrack Mountain. It was nearly midnight and still daylight by the time I got my tent set up. The everlasting Alaskan days had begun.

The next day was so hot that I couldn't resist swimming twice, despite water temperatures hovering in the low 40s. We paddled north across Beartrack Cove and along a shoreline packed with eagles. By late afternoon, we crossed an open expanse of water to reach the southern tip of Leland Island, where we set up camp and cooked a hearty meal.

Across another short stretch of open water was South Marble Island, a haul out spot for several hundred sea lions. These sea lions, researchers had told us, were made up entirely of males who had been out-competed on the breeding islands. It was a bachelor pad, and it certainly sounded and smelled like one! The roars of the sea lions echoed across the water. The wind was out of the west and pushed an unfamiliar odor my way. Oddly, it proved to be a lure greater than I could overcome. By eight o'clock, I was paddling toward the island, bouncing in the waves, enchanted by its wildness. The closer I got, the wilder it felt. Several sea lions surfaced close to me, roaring and rolling in the waves. A single sea lion is usually nothing to be concerned about. However, when in a group, sea lions tend to be aggressive and have even been known to bump kayaks repeatedly until flipping them over. Consequently, I kept my distance. Thousands of gulls clung to the rocky cliffs of the island and circled around with the wind, their cries filling the air. Tufted puffins flew above, their wings beating fast to keep their plump-looking bodies barreling along. The sun set brilliantly over the Fairweather Mountains, but darkness never came. That night, I lay awake as long as I could. The sea lions were roaring, the gulls crying, humpback whales spouting…it was truly an enchanted island.

When I stepped outside my tent early the next morning, I was astounded by the beauty that met my gaze. The forever snowy Fairweathers were brilliant pink in the rising sun. Beth and I hopped into our kayaks and continued north, while Marylou returned south. This day, number three of our trip, was even hotter. I found myself paddling in shorts and swimming every chance I got. We paddled into remote coves with glacier-fed rivers emptying into the turquoise water of the bay. We glided along the base of towering cliffs, cascading waterfalls plunging hundreds of feet down the mountainside. By evening, we had set up camp at the southern tip of Garforth Island. Our tents and kayaks were dwarfed by the towering image of Mount Wright, no more than half a mile away. Its 5,139 foot bulk rose straight out of the ocean at an impossible angle up to a jagged, snow dappled summit.

As we sat back along the rocky shoreline, Beth introduced me to a fascinating backcountry game. This is probably something you don't want to try in public, but it's a great way to pass an endless Alaskan summer evening or a long afternoon on the trail...

"Have you ever played fart tennis?" Beth asked with a straight face.

"Fart tennis?" I repeated slowly. "No...do tell."

She smiled and proceeded to let out a fart so loud it must have startled the grazing mountain goats several thousand feet above us. "Serving Mike," she said triumphantly. "Now, if you can't fart back at me within the first minute, you'll be down 15-luv. Whoever gets to 50 first, wins!" I was laughing so hard, I couldn't concentrate. "Oh by the way," she continued sweetly, "if you poop your pants, you're automatically disqualified!"

Normally, I can hold my own in the world of farting, but never before had I encountered someone like Beth. Perhaps it was the dried fruit she had been eating all day or maybe she's just a really good farter, but for whatever reason, I was easily defeated that evening. She farted nearly non-stop for two hours and left me laughing so hard my stomach hurt.

The next morning, there were a few stray clouds swirling around the summit of Mount Wright, but they soon burned off underneath another blistering sun. We paddled across to Sebree Island and by mid morning were picked up and transported back to Bartlett Cove. Never again would I experience a Glacier Bay kayak trip with so much continuous sun.

Of Bears, Family, and Fog

The long days of June merged imperceptivity into July. There was an adventure to be had every day, whether I was aboard a cruise ship, kayaking in the bay or leading a hike in the forest. Often, the adventures centered around wildlife. On July 7th, I stepped out my door at midnight and heard an incredibly loud "whoosh" from the direction of the cove. The sound echoed back and forth across the silent hills. For the next hour, I listened to the humpback whales breathing and spouting in Bartlett Cove. The next day, while leading a hike for 15 people, I came face to snout with an agitated black bear. Fortunately, he ran the other way and disappeared in the tangled understory of the rainforest. The day after that, I nearly stepped on a baby porcupine while walking along the trail to the lodge to meet up with my first guest in Glacier Bay, my brother John.

Several days later, John and I were in the midst of the Beardslee Islands. A warm sun filtered through a few scattered clouds. We paddled up to a small island fronted with a flower-filled meadow. We were just about ready to set up the tent when John noticed movement along the shore a little ways away. "There're some people on the shore," he said nonchalantly.

"Oh, I doubt that," I countered with a little laugh. "It's probably a bear." Seeing people in "my backyard" islands was a novelty. It was much more common to see bears. I grabbed my binoculars and looked in the direction John was pointing. "They *are* people!" I said with awe. "Hmmm… I wonder if we should hide."

John laughed. "Maybe you've had too many solo trips out here!"

"Shhh…" I whispered. "They may hear us!" We stood silently for a few minutes in the tall grass of the meadow. The intruders were digging a few things out of the storage areas of their kayaks. "Oh no," I whispered again. "What if they set up their tent on our island?"

"Maybe we should make some noise," said John.

"Good idea!" I said. "Maybe that will scare them away!" We began talking loudly and banging our equipment around. I hoped that would work, but I had very little experience with human beings in the backcountry. If it had been a bear, I would have known exactly what to do.

"I think it's working!" said John, obviously enjoying our little game. Just then, the intruders on shore waved in our direction.

"Oh, great!" I said, as they began to walk toward us. "Now what?" Cautiously, we walked toward them. I grabbed my bear spray just in case.

"Hey, Mike!" called one of them, not a stranger after all. It turned out to be people I had worked with in Glacier Bay the year before. We chatted for a few minutes before they headed back to their kayaks to paddle to a different island.

As the sun set that evening, the clouds formed above the horizon just enough to set the sky ablaze with color. A calm, quiet bay reflected the red, pink and purple of the clouds. We walked slowly along the pebble-filled beach, each lost in our own thoughts.

Finally, I broke the silence. "You know, sometimes it's hard for me to deal with humans. That probably sounds funny because I work with people all the time, but out here, the rules are different. The norms of society are gone. Out here, life is so simple, so pure and easy. When I have to deal with people out in the wilderness, I find myself tongue-tied and awkward."

"I know what you mean," said John. "There are two different worlds here. When they mix, things feel a little weird."

The next day, a relentless, bitter rain convinced us to paddle back a day earlier than planned. The cold front lasted a few days, but nicely cleared up for my next guests, who arrived on the 17th of July.

That afternoon, I walked down to the dock, feeling anxious as I watched the ferry from Juneau pull into port. I was in full uniform with my head held high. Along the railing stood my dad, camera in hand. Moments later, my parents stepped off the boat with big smiles on their faces and excitedly hugged me.

I was incredibly proud to tour them around my new world. They joined me for a guided walk through the rainforest and later, a slide show program about humpback whales.

Over the next few days, we gazed at glaciers and mountain goats, hiked the seven miles of designated trail in the park and kayaked in the Beardslee Islands. The weather was warm and sunny, more like a Michigan summer than an Alaskan one. I realized where my love of swimming in the wild came from…my dad. Not only did we swim in the relatively warm water of Bartlett Lake, but also in the brutally cold ocean where waters barely reached a temperature in the low 40s. We repeatedly dove into the frigid water, enjoying the reflection of majestic evergreens and snow covered peaks on its surface.

The day we went kayaking, the clouds began to build over the Fairweathers and a strengthening wind rose out of the south. That evening, the rain returned with a vengeance. A chill in the air seemed to hint at an early fall. Fog as thick as pea soup covered most of Southeast Alaska and a bitter rain fell for days. The day after the storm hit, my parents surprisingly made it back to Juneau on a tiny plane through a brief window in the clouds.

On the fourth miserable day of the storm, I boarded a small tour boat for a day in the upper bay. I couldn't help but feel bad for the visitors onboard during a rainy, gloomy day. For most, that one day would be their only opportunity to see Glacier Bay. But something was different about that day and by the end of it, I would have a whole new appreciation for cold, foggy weather in Glacier Bay.

Immediately, I knew I had a great group of visitors aboard. Despite the dreadful weather, they appeared to be loving every second of the journey. Many of the 60 passengers hung out with me on the deck of the boat and listened intently to my stories. There was at most 30 yards of visibility on either side of the boat much of the way up the bay, but that didn't diminish the number of wildlife sightings. A peregrine falcon flew right next to the boat for several minutes, a large brown bear and cub ambled along the shore of Tidal Inlet and a tiny break in the clouds at Gloomy Knob revealed a stately mountain goat.

The wildlife was amazing that day, but it was the approach to Margerie Glacier that I will never forget. The tour boat purred slowly through a mine field of floating chunks of ice. A constant clinking sound reverberated around the boat as it gently pushed the ice aside. Thick fog hung in the air. Out of nowhere, the low rumble of thunder met our ears. Margerie was talking.

I stood transfixed on the bow of the boat. Ever so slowly I looked around at a crowd of wide-eyed, open-mouthed, silent visitors. Behind us came the ominous sound of a foghorn from an unseen ship.

Another loud crack, followed by a deafening boom, rocked our small boat in the swirling mist.

Every visitor was speechless. We stood in silence, listening to one of the most powerful phenomena in nature. Our boat slowed to a stop in the midst of a sea of floating ice, only a quarter of a mile away from Margerie Glacier. The foghorn of the big ship behind us indicated that it continued to inch closer. I felt like one of the early explorers to Alaska. We still couldn't see the glacier, but it was obviously right in front of us, as wild and alive as could be. Perhaps this was how John Muir saw his first tidewater glacier. What a feeling, to approach something so wild and ominous, hidden beneath a cloak of invisibility.

A few minutes later, a tiny window in the fog revealed a massive wall of blue and white ice. Like magic, the curtain of fog lifted for a few minutes to reveal the entire face of the enormous glacier. We floated in front of the glacier for more than an hour. Finally, it mysteriously slipped back into the fog.

Less than an hour later, as we motored back toward Bartlett Cove, the fog dissipated. Jagged mountains loomed around us, their peaks hidden in the swirling clouds. Rays of sunlight pierced through the clouds and sent a blinding light onto Lamplugh Glacier, which glistened radiantly in response. We had entered a heavenly realm.

Never again would I feel sorry for someone who arrived in Glacier Bay on a foggy day.

The Storms of September

The summer was progressing quickly. The storms became more frequent throughout August and seemed to take longer to clear up. Fall was just around the corner.

Soon, the rains of September had arrived. Day after day, the sun would try desperately to break through the clouds, only to be overcome by another rain squall. The cottonwood trees turned yellow, the moose were more agitated and a sense of wildness hung in the air.

Despite a steady rain, the lure of one last kayak trip was strong. A cold, salty breeze caressed my face as I paddled away from the Gustavus dock toward Pleasant Island. For the first time, I was kayaking outside of the protected water of Glacier Bay and in the open, exposed water of Icy Strait. With great relief, I paddled into the lee of the island and began my exploration. The island looked much different than the land within Glacier Bay because it hadn't been covered by glaciers in the last Ice Age. Hemlock trees had replaced the spruce in the natural stages of an aging forest. Thick green moss covered everything. The island seemed ancient and enchanted. Once inside the forest, I could almost imagine gnomes wandering about, peering at me from the cover of shadows. A chill ran up and down my spine as I thought about the secrets that lay hidden deep inside the impenetrable layers of moss.

As the afternoon progressed, I paddled east along the cliffs and forests of the north shore of the island. The rain stopped and the sun looked ghostly through the fast moving, wispy clouds above. It was late afternoon when I turned around and noticed a menacing cloud approaching from the west. I could see the squall line and churning water near the storm front. The infamous "*white wall of death*" was barreling toward me.

Within seconds, the waves began picking up around me. Quickly, I scanned the shoreline for an escape. My eyes were met with indifferent cliffs and tangles of impassable forest. My pulse rocketed as I paddled onward, hoping desperately to find a safe landing zone. Just then, I noticed a brilliant, white spot in the midst of a shaggy green hemlock tree. A bald eagle sat, nearly hidden, looking intently in my direction. I took a deep breath, and a sense of peace enveloped me.

Onward I paddled, hoping to find a safe take-out place. Around each corner, there was another bald eagle peering calmly at me, guiding the way to safety. Oddly enough, the storm seemed to have stalled near the entrance of Glacier Bay, only a few short miles behind me. It took nearly an hour to find a safe spot to land. During that hour, there was never a time that I couldn't see an eagle.

I set up my tent out of the wind nestled among several large boulders. The storm never materialized. After dinner, I wandered along the rocky shore of Noon Point. The rock-strewn inlets, lichen covered stones and small cliffs were incredibly similar to Isle Royale scenery. Waves crashed against the shore with a hypnotic quality. I closed my eyes with the overwhelming feeling that I was back on my beloved island. Just then, a loud "whoosh" knocked me out of my trance. "That's definitely not a sound from Isle Royale," I whispered.

Quickly, I scampered to the small cliff at the edge of the shoreline. Beneath me, somewhere deep in the dark water of Icy Strait, was a giant. I stood breathless for a second. Like a rising submarine, a massive head exploded from the water not more than 100 feet off shore. A huge humpback whale opened its mouth wide, gulping down thousands of unsuspecting herring and krill, and then disappeared as quickly as it had come.

The rest of the evening, I watched as the whale swam back and forth along the point, feeding intensely. At times, he was so close to the shore, I had the overwhelming urge to take a running leap off the cliff just to see if I could land on its back. Fortunately, common sense won out and I contented myself with just watching from my cliff-top hiding place.

Several days later, I found myself in the upper bay on the last cruise ship of the year. New snow, which is often called "termination dust," had fallen from a recent storm and seemed to be advancing farther and farther down the mountains. It was a constant reminder that an Alaskan winter was not far off.

As we slowly pulled away from the magnificent face of Margerie Glacier, I wandered up to a frail, old man who stood quietly by himself gazing out at the mountains. He looked at me and smiled. For a couple of minutes, we stood silently by each other, transfixed by the beauty.

"You know," he said finally, "I've always dreamed of coming to Alaska." His old eyes were wise and content. "I've been all over the world, but have never seen anything like this." He waved a gnarled hand toward the mountains then whispered, "I can't believe a place like this really exists."

We chatted for a few minutes about Alaska and making the most out of life and one's personal dreams. I was deeply moved and wished I could stand and talk to him for the rest of the day. He had more stories from his life than could possibly fit into a book. As silence fell over us, I knew he wanted to be alone. He was once again gazing out at a landscape that defies reality. As I turned to leave, he said one last thing to me. "Thanks for what you do. This world needs people who strive to protect what's pure and wild and beautiful."

I was still deep in thought a few minutes later when I nearly ran into Jodi, the Port and Shopping Guide. She cocked her head and looked at me with a blank expression on her face. "What are you doing for the winter?" she asked.

"I'm going to see the world," I replied with a growing smile on my face. "How about you?"

"I usually spend my winters in Miami," she said.

"Oh really?" I replied. "I spent the last three winters working in Everglades National Park."

The blank look returned. "Where's the Everglades?" She cocked her head once again, her blonde hair covering her shoulder.

"I'm going to miss you, Jodi!" I said with a laugh. "We should keep in touch. Do you have an e-mail address?"

"Sure," she said. "I have six of them. Which one would you like?"

On September 19th, I turned in my badges and official work gear. It was my last day of work for the next seven months. I really was going to see the world. It didn't fully hit me until the following day when I was packing several boxes which would remain in Gustavus until the next April. On one side of the room were the boxes for storage and on the other was my backpack for travel. When I picked up my alarm clock, I hesitated. "Could it possibly be that I don't need this until next April?" I asked myself in disbelief. With a laugh, I dropped the alarm clock in the storage box and taped it up. "I'll see you in seven months!"

The Spark that Grew into a Flame

A cold, December sun dropped below the frozen horizon of snow covered fields in central Wisconsin. "Stevens Point, 29 miles," I said to myself as I read the tall, green sign on the side of the road. I had left Glacier Bay more than two months earlier and already had enough adventures to fill a journal. My meticulous mind was going over every detail, sight, sound and feeling.

I thought about what life must be like now in northern Alaska. In early October, I had stood on top of a small hill in Circle Hot Springs, Alaska, just 70 miles shy of the Arctic Circle. As I looked to the northeast on that frosty morning, a shiver of excitement had run up and down my spine. More than likely, if I had started walking in that direction, I would have been able to walk to the Arctic Ocean without seeing any signs of human beings.

The last couple of months continued to play through my mind as I drove toward Stevens Point. I had already been in 23 different states and I didn't want to forget a thing. I thought about the stunningTatoosh Range of Mount Rainer National Park in Washington, the silent red rock canyons of Capital Reef National Park in Utah, the long train journey from Needles, California, to Grand Rapids, Michigan, the November colors of the Old Loggers Path in Pennsylvania and the early snows in the White Mountains of New Hampshire.

Somewhere deep in my mind, I felt sure that the greatest adventure was yet to begin.

When she opened her apartment door, I knew immediately that something was different. She looked at me deeply and fell into my outstretched arms. We hugged each other as if we were the last people on earth, and then looked around with sheepish smiles on our faces. Susanna was as beautiful as I had ever seen her. Her curly blonde hair fell just below her shoulders. Her chestnut brown eyes sparkled in the soft glow of a lamp and her smile lit up the room more than any light could ever do.

That night, we stood in the softly falling snow in Iverson Park, a short walk from her apartment. Ever so slowly, I put my arm around her. A great horned owl called from a nearby white pine. She cuddled close to me, her head buried in my shoulder.

"Let's go camping this weekend!" Susanna said suddenly.

"You want to go camping this weekend?" I asked to clarify. "You do know that the temperature is supposed to get down into the single digits on both Friday and Saturday nights, right?" As soon as I said it, I began kicking myself. What if I had just convinced her *not* to go camping?

"Sounds like an adventure!" she said, not missing a beat.

I was in love. She was every man's fantasy and she was standing there with me. We spent much of the next three days along the shore of Lake Michigan in Door County, Wisconsin. We camped at Potawatomi State Park and spent the evenings huddled together next to a roaring fire under a dazzling, star-filled sky.

Our parallel worlds collided for a moment that weekend. But the timing was still not right. When the weekend ended, we went back to our separate lives... but *this* time, the spark had grown into a tiny flame.

Chapter 7:

2003: The World Awaits...

With a sudden burst of power, New Zealand Air flight number six rose from American soil, bound for the other side of the world. A deep red sun fell slowly into the vast blue cauldron of the Pacific Ocean. From Los Angeles to Auckland, this flight would cover more than 6,000 miles over land and sea, take 12 hours to complete, and would eliminate an entire day. By crossing the International Date Line, January 6, 2003, never existed for me. I sat quietly in the middle of the jet, but inside I was bursting with excitement. "New Zealand, here I come!" I whispered.

In the early morning hours of January 7th, I landed in Auckland. My arrival didn't truly hit me until I took a step outside. It was sunny, and the temperature was in the low 70s. Giant red and white flowers erupted from thick green stalks like a fourth of July fireworks show. Strange looking birds flew about, singing in the warm breeze. I looked at a waiting bus and quickly did a double take. The steering wheel was on the "wrong" side of the bus. I casually stepped onto the bus through the "driver's" side as if I had done this a thousand times. The bus took off and I winced as we proceeded down the "wrong" side of the road!

By the afternoon of the next day, I had worked my way south by bus on surprisingly twisty roads, through rolling, green pastures filled with sheep, to Tongariro National Park. I walked up confidently to the visitor center and inquired about a campsite.

"Yes," said the pleasant young female ranger, "there are campsites just up the hill."

"How much do they cost?" I asked.

"Teen dollars," she replied.

"Excuse me, how much?" I asked again.

"Teen dollars," she repeated calmly.

"Hmm…" I spoke slowly, with a confused look on my face. "How much is that?"

"How much is teen dollars?" she asked, suddenly as confused as I was. "What do you mean?"

"Like, does that mean it costs thirteen dollars for a campsite?" I asked.

She looked at me as if I was an alien that had just fallen out of the sky. In a way, I was! "Nooo," she said very slowly as if I was hard of hearing. "You don't know how much teen dollars is?"

Suddenly, the connectors in my brain began to function. "Oh!" I said, embarrassed. "You mean *ten* dollars!"

"What?" she asked with growing frustration.

"Never mind!" I said and quickly vanished out the door. For the first time, I had experienced the foreign language of New Zealand English.

The next morning, I awoke to the sound of rain thundering on my tent and wind roaring through the trees. According to the rangers, the wind was blowing 85 kilometers per hour (53 miles per hour). My curiosity, however, didn't allow me to stay sheltered in my tent for long. Rain or no rain, I was going to explore this new land. Throughout the day, I made several short forays into the inviting landscape. Frequently, I stopped and peered inquisitively at the vegetation or at birds passing overhead. They looked similar to those that I was used to seeing, but an odd splash of color or crest of feathers added an exotic twist to otherwise familiar birds and plants. The main focal point of the park was a collection of tall, recently active volcanoes. The lower slopes of the volcanoes were covered with green trees and low bushes, but the higher I ascended, the more barren it became.

In the evening, I snuck into the luxurious Chateau Grand Hotel, a short walk from my tent. The hotel was exceptionally fancy, at least for a dirty backpacker who had recently been living in the wilds of Alaska. Strangely, nobody looked at me as I wandered over to the most comfortable couch around. While rain and wind pummeled the windows outside, I remained warm and dry, listening to a tuxedo-clad man playing the piano and singing love ballads.

Dawn held a promising window of blue sky, but thick clouds still hung around the volcanoes. With a triumphant smile, I set off into the New Zealand backcountry. Within a couple of hours, the rain and fog had returned.

In the late afternoon, I rounded a rocky corner and saw the ghostly image of a structure in front of me. This small, tin-roofed building, Uterere Hut, would be my home for the night. Unique formations of lava surrounded the hut. The fog danced around them in an eerie fashion, adding an element of mystery to the land. Some of the formations were tall and looked like proud kings and queens of ancient times surrounded by a massive army of lava soldiers. It was easy to imagine that I was walking through an enchanted fairy tale.

It wasn't until the middle of the next day that the fog began to lift. I was slowly trudging up a steep, barren, lava-strewn landscape when a hot sun broke through the thick mantle of fog above. At that moment, I noticed a startling drop-off with steam rising from it no more than five feet to my left. Tentatively, I crawled over to the edge and gazed down into a deep red crater with sulfurous gases rising from its depths.

A volcano loomed ominously on the horizon. Steam rose from its conical crater, its sides barren and lonely. I was intrigued. Somewhere in the back of my mind, I felt that I had seen this image before.

That evening, I sat on the porch of Mangatepopo Hut gazing up at the volcano. Its sides were bathed in a soft pink light from the setting sun. For some reason, the mountain held an incredible allure.

"Did you climb Mount Doom today?" asked a young hiker from Germany.

"Mount Doom?" I asked.

"Ya," he continued while pointing up at the volcano. "You're looking at Mount Doom… from the Lord of the Rings movies."

Suddenly it all made sense. "No wonder I've felt drawn to that mountain!" I said. "I haven't climbed it, but now that I know it's Mount Doom, I'll have to!"

"I was talking to the hut warden earlier and he showed me the hut log books from last year," continued the young German. "It's really funny to read what people wrote during that timeframe. One of them read, *'hiked from Ketetahi Hut today…bit of rain…Red Crater very beautiful…saw an army of orcs and think I may have caught a glimpse of Sam and Frodo!* ""

"I'm definitely going to climb it tomorrow!" I said with determination.

"Welcome to Middle Earth!" he laughed.

As I climbed up the flanks of Mount Doom the next day, it seemed as if I really was in Middle Earth. The weather had turned once again. Thick clouds obscured the summit and a strong wind threatened to blow me off the mountain. I was climbing on all fours up slippery slopes of volcanic pebbles. For every step up, I slid back half a step. It was almost as if the mountain didn't want to be climbed. The suffocating fog enveloped me, reducing my world to an enchanted bubble. Higher and higher I climbed until suddenly the other side disappeared. In the hazy void, I knew I had arrived at the summit crater. A sizzling vent of steam leaked out of the rocks with a soft hiss. The bitter, stinging wind whipped across my face, slinging tiny volcanic pebbles into my eyes. The smell of sulphur seemed to penetrate my skin.

An overwhelming urge came over me to throw something into the depths of the crater. If I had had a ring on, I may very well have thrown it in. Hesitantly, I picked up a rock and heaved it into the abyss, half expecting the world to fall apart. With that, I turned and slid back down the steep slope.

The Three Travelers

My adventures in New Zealand began piling up like snow in an endless Michigan winter. I found myself hitchhiking from trailhead to trailhead with a day in between to re-supply my food and take a hot shower.

In the end of January, deep in the backcountry of Nelson Lakes National Park, I met three travelers who quickly spiced up my experience in New Zealand. It was so rainy and cold that morning at Blue Lake Hut that I decided to spend a lazy day inside.

"You want to play some cards?" asked a strong, young guy with a thick Australian accent.

"Sure," I said. "Nothing else to do today!"

"My name is Tristan," he said, and then pointed to a young, attractive woman. "This is my fiancée, Blaine."

Another guy, who was in the bunk below mine, joined us. "My name is Omer," he said with a big, infectious smile. "I come from Israel." Omer had a quiet, calm disposition and was immediately likeable.

It didn't take long to feel as if we had known each other our entire lives. We laughed, told stories and played cards all day. Thus began an unlikely friendship between two Australians, an American and an Israeli.

We ended up spending much of the next week and a half together and never tired of laughing at the differences in the way we spoke the English language. Tristan and Blaine had bought a car when they arrived in New Zealand a month earlier, so my transportation became much more reliable. After leaving the backcountry of Nelson Lakes National Park, we journeyed together along a curvy road with thick, lush forest on both sides. A rushing river thundered down a steep cleft to our right. Finally, the road smoothed out and dropped toward the sparkling ocean on the west coast. With a sigh of relief, we stopped the car in the quaint town of Westport and set out to find lodging and a restaurant.

Several hours later, we were finishing up a fantastic restaurant meal when Tristan asked if anyone was interested in dessert. Being forever budget oriented, I decided to forgo dessert in the restaurant and eat my leftover cookies from the trail. "Mind if I run out to the car and grab my cookies from the trunk?" I asked innocently.

"*What* did you just say?" Blaine asked, swallowing her laughter.

"I asked if you would mind if I grabbed my cookies from the trunk of your car," I repeated a bit defensively.

"The *cookies* from the *trunk*!" she squealed in a frenzy of laughter. "That should be the *biscuits* from the *boot*."

"The *biscuits* from the *boot*?" I said, beginning to laugh. "Now *that's* funny!"

We continued on like this for several minutes covering everything from being nackered (tired) to moseys (mosquitoes). Finally Tristan turned to Blaine and said, "While you figure out what you want for dessert, I'm running over to the dunney."

"What on earth is a *dunney*?" I asked, tears of laughter streaming down my face.

When we went our separate ways in Queenstown on the first day of February, we promised to meet up again soon. It was an amazing feeling to be so far away from home, but to feel so close to these good friends.

The Wildest Track in New Zealand

"It's labeled the wildest track in New Zealand," stated the ranger, a bit arrogantly. "It starts along two of our largest lakes, ends at the longest fjord in the park and traverses three major valleys and two mountain ranges. To complete the entire journey, we recommend at least six days with enough food for eight to nine days just in case you're stranded by the perpetual rains. If you don't mind all-day rain and mud up to your waist, we can continue issuing your permit." She paused as if waiting for me to admit the adventure was way over my head.

"That sounds fantastic," I said happily. "When can I start?!?"

The route was called the Dusky Track. It looked like an upside down Y. The bottom two sections of the upside down Y were the access lakes and the top was a large fjord called Dusky Sound. My goal was to get dropped off at the far end of Lake Hauroko, hike to the middle of the Y, spend an extra day hiking to Dusky Sound and then finish at the end of Lake Manapouri. My backpack was stuffed with eight days worth of food, but I figured I could do it in five without too much difficulty.

It was the middle of February when I was dropped off by boat at the far end of Lake Hauroko, a beautiful, glacially scoured lake surrounded by impenetrable forest and rocky cliffs. A faint trail led to a small backcountry hut. The other hikers stepped off the boat and disappeared into the bush and the boat returned to its port. I was once again alone in the wilderness of New Zealand. Light rain drizzled from the gray sky and a thick cloud of tiny, biting flies called midges swarmed in frightening numbers.

I stood for a long time, soaking up the feeling of pure wildness. Finally, I ventured into the forest. Right away, thick mud threatened to yank off my boots and the midges descended upon me like miniature fighter jets in a massive aerial attack. It didn't matter though; it added to the sense of wildness.

All day I walked through the forest, higher and higher into the mountains. The trail traversed several raging rivers. The only way across was to inch myself along a walkwire, which consisted of three narrow wires attached to trees on either side of the river. Two of the wires were for your hands and the third, for your feet. By evening, I had climbed above tree line into the windy alpine zone and with a sigh of relief, left the midges to lurk in the depths of the forest. Soon, I could smell wood smoke and knew I was nearing my destination.

With relief, I stepped into Lake Roe Hut. It was warm, dry, and currently home to several other hikers. An older couple from Auckland handed me a steaming cup of tea and proceeded to tell me some amazing stories of life in New Zealand. I sat back with my mug of tea and contentedly listened to their stories while the wind and rain pelted the outside of the hut.

I woke up the next morning to a dazzling blue sky. During breakfast, my eyes were drawn to a towering, jagged mountain behind the hut. Soon I began climbing toward the mountain, with the intention of hiking just a short distance. Each time I reached my goal, I looked farther up the mountain and decided to climb just a little higher. Soon, I was among the snowfields and finally scrambled up the last few nearly horizontal rocks to the summit.

The view was astonishing. Mountains stretched to the horizon in every direction. Snowfields angled like glistening ribbons from serrated peaks into emerald lakes below. In the distance, I could see Dusky Sound, its turquoise water glistening in the morning sun.

Ever so slowly, I turned around. My arms were stretched out in the light breeze, the bright, southern hemisphere sun warming my face. It felt like the exclamation point of my journey. "This is living!" I yelled to no one in particular. I imagined I was an early explorer finding an unknown land. "I've done it!" I exclaimed triumphantly. A kingdom of forgotten mountains, lakes and forests looked up at me indifferently, laughing at my small victory.

That evening, I stumbled into Loch Maree Hut at the junction of the Y. This hut sits on a small, forested hill between two swift flowing rivers which empty into a narrow lake full of old tree stumps. Impressively steep, forested hills rise on either side of the lake, which was formed some time ago when a landslide blocked the river on the far side. Old tree stumps rise menacingly out of the dark water. In the gray light of evening, it looked haunted. The next morning, a thin fog hung above the lake like a mysterious veil. I imagined that time had reversed itself, delving back into the lush, tropical, prehistoric times where a dinosaur could appear out of the mist at any moment.

My plan was to spend two nights at the hut, day hiking to Dusky Sound on the middle day. I had hiked several miles and had nearly arrived at Dusky Sound when the brilliant blue sky switched abruptly to a deep gray. Not long after, the rain hit. It began slowly, but intensified throughout the afternoon. It was a torrential downpour by the time I arrived back at Loch Maree Hut in the early evening. The rain was so loud on the tin roof that it was difficult to talk to the other campers. All night long, the rain thundered down, like a brigade of soldiers attacking the roof.

When I stepped outside the next morning, I was stunned; not by what I saw, rather by what I didn't see. The tall tree stumps in the lake were completely gone! I scampered down to the river and realized it had become, overnight, part of the lake. The water level had risen by more than six feet! On the hillside, a surging waterfall shot a thick spray of water over a cliff like a broken fire hydrant. Quickly, I ran to the other river. It looked the same. We were completely flooded in! The hill which held the hut was now an island. There was no way anyone could leave until the water level dropped.

Fortunately, a hot sun burned off all the clouds by midday and the water level began to go down. It wasn't until the morning of day five that I was finally able to leave the hut. The trail was still under water in places. At times, I found myself wading through silt-filled, waist deep water, my pack balanced precariously on my head to avoid getting it soaked. Finally, I climbed out of the river drainage and over Centre Pass. At dusk, I arrived at Upper Spey Hut, less than a day's walk from the end of the trail.

The next day, after finishing the route, I rode a boat across Lake Manapouri, then hitchhiked into Queenstown. There, with huge smiles on their faces, were Omer, Tristan and Blaine. It had been several weeks since we had seen each other and there were many stories to tell.

"I'm starving," I said, "Where do you guys want to eat?"

"We have some food in the boot if you want some," said Tristan.

"I know of a really great booger place," said Omer in his thick Israeli accent.

"A booger place?" said Blaine with a little laugh. "Sounds a bit dodgey to me."

"It a really good booger place," continued Omer. "Best boogers in town!" By this time Tristan, Blaine and I were nearly falling over with laughter. "What?" asked Omer. "You no want boogers?"

"I think you mean burgers," said Blaine while clutching her stomach.

"Bur...ger," repeated Omer slowly. "Then, what is booger?"

That afternoon, I checked my e-mail for the first time in over a week. There was a message from my mom that was simply entitled, "Dad." My heart skipped a beat as I clicked on the link. I couldn't believe what I read. After cross country skiing on a cold Saturday afternoon, my dad had had a massive seizure and was now in the hospital. I immediately tried phoning home, but no one answered.

That night, I got incredibly sick. I laid half in my tent and half outside of it in a groggy state of consciousness. I threw up more times than I could count and felt as if I was near death. My mind returned to my dad's first visit to Isle Royale back in 1997. With haunting clarity, I remembered Smitty's words: *"Always appreciate times like these that you spend with your father. You won't always have these opportunities."*

Fortunately, I talked to my mom the next day and found out that he was doing much better. There was no explanation for the seizure, but at least he would return to a normal life. It was a helpless feeling to be so far away, unable to help my parents in any type of emergency. My mom assured me that my dad was fine and that I should continue my travels.

I followed her advice, but began phoning home any chance I got. Tristan, Blaine and Omer proved to be true friends during this difficult time. We traveled together for the next week and a half, laughing at our differences and exploring the incredible countryside of New Zealand. We talked about life and how we each planned to live it to its fullest.

On the evening of February 26th, I said a sad goodbye to my trio of friends. We hugged and promised to keep in touch. I looked over my shoulder as I boarded an overnight train bound for Auckland. Omer's happy face had already disappeared. Tristan stood tall and strong with an arm around his fiancée. A tear ran down Blaine's face. We would each return to our separate lives in far-off corners of the world. Deep down, we knew that we would never be together like this again.

My time in New Zealand had come to an end. The next day, I would hop on a plane bound for Australia. As the train rattled along just north of Wellington, I began to think back on nearly two months in this backwards world. I rested my head against the window and looked out at the setting sun. The sky turned pink and red and settled into a deep purple. My eyes grew heavy and I fell into a peaceful dream. Once again, I was walking along a ridgeline trail, alpine grasses blowing in a strong wind all around me. I was scaling unnamed peaks with snowfields above and emerald lakes below. I was jumping into the cold waters of a rushing river on a warm summer day, the sense of wildness permeating my skin. There was no rush. No deadlines. No place to be but there.

The Land Down-Under

A young, oriental man stepped off his motorcycle at the town square in Port Augusta, South Australia. A light, salty breeze blew off of Spencer Gulf and several ravens called raucously from the treetops nearby.

"Where are you coming from?" I asked him.

"Just came from the Outback," he said quickly while looking around him as if someone or something was after him.

"How was it?" I asked curiously.

"Too many fries," he said in a thick oriental accent, then hopped back onto his motorcycle and sped away.

"What on earth does that mean?" I wondered. I imagined a McDonalds around every bend in the Outback selling fries. "Weird." Within 24 hours I would have a really good idea what the young Asian man meant by '*fries*.'

At midnight on March 15th, I boarded a bus heading north into the wild center of Australia, often called the Outback. A seemingly endless, flat road stretched into the wildest open space imaginable. I tried to stay awake as long as possible, staring out on a lonely land bathed in starlight. The Southern Cross, a small but beautiful constellation in the shape of a cross, hung in the sky above, reminding me of how far away from home I was.

The eastern sky was just showing streaks of pink when I stepped off of the bus at the tiny frontier town of Coober Pedy. Moments later, I was walking through this very odd town. The houses and businesses were mostly underground. The only evidence of habitation came from the small doors at the base of the sandy hills. I checked into an underground hostel and walked up a small hill at the edge of town.

As dawn broke, I found myself looking out at the most desolate landscape I had ever seen. Brownish-red dirt hills stretched to the horizon in every direction. With the sun came the *'fries'* which I immediately discovered were actually *'flies.'* They were utterly relentless. They swarmed me, landing on my face and arms and legs with such intensity that my legs turned black with their numbers. They crawled around my ears, into my eyes and, if I shooed them away, they were replaced by countless others waiting their turn.

All day, I explored the town and the land around it. The people were as unique and intriguing as the landscape. In the local cemetery, I found a long, cement grave site with a wine bottle on one side and a keg on the other. Written on the keg were the words, *'Have a drink on me.'*

Later that afternoon, I stood alongside a short fence that stretched in both directions over rolling hills to the horizon. "So this is the world-famous dingo fence," I said aloud. The fence was built to keep the dingoes, a short, stocky member of the dog family, in the center of Australia and away from the sheep and cattle farms on the edges. According to the sign, the fence was 5,530 kilometers (3,436 miles), the longest on the planet, and circled around what many people called the Red Center.

The next morning, I hopped on another bus heading farther north. The sun rose like a blazing inferno. It was so hot in the bus that I wondered if I would pass out. Mile after mile, we traveled north over red-rock roads in flat, endless, sizzling bush country. Unexpectedly, the bus slowed and then stopped at a dirt crossroad. The driver got out, walked across the road to a mailbox, put something in it, took something out and then returned to the bus. I craned my neck out the window trying to see where the house was. The dirt road just disappeared around a bend surrounded by low bushes.

As we continued north through uninhabited country, I thought more and more about that lonely little dirt road. Who lived there and what did they do all day?

Hour after hour, we cruised north. The endless brush land was replaced briefly by a stunning section of red cliffs and silent canyons. Too soon, that was gone, replaced once again by the endless flat land of scrub bushes and red sand.

In the middle of the afternoon, we entered the surprisingly populous town of Alice Springs. I immediately went for a walk in the beautiful desert environment. My feet mindlessly leading the way, I slipped into deep thoughts. The landscape was very similar to areas of the American Southwest. I almost forgot I was in Australia until a kangaroo hopped by. Interestingly enough, the more I looked, the more kangaroos I saw. They were everywhere, standing in the shade behind bushy trees or reclining in the cool, damp caves and overhangs or peering at me from behind rocky walls.

I spent the next five days exploring the Red Center of Australia, mainly with an organized tour group of 20 travelers from all over the world. We explored the depths of Kings Canyon with its refreshing swimming hole at the bottom. We walked along the intensely red walls of Uluru, the great symbol of the Australian Outback, at sunrise. We explored the twisted red-rock mounds called the Olgas. But the most memorable moment of the entire Outback experience occurred in the wee hours of my final night in the Red Center.

"Dude," came the hushed voice of one of the French guys on the tour, "I think a dingo just stole your boots!"

Groggily, I looked at my watch. It was four o'clock in the morning. A brilliant full moon illuminated the other travelers sleeping soundly under the stars. Sure enough, my boots were gone!

My French friend was wandering at the far side of the campsite near a string of trees. "Here's one!" he said unexpectedly and produced one of my lost boots. We continued looking around for a few minutes without any luck.

"You may as well go back to bed," I said. "I'll keep looking."

At the far side of camp, I slipped silently into the trees. I ducked underneath a couple of branches and then crept slowly out of the trees on the far side. Time seemed to stand still as I stood in the midst of a silvery world. It was totally calm, quiet and perfect. A sense of wildness saturated the air. The scene repeated itself for miles to the horizon and then hundreds of miles beyond that.

Just then, I looked down and saw my lost boot standing upright next to a newly dug hole. The dingo must have been getting ready to bury it! As if on queue, another image materialized. A dingo trotted out of the trees and passed right next to me. The stocky, powerful, wild dog didn't even look at me but was so close I could have put a hand down to touch him. Within seconds, he had disappeared into the silent, silver wilderness of the Outback.

Steamy Southeast Asia

The outside world turned pink as the sun set to the west. British Air flight ten rose to 39,000 feet and sailed through the clouds to the northwest. We crossed high over the Outback and above places with exotic names like Timor Sea, Makassar Strait, South China Sea, Ho Chi Minh City and Phnom Penh. Finally, we descended into Bangkok.

As the plane touched down, I became slightly apprehensive. It was ten o'clock at night; I didn't speak the language, didn't know the local culture, and didn't even have a place to stay. I held my Thailand Lonely Planet book in front of me like a shield and walked off of the plane into the bustle of a third world country.

Somehow, I found my way to Khao San Road, a street packed with tourists, sizzling food and old hotels. It was nearly midnight, but my adrenaline and the deafening music wouldn't allow me to sleep. For the next couple of hours, I walked the streets, watching the people and breathing in the atmosphere. Somehow, I found myself alone among a sea of people on the streets of Bangkok in the middle of a steamy, Southeast Asian night.

The following morning, I set out to explore the city. I spent the day wandering around streets littered with people, noise and filth. The words *"Taxi! Taxi!"* were constantly being tossed through the thick air in competition with the sounds of blaring car horns. I wandered along the Chao Phraya River, a bustling, muddy brown transportation route. I was fascinated by this new land.

The tuk-tuks, three-wheeled taxis with a shaded roof and open air on the sides, intrigued me. I took two tuk-tuk rides, marveling at the golden Buddhist temples, the ancient stone towers and the third world houses constructed with thin walls of tin, backed by a modern scene of tall skyscrapers.

By the end of my second full day in Bangkok, I had a sore throat, a headache and a raspy voice from breathing in more exhaust and pollution than my typical yearly allotment. I bought a ticket out of the city, with the goal of reaching the little island of Ko Tao, nestled in the turquoise waters of the Gulf of Thailand. The travel agent spoke broken English but seemed happy to do business with me.

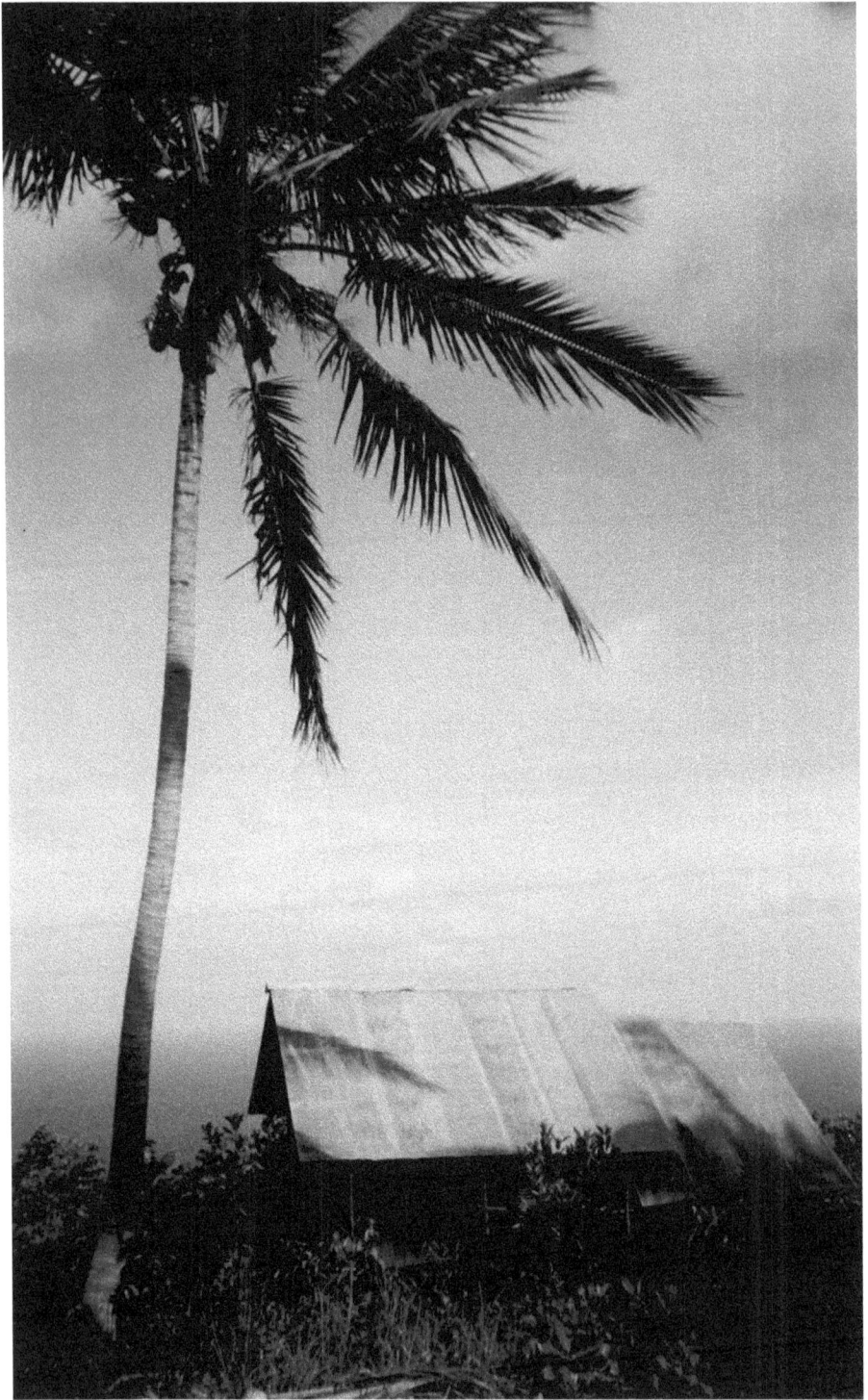

"This ticket," he said, as he handed me a wad of paper, "get you all way to island Ko Tao."

I waited for him to continue with instructions as to how this would all work, but he seemed content to sit back and smile at me. After a moment of silence I asked, "So, I catch a bus from here and then what?"

He looked at me as if I had asked a very obvious question but decided to answer me anyway. "Bus drop you off in Chumphon at six in morning. Then you catch ferry to Ko Tao at seven." It all seemed very simple in his mind but it was still a bit cloudy for me.

"So, I get dropped off in the town of Chumphon and can walk over to the boat which leaves at seven?" I asked in clarification.

"Yes, yes, of course," he said impatiently.

When the bus failed to show up at the proper time and place, I should have become suspicious. Somehow, though, I found the right bus and was soon heading south out of the city. A deep red, hazy sun dropped below the steamy horizon and slowly the tropical night deepened.

It was well after midnight when I drifted off to sleep. At two thirty in the morning, the bus came to a standstill along a black, lonely section of the road. In the back of my mind I heard the words, "Chumphon! Chumphon!" The ticket master came back to me and said something in Thai then pointed emphatically out the window. "Chumphon! Chumphon!" he repeated. When I didn't move, he tapped me on the shoulder and motioned for me to follow him.

I cautiously followed him. Strangely, I was the only passenger getting off the bus. He pulled my backpack from a hidden compartment and said something in Thai to a man on a motorcycle next to me. I was still half asleep and thoroughly confused when the bus revved its engine and left me in a cloud of dust in the darkness. Instantly, I was wide awake and terrified. As the taillights disappeared, I looked around at the black tangle of trees and then at the man on the motorcycle.

I whipped out my Thai dictionary and tried to ask where the town was. "Yuu thii nai Chumphon," I said slowly. It became obvious immediately that I had pronounced it all wrong because he just looked at me as if I had spoken Swahili. He said something again in Thai and then pointed to the back of his motorcycle.

With a feeling of dread, I strapped my backpack tightly to my back and hopped on the back of his motorcycle. We sputtered away from the paved road and onto a rut-filled gravel road. There was not a single sign of civilization anywhere. The black, sticky Southeast Asian night enveloped us like a cocoon. Visions of being held captive in the jungle filled my mind. My hopes sank even lower when we drove off the gravel road and onto a narrow dirt path in the midst of a banana plantation.

I had just about given up hope when we climbed a rickety, wooden bridge and the lights of a town beckoned us toward the horizon. A few minutes later, we drove from the dirt path onto a gravel road and soon a well-illuminated paved road. When he stopped in front of a bus station, I felt so relieved that I paid him whatever money he wanted and began the wait for the ferry. I took a short walk around the area and could find no evidence of the Gulf of Thailand. The adventure was far from over.

At five in the morning, the motorcycle man returned and somehow communicated to me that he needed to take me to another place in the town where I would catch a bus in thirty minutes which would take me to the ferry dock. As the roosters began crowing and a faint, hazy light spread along the eastern sky, he dropped me off at an old, rundown house in the middle of town.

"You go to Ko Tao?" asked a raspy voice from the inky darkness of an open door in the house.

"Yes," I said hesitantly, wondering what else could possibly delay my arrival to Ko Tao.

"You wait here 20 minute," he continued in broken English, "bus pick you up, take you to boat."

The "bus" that arrived in 20 minutes was an old army truck with a covered back. The benches in the flat bed were already filled with locals all looking at me and my big backpack as if I were a strange being from an ancient legend. I climbed onto the back bumper and held on as we motored away. I kept my backpack on my back, assuming we would arrive at the coast momentarily.

A hazy dawn broke over a foreign world. We rattled past tin houses with thatched palm roofs; smiling workers wearing cone-shaped hats walked through a banana plantation; bright white egrets pecked among the black, powerful legs of water buffalo in soggy green wetlands. It took nearly an hour to pass through the countryside to the edge of the Gulf of Thailand.

A couple of hours later, with a great sense of relief, I found myself wandering along a peaceful beach lined with coconut palms swaying in a light, tropical breeze. For the next week and a half, I explored several local islands. I often went scuba diving in the morning and walking in the afternoons. During the evenings I relaxed, sipping mango shakes and listening to the hum of crickets in the thick, tangled coastal forests.

My lifestyle in Thailand was the stuff that dreams are made of, but even while surrounded by warm breezes and crashing surf, I found myself longing for my life back in the cold wilderness of Alaska.

I was awakened at one o'clock in the morning with the words, "Mike, Mike, the lights are out!" Half thinking it was a dream, I stepped outside my Glacier Bay cabin into a world illuminated by white, shimmering lights. Several of my friends were already outside enjoying the northern lights. I ended up staying out for nearly two hours, mesmerized by dancing and pulsing green and white lights. I rested in the grass near the ocean and gazed up at a million angels dancing joyfully in the heavens. It felt as if God was right above me, once again proclaiming His dominion over the Alaskan wilderness. I was home at last.

Several days earlier, I had returned to the land of dreams. It had been seven months since I had had a home and I was ready to melt back into life in Glacier Bay. It was hard to fathom all that had occurred since I last gazed up at the northern lights of Alaska. After the flight back to the United States from Thailand, I had taken the Great Northern Railroad from Michigan to Washington. On the way, I had visited Susanna in Wisconsin. The magic was still there, burning stronger. Ever so slowly, our friendship was blooming into love.

The Alaskan spring inched along. Occasional rain storms were quickly replaced by deep blue skies and a warm sun. The whales returned and were concentrating in the lower bay like never before. Bald eagles silently glided overhead on a daily basis. Soon, we were back aboard the cruise ships and tour boats explaining the story behind the incredible scenery.

On one of my first evening programs of the year, I had a rather memorable encounter which left me realizing how different my world had become. I had just gotten through my safety messages, which included advice on what to do if a person encountered a bear or a moose. A gentleman in the back row seemed concerned about certain wildlife encounters.

"Ranger Mike," he said while raising his hand, "I know you said we should make some noise when hiking in a place that is thick with vegetation to avoid a surprise encounter with a bear, but what if the bear still doesn't hear us coming?"

"Well," I said, "chances are very good that the bear will smell you long before it can hear you. But if you really think you may surprise a bear despite making noise, you could just turn around and hike back or find another route."

"Okay," continued the man, his hand still raised, "what if we run into a bear while trying to find another route?"

"I've had a lot of experiences with bears," I said calmly, "and have realized that, by far, the vast majority of bears are terrified of us. If they do seem curious and approach us, which is *very* rare, simply making some noise often works to scare…"

"But you were telling us what to do if we think we are getting charged or are about ready to get hit by a bear!" The man's voice had risen an octave and he seemed rather anxious. "Does that really happen?"

"Well, yes, but…"

"So it *does* happen!" cried the man, as he began looking apprehensively at the open door of the lodge as if considering an escape route.

"Consider this fact," I replied as calmly as possible, "In Juneau, over the past 20 years, the city police have gotten reports of over 300 people being injured in attacks by domestic dogs, over 500 people being attacked and injured by another human being and just one single report of a human being attacked and injured by a bear. Supposedly, that one 'attack' was from a bear that got spooked by people, was running away, rounded a bend in a trail and ran over a person. That person's injury was a gash on his head due to a jagged rock he fell on when the bear ran him over. The bear continued running without another look at the fallen person."

"So, let me get this straight," said the man, not missing a beat, "that person was *run* over by the bear! This land is way too frightening! Ranger Mike, how on earth do you dare *live* here?!?

I really had no idea what to say at that point, so I decided to change the subject. "So, where are you all from?" I asked the crowd, many of whom appeared to be in the midst of a Halloween haunted house, expecting monsters to jump out at any moment.

"Oh, I'm from the outskirts of Chicago," lamented the same man from the back row. "The traffic is horrible! I have to drive an hour and a half in rush hour traffic to get to work! People drive like maniacs there. They either drive 80 miles an hour or they're in standstill traffic!"

For a moment, I looked at him, speechless. Finally I said, "How do *you* dare live *there*?"

It's all a matter of perspective. Give me a forest full of bears any day over a road full of crazy drivers.

Rosie's Bar

On May 24th, I was offered a unique opportunity to explore one of the tiny communities south of Glacier Bay. After work, I raced down to the dock and hopped into a boat owned by my friend, Bill. Sean, Kerry, Julie and Whitney were already eagerly waiting inside the cabin of the boat. We cruised through the lower stretches of Glacier Bay and into Icy Strait. Rain pelted down and low clouds passed overhead like silent ghosts on patrol.

We motored west through South Inian Islands Passage, past George Island and Three Hill Island, around Column Point and finally into Lisianski Inlet. Waterfalls were slithering down the steep, rocky slopes and cascading into the ocean. Rugged, rocky pinnacles dotted the coast and thousands of gulls circled and cried in the cool, damp air.

Just before the tiny village of Pelican, we found our destination: a beautiful log cabin owned by our friend, Ron. We happily walked out of the chilly dampness of a Southeast Alaskan evening and into a warm, dry cabin.

Pelican is a tiny, backwards town of about 100 inhabitants. They have no cars, no roads and their only connection to the outside world is by seaplane (which can only arrive or depart when it isn't foggy, leaving few possibilities) or by a very long, difficult boat ride.

"The people who live in Pelican tend to keep to themselves," said Ron with an amused, yet stern, look on his face. "They're a tough, redneck breed of people who don't want any questions asked about them. There's no law here and many of them are just trying to escape something in their past. It's safer not to ask questions about where they came from or how long they've lived here or how long they plan to live here. Most people around here are very suspicious of any outsider asking questions."

In the early evening, we jumped into Bill's boat and motored slowly into town. Ron was more than happy to tell numerous colorful stories of this town that he called home. He obviously loved living in Pelican. It was wild and had the feel of being one word away from an old fashioned gun fight. Brown bears were common intruders into people's yards. The natural beauty was astounding. Every one of Pelican's inhabitants could probably write a best selling book about life in this fascinating town at the edge of the bush in Alaska.

We tied up at the main dock and walked around town on the boardwalks. A light drizzle was falling when we stepped into Rosie's, the local bar. Ron joked around with the bartender, a gruff-looking woman who looked like she could easily win an arm wrestling competition. She warmed up to us slowly and decided to fire up the grill and bring out some cheesy French fries dripping in grease.

It was nearly midnight when a gnarled old man with a thick, white beard dripping from the relentless deluge outside, came stomping into the bar. He looked around briefly with his thick, wire rim glasses and then staggered over to the counter. The bartender was nowhere to be seen. Just then I noticed a large bell on the counter that read, "Ring Bell for Service." The bell must have been three feet high and had a large mallet next to it. The old man was also peering at the bell. Suddenly, he grabbed the mallet, lifted it high over his head and slammed it down onto the bell with surprising power. An earsplitting sound reverberated through the bar and everyone stared with mouths agape at the old man.

"What's a man got to do to get a little service around here?" growled the old man as he swayed about in an obvious drunken stupor.

The locals thought this was funny. Their laughter only encouraged the old man. He was just about to slam the mallet on the bell again when the bartender came scurrying out. According to Ron, things would only get wilder in Rosie's Bar as the night wore on into the wee hours of the morning. We took it as our cue to leave.

A soft rain fell on the roof of the lodge in Bartlett Cove. I stood anxiously at the visitor center desk, on the second floor of the lodge, the minutes feeling like hours. Finally, a van pulled up to the front doors of the lodge and a beautiful blonde girl stepped out. Susanna had arrived for a month-long visit!

Within minutes, it was as if we had never been apart. We laughed and told stories, making the most of every millisecond of life together. That evening, the rain continued to patter on the roof. We sat in my little cabin and talked for hours, the candlelight flickering on the wooden walls. I couldn't help but think about that little candle in the cabin window on the island in Isle Royale. I had dreamed of a life with Susanna in a cabin like that. Now, right before my eyes, that dream was edging toward reality.

Our time in the cabin was wonderful, but it was in the backcountry that our bond was strengthened. We spent 12 days of that month deep in the heart of Glacier Bay's wilderness. We saw humpback whales at Point Gustavus catapult themselves out of the glistening late afternoon waters, we stared into the beady eyes of a black bear along Strawberry Island, we held each other close under soaring bald eagles and through never-ending sunsets.

The greatest moments came while we were "up bay" on a three-day kayak trip. We had been dropped off by a ferry at Blue Mouse Cove under a piercing blue sky in mid June. Clouds swirled in the high peaks. With whales spouting nearby, we kayaked across the bay and landed beside a two thousand foot gray slab of rock called Gloomy Knob. Our eyes were drawn to the cliffs just above us where eight mountain goats greeted us with curious, yet strangely intelligent looks.

Throughout the afternoon, we scrambled higher and higher up Gloomy Knob, far into the land of the mountain goats. Vivid Lake, appropriately named, sat like a hidden jewel behind the massive bulk of Gloomy Knob. We climbed ever upward, at times using all four limbs to scale the sides of the slippery rock walls. When we reached the top, I was so overcome with awe that I couldn't speak. The fjord lay far below, a million diamonds sparkling along the surface of the water in the afternoon sun. There were more mountains than I could count, all as wild and untouched as anyone could imagine. If heaven is even half this beautiful, we're in for a treat.

We scrambled back down in the late afternoon warmth and cooked a big dinner along the beach at the bottom. The wind began to pick up from the south as we pushed off the shore in our kayaks and thankfully, turned north. Just before we turned the corner, we glanced back and saw several mountain goats silhouetted against the sky, peering down, as if they had been watching us all along.

For the next hour, we drifted along the towering cliffs of Gloomy Knob. Several times, we passed mountain goats only a couple dozen feet away. They peered at us without a fear in the world, their thick white fur blowing in the evening breeze. The sound of the wind and the waves coupled with the stunning views, the curious mountain goats, and the easy paddling made me wonder if we had somehow shifted into a different dimension.

Susanna and I set up our tent after ten o'clock among bushes and cottonwoods. Beyond our tent lay massive, glacial scoured valleys.

The next morning we caught a classic image of the Alaskan wilderness. "Bear!" whispered Susanna. A giant golden brown bear had just ambled out of the bushes nearby and was slowly walking along the alders near shore. Within moments, he silently disappeared back into the bushes.

We paddled slowly north into Queen Inlet. Rays of sunshine filtered through holes in the clouds and the water was the color of turquoise. We passed cliffs that seemed to rise into oblivion. Soon, a wide outwash plain came into view, nestled between enormous mountains. Behind it, a hanging glacier capped a 3,500 foot vertical wall. Several milky colored streams tumbled over small boulders and arctic terns zipped through the air.

"Are you ready for lunch?" I asked.

Susanna glanced across the landscape as we glided the last few yards into shore. Her sudden stillness caught my eye. I followed Susanna's gaze toward a brown bear sow standing on her hind legs, peering at our kayaks. Her shaggy brown body swayed slightly as she balanced her weight. Her yearling cub mirrored her curiosity. A third bear, beautiful and golden, pulled our attention away from the others. When he stood to sniff the air in our direction, his height humbled us. He must have easily stood 10 feet tall!

Swiftly, the sow and cub dropped to all fours, wheeled and ran into the thick brush nearby. Moments later, the giant golden bear did the same. We looked at each other with wide eyes and astonished smiles. I slowly exhaled, realizing I had been holding my breath as the National Geographic moment played out before us.

"Maybe we should wait a little while to have lunch," Susanna said, with a smile.

"Good idea," I replied. "Last year, when I paddled by this valley I saw four brown bears ambling around near the rivers and shoreline. There must be a really high concentration of bears here."

"That last bear was huge!" Susanna said, her voice full of wonder.

"I bet he'll top 1,000 pounds by fall!" I replied. "If it's a good salmon season, he'll gain several hundred pounds before then. I wouldn't want to run into him in a dark patch of alder!"

In the early evening, we left Queen Inlet and made a long crossing to the western shore of the bay near Gilbert Peninsula. Our voices and laugher mingled with the sound of the wind and waves until I felt as if they were one. Sun crystals danced across the surface of the water, nearly hypnotizing us with their beauty.

When we finally set foot on dry ground near Gilbert Peninsula, we pulled out the stove to cook dinner. A disturbance in the water caught our attention. As we watched, a six-foot tall, jet black dorsal fin rose out of the deep blue water where we had crossed in our kayaks just a few minutes earlier. A loud whoosh echoed off the nearby cliff. Five more dorsal fins rose out of the water, followed by the sound of quick breaths. Of all the wildlife sightings we had witnessed during this trip, this one was the one that will remain forever etched in our minds. We sat in stunned silence as the pod of orcas swam by, all powerful in their underwater kingdom.

A couple of hours later, the sun dropped below the jagged peaks to the northwest. We set up camp near Scidmore Cut and warmed our chilly fingers next to a small campfire. The flames licked the driftwood and the smoke curled into the Alaskan night. The surrounding mountains were purple in the everlasting summer twilight. At midnight, the rising tide swallowed the fire and we slipped into my little blue tent.

At times, the month that Susanna spent in Glacier Bay felt like a never-ending dream; most of the time, though, we realized it would pass in the blink of an eye. As June gave way to July, a knot began to form in my stomach. Our remaining time together had dwindled to a few precious days.

The morning of Susanna's departure, I walked into my bedroom and saw a card on my pillow. My eyes misted over as I read it. It was nearly a carbon copy of the card I had given her all those years ago on Isle Royale. She had carefully listed all of our adventures together, but it was what she wrote at the bottom that made the tears start to flow. It was a Bible verse from Ecclesiastes which read, *"He has made everything beautiful in its time."*

Crossing the Narrows

When Susanna left in early July, a huge void developed in my little home. It felt empty and incredibly lonely. I couldn't imagine life without her, but now once again, my life *was* without her.

Her adventurous spirit had taken her to Japan for the next six weeks. In the fall, she would be back in Wisconsin. Were we still just two kindred souls that lived parallel lives, destined to never truly be together? I didn't see how we could possibly merge our lives, yet I couldn't imagine continuing this way.

As always, my world remained centered in the backcountry. Consequently, I escaped to the wilderness every chance that arose.

The backcountry of Glacier Bay has a way of humbling a person. No matter how much experience or how much comfort you have out there, disaster is often just inches or seconds away. That is when the sense of wildness reaches its peak. Two events in mid-summer brought that home to me.

The morning of July 13th was cloudless. The water was so calm and silent that I could see the mountains' reflections and hear the marine mammals breathing for miles around. It was a good thing, too, because I had a long, open crossing of Sitakaday Narrows in front of me.

Sitakaday Narrows can be a terrifying section of water. This area is just under three miles wide and five miles long. The depth of the water ranges from a couple dozen to two hundred feet. All tidal water that moves in and out of the entire bay must pass through the Narrows. A bit farther north, the bay is more than 15 miles wide and over 1,000 feet deep. The tidal change can be as much as 25 feet every six hours. That's a lot of water shifting in and out of the Narrows! At peak flood or ebb, the current in the Narrows can reach eight knots, causing whirlpools and frightening waves.

I had never crossed the Narrows in a kayak before, but I had paddled along its shore. Even that can be foolhardy in the wrong tide or weather. My friend Sean and I had camped the night before in Fingers Bay, a beautiful, forested cove a few miles northwest of the Narrows. Our goal was to wait for a favorable tide and paddle down the center of the Narrows until getting south of the Beardslee Islands, where we could then paddle east and then north into Bartlett Cove. Given the favorable forecast and a strong ebbing tide in the early afternoon, it looked like our best chance to cross.

We had worked our way south against the tide in the morning until arriving at Lars Island. We waited until the tide changed and then made a break for it. At first the water was calm, gently moving toward the open ocean. As the minutes ticked by, the water velocity increased substantially. I barely paddled, letting the current push me along faster than I had ever kayaked.

Suddenly, I saw a white line on the horizon dead ahead. A tiny breath of wind from the south caressed my face. "That doesn't look so good," I said as we drifted on.

"No, it doesn't," replied Sean, a bit apprehensively. "Let's start paddling more to the east. Maybe we can find calm water near Young Island."

The white line on the horizon grew wider by the second. A strong southerly wind hit the ebbing tide and created a section of standing waves and swirling water. Even large boats with motors can be destroyed in conditions like that. The story of the '*white wall of death*' told by our park whale biologist kept popping up in my mind. She always booked toward home as soon as she saw that line. Without a motor to whisk us away, our greatest abilities and prayers would be tested.

I began to paddle hard toward shore, but the current was too strong. Within minutes, we hit the white line. Our calm sea evaporated almost instantly and became an angry, four foot chop. The waves crashed over the bow of my kayak and a howling southerly wind made it impossible to communicate. As the waves grew to six feet, Sean and I separated to avoid the possibility of an accidental collision. We were alone in the jaws of a brutal sea.

All of a sudden, directly in front of me and no more than 100 yards away, a tremendous humpback whale breached, flipping itself completely out of the water, crashing down among the waves. Seconds later, Sean appeared at the top of a wave, paddling furiously, and then disappeared again in a trough. I paddled hard and non-stop, trying not to think of the whales beneath me.

Time stood still. A parasitic jaeger, a large seabird so well suited for the ocean, flew within a couple feet of my head. Moments later, a common murre, another bird of the sea, did the same thing. I was jealous of the fact that they looked so calm and confident. We were in a world where no human should ever be, but a world that was so normal for these birds.

For some reason, as the conditions worsened, my hope and confidence increased. I was alone with my thoughts and strangely at ease. I thought about the times when I was scared as a little kid. My mom was always there for me. She would hold me in her arms and quietly whisper Psalm 46: "*God is our refuge and strength, an ever-present help in trouble. Therefore we will not fear, though the earth give way and the mountains fall into the heart of the sea, though its waters roar and foam and the mountains quake with their surging.*" It was always the words from verse ten that fully calmed me: "*Be still and know that I am God.*"

"God is always with us," she would say. "You don't ever have to fear, because God is in control."

As I paddled on, I felt as if my kayak was a simple extension of my body. We were a team and no wave could break us. With a smile, I thought back to those first few shaky kayak outings in Glacier Bay. That day, in the midst of an angry sea, in a world somewhere between earth and heaven, I felt an absolute peace and tranquility. Not once did I feel like my kayak would flip. When I finally made the turn east and then north into Bartlett Cove, I was almost sad to see the waves flatten into the calm waters of the bay.

There's Something Drooling on My Tent!

The second humbling event occurred in early August and in many ways, was far more frightening. A close encounter with an Alaskan brown bear is perhaps the ultimate primal fear.

Rain hammered the front windows of the Baranof Wind, Glacier Bay's day tour and camper drop-off boat, as we surged through the Narrows. By the time we reached South Marble Island, the rain had slowed and through the clouds we could see the imposing glacier-covered side of Mount Bertha.

"That's a good sign!" I said to Randy. "Whenever I see one of the mountains in the Fairweather mountain range, I know it's going to be a good day!"

Randy had arrived in Glacier Bay a couple of days earlier after several long flights from Michigan. "I can't wait!" said Randy while rubbing his hands together in front of him, as excited as a kid in a candy store.

The last little sprinkle of rain evaporated just before Rendu Inlet, our drop-off cove. Within moments, we were standing on shore with our kayaks, waving goodbye to what felt like the last people on earth. The boat disappeared around the rocky corner and a primeval silence descended upon us.

Never in my life will I be able to fully describe the feeling of being dropped off in the middle of nowhere in Glacier Bay. One minute, you're sitting on a warm, comfortable boat talking to people; the next minute you and your companions are alone in one of the last wild places on the planet.

We both stared at the vacant spot where the boat had been just minutes earlier. "Now it's just us and the bears!" I said while mimicking Randy's excited hand rubbing. Little did I know just how accurate my statement would be.

We paddled northwest into the upper reaches of the bay. Clouds swirled around the peaks above and harbor seals poked their heads up from the depths below. We stopped for lunch along Russell Fan and promptly saw a brown bear ambling about. Two bald eagles sat in a small spruce tree nearby.

As evening progressed, we drew closer and closer to the thundering glaciers at the end of Tarr Inlet. The chocolaty water was choked with floating ice and circling gulls. At dusk, we set up camp right next to Grand Pacific Glacier and quietly listened and watched as day turned to night.

"Sounds like a classic mid-western thunderstorm," said Randy, his voice full of awe. "I have no idea how to even begin to write about this in my journal."

"Even after all this time spent in Glacier Bay," I said quietly, "I still can't believe it's real. It's almost too perfect."

Dawn broke, sunny and warm. We spent the morning weaving through the ice flows in front of the two massive glaciers. Periodically, pinnacles of ice would crash into the sea, the thunder echoing back and forth across the inlet. As far as either one of us could tell, we were the only human beings left on the planet.

We paddled south throughout the afternoon and arrived at the southern tip of Russell Island just as dusk began to settle.

"This is where John Muir camped when he was exploring Glacier Bay way back in October of 1879," I said proudly. "It's a perfect campsite for us! We can pretend we're on John Muir's expedition way back then, discovering the world of glaciers for the first time."

Within moments, I could tell it wasn't a perfect campsite. Bear tracks littered the soft sand and a few late season strawberries clung to the tiny green plants. Silently, I weighed our options. There were very few places to set up a tent in the area. Most shorelines were either sheer cliffs or prime bear habitat. On the nearby mainland was an active salmon stream; definitely not where we wanted to camp. The bears there would be gorging themselves and actively defending their territories with brute force. South of Russell Island there were several small rocky islands, but, full of bird colonies, they were off limits to camping. Besides, they were too rocky and rugged for tents.

Many times in the past, I had set up my tent late in the evening in a completely different place than where I had eaten dinner, and taken down camp early in the morning to avoid as many bear encounters as possible. There was no reason to believe this night would be any different.

At five thirty in the morning, I was awakened from a deep sleep by the sound of a heavy snap. Instantly, Randy and I were jolted into consciousness and looked nervously at each other. My heart pounded so hard that I feared it would erupt through my chest. Something large broke a branch near the tent. My mind raced through the possibilities. We were too far north in the bay to find moose and wolves would never make a sound like that…I could find no other explanation than the unthinkable. Some rustling and a second snap confirmed a rapidly rising nightmare. My lips became absolutely dry.

"I think there's a bear out there," whispered Randy in a shaky voice.

A giant shadow descended toward the other side of the small vestibule, only inches from my face. The silhouette of a snout touched the other side of the nylon followed by the loudest sniff I could have ever imagined. Never before had I felt so small and insignificant. Man is nothing compared to an Alaskan brown bear. With one swipe of its enormous claws, we would cease to exist.

The bear stood frozen in place for what seemed like an eternity before finally shuffling over to Randy's side of the tent. Deep, heavy breathing came from the giant outside. Once again, the bear stood panting quietly, almost expectantly. My heart was now pounding so hard I imagined the bear was listening to it. Randy and I remained utterly silent.

Finally, the silhouette moved away and we both exhaled for what felt like the first time ever. A few minutes passed without any further sound. Ever so slowly, I unzipped the tent. Our visitor was nowhere to be seen, but the evidence was everywhere. An ominous line of drool, complete with strawberry seeds, streaked the side of the rain-fly and a steaming pile of scat lay on the ground nearby.

All of a sudden, an eagle flew overhead and landed in a large spruce tree. A second eagle stood calmly on a rock nearby, gazing intently at us. A chill went up and down my spine and a tear formed in the corner of my eye. *"God is always with us,"* came the whisper from my mother. *"Don't be afraid..."*

An hour later we paddled by a rocky, exposed island with two young eaglets on top. They were flapping their wings awkwardly but continuously. Just then, we spotted an adult eagle with a full white head just beneath the eaglets on a tiny rock ledge. The adult slowly flapped its wings. The eaglets copied their parent in an ancient lesson of flight.

The Baranof Wind picked us up in a driving rain later that morning. The boat sped up the coast, re-tracing our route almost exactly. It no longer seemed like a difficult journey. At Margerie Glacier, people fought for a spot along the railing and took pictures with unknown people in them. Randy and I just shook our heads and thought about the front row seats we had for hours the day before.

Several mornings later, I tried desperately to start the tiny silver car owned by my friend Jim. I had to get Randy to the airport in Gustavus and return in time to catch a cruise ship in mid morning. "If it's cold out, it will be all you can do to get the car started and keep it going," Jim had said the evening before. "Once it starts, don't bring it to a complete stop or you'll never get it going again."

Sure enough, it was cold and clear. Fortunately the car, nicknamed *The Silver Bullet*, started and we sputtered toward the top of the hill. By the time we reached the crest, we were barely going five miles per hour. We cheered as we crested the hill and began barreling down the other side at almost 30. When we reached 35, the steering wheel began to shake so badly that I had difficulty controlling it. A few minutes later, I slowed the car as Randy dove out onto the gravel parking lot of the airport with his backpack in tow. Even in the civilized parts of Southeast Alaska, there's always an adventure to be had.

Where the Wildness Remains

With confident strokes, I maneuvered my kayak through the frigid, ice choked water of McBride Inlet. The ice flows were exceptionally thick. At times, the big ones would collide into each other with a deafening crunch. At other times, they would open up a deceptively easy path in the churning water and then close in with surprising speed. House-sized icebergs, stranded by the lowering tide, glistened in the weak sunshine and then illuminated a deep, indescribable blue when the sun disappeared behind a black cloud. Dark, towering mountains rose on either side of the inlet and an immense, sparkling blue glacier emptied into the sea at the far end.

September was already well established. The cottonwood trees shimmered a golden yellow in the light breeze. The wildlife seemed restless. It was nearly time for many of them to journey south, which meant the same for me.

With each opening in the ice, I inched closer and closer to the thundering glacier at the far end. Gulls circled overhead, their cries piercing the cold, morning air. Inquisitive seals poked their heads out of the narrow openings in the shifting ice and eyed me warily. Finally, I came to an impenetrable barrier of ice.

My kayak and I sat alone, gently rocking with the ice, gazing at the towering face of McBride Glacier. Somehow, this awesome wilderness deep in the heart of Alaska had become my home. This was my backyard and I had grown to know it like the back of my hand.

Finally, I turned from the great glacier and began paddling south. The rain caught up to me that afternoon and began dumping in buckets. Somewhere deep in my soul, I knew that this was my final kayak trip in Glacier Bay. My heart ached with the thought of leaving, but also began to soar with the thought of a new adventure.

The rain continued its relentless soaking throughout the afternoon and evening. It was nearly dark when I finally set up my tent at Caroline Point and snuggled down into a dry sleeping bag. Raindrops pattered the tent in a slow, hypnotic dance.

Dawn was cold and gray, but thankfully, dry. The last of my bags were packed, and my kayak sat waiting near the shore. Two loons floated by, singing a mournful tune.

"Where shall I go next, my friends?" I asked quietly. Were they calling me back to my island? I smiled as I looked around. "I'll miss you...but you'll always remain in my dreams."

Two eagles balanced on a barnacle covered rock nearby. Suddenly, a wild sound broke the silence. A deep, barrel-chested howl rose from the mist shrouded forest nearby. Perhaps it was a wolf, perhaps it was the wilderness, or perhaps it was the Creator himself. Surely, this is His domain. In this land that is much closer to heaven than earth, God is present everywhere.

All those years ago, I had set out from college in a desperate search for those forgotten corners of the world that only legends speak of. I wanted to feel like a part of the earth and become one of its ancient stories. I wanted to be like my ancestors and live with the land, not against it. What I found was even better than I could have imagined.

One of the most precious feelings in the world is to come to a place where the sense of wildness takes your breath away, a place where you feel the heartbeat of the earth. This sense of wildness does not necessarily come from a National Park or even a designated wilderness. It is much rarer than that, but it *does* still exist. It is in these places that we feel awed by the world. It is in these places that we feel like children again, discovering the world for the first time. It is in these places that we feel the angels soaring above.

There are a certain few people who have discovered where the wildness remains. We whisper the secret quietly in certain circles. We soak the wildness into our veins, laughing in the joy of life. We dance in utter ecstasy under the Aurora-filled sky.

Epilogue:

Gothic Peak stood like a mighty sentinel over a vast valley fast approaching autumn. Dozens of other mountains towered around the valley, disappearing into a purplish horizon. A cool wind whispered through the restless trees. Swirling clouds poured over the summits like giant waterfalls.

I stood alone, watching the grand spectacle unfold. The immensity of the situation had hit me long ago, but an odd sense of peace enveloped me. For a moment, I closed my eyes and thought about all that had happened over the last year and a half. Could it really have happened to me?

Just then, the music began to play. I walked slowly over the hill and saw a small group of smiling friends and family gathered at the edge of the meadow. The words of the music pierced my soul: "...*like a fairy tale come true*..." My mind began to swim as tunnel vision took over. "...*you're the answer when I prayed, I would find someone*..."

I walked up to the minister, his white robes billowing in the light breeze, an image of a biblical Moses on top of a windswept summit coming to mind. "...*Watching as you softly sleep*..." Just then, she emerged from the trees at the far end of the meadow, walking arm and arm with her father. "...*What I'd give if I could keep, just this moment, if only time stood still*..." Her radiant smile must have been evident from a mile away. "...*All I want is to hold you forever. All I need is you more every day. You saved my heart from being broken apart. You gave your love away...and I'm thankful every day...for the gift*..."

As the music ended, I looked deeply into the eyes of the most beautiful woman on the planet. She looked directly back into mine. She had chosen me to be her husband. Deep in the wilds of the Elk Mountains of Colorado, Susanna, my soul mate of so many years, became my wife.

Acknowledgements:

There are many people I would like to thank for their support, friendship, and love. Without each of them, this book would never have been possible.

First of all, I would like to thank my mom and dad for bringing me up to love wild places and to have a firm belief in God.

To my close friends Randy, Tracy, Al, Smitty, and Shawn, thank you for our adventures together throughout the past decade.

My brother John has always taken the time and energy to visit me in these far off lands, encouraging my dreams along the way. For this support I will always be grateful.

Most of all, I would like to thank my wife and soul mate Susanna. She has been, and continues to be, the most amazing partner I could ever imagine. May the adventures continue…

— · — · — · — · — · — · — · —

Editing and Formatting: Susanna Ausema

Wedding Photo: Erik Hays

Author Photo: Susanna Ausema, Lamphier Lake, Colorado

Song Quoted in Epilogue: "The Gift" by Jim Brickman

Chapter Photos: Michael P. Ausema

National Park Maps: drawn by Michael P. Ausema

About the Author:

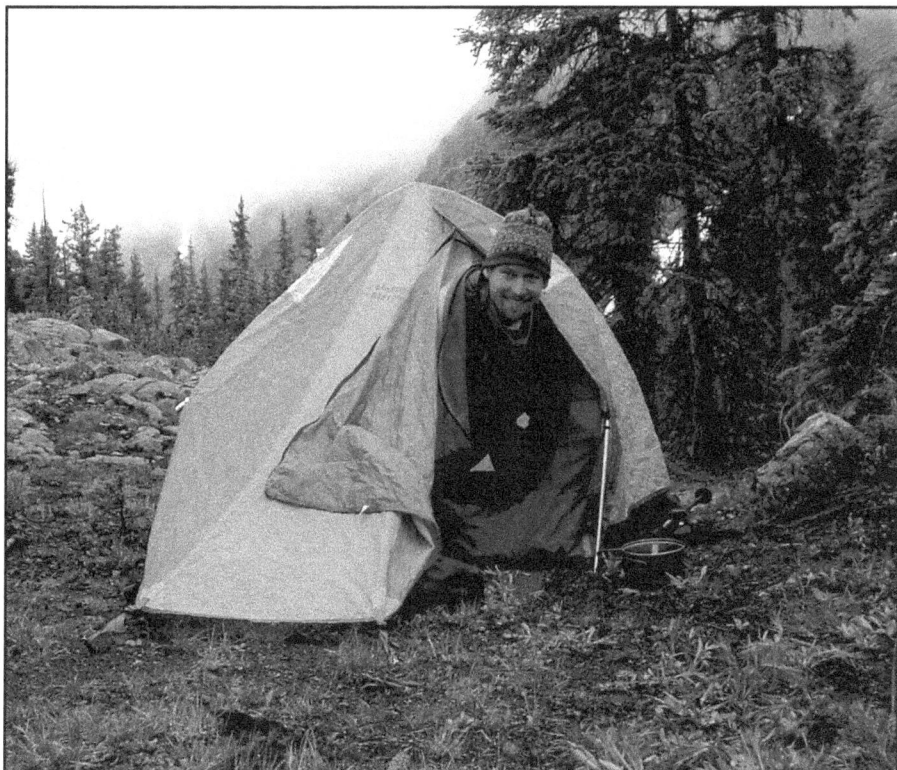

Michael Ausema has worked for the National Park Service since the summer of 1997. His adventures have taken him to some of the farthest corners of the world. He continues to work as a park ranger in western Colorado today.

www.ingramcontent.com/pod-product-compliance
Lightning Source LLC
Chambersburg PA
CBHW031831090426
42741CB00005B/197